Georges Perec's Geographies

Georges Perec's Geographies

Material, Performative and Textual Spaces

Edited by Charles Forsdick, Andrew Leak and Richard Phillips

UCLPRESS

First published in 2019 by
UCL Press
University College London
Gower Street
London WC1E 6BT

Available to download free: www.uclpress.co.uk

A CIP catalogue record for this book is available from The British Library.

ISBN: 978-1-78735-443-2 (Hbk.)
ISBN: 978-1-78735-442-5 (Pbk.)
ISBN: 978-1-78735-441-8 (PDF)
ISBN: 978-1-78735-444-9 (epub)
ISBN: 978-1-78735-445-6 (mobi)
DOI: https://doi.org/10.14324/111.9781787354418

Contents

List of figures

List of tables

Notes on contributors

Kevin Boniface is a postman, artist and blogger. For the last eight years he has been writing succinct descriptions of events and incidents that have taken place while out and about on his postal round, his daily route taking him from the main sorting office to the streets and outlying neighbourhoods above the town. In these commentaries and records nothing seems to be typical. Engaged and disconnected conversations, the observed and the overheard are all part of the everyday activity of life on the move. These observations form the basis of Kevin's most recent book, *Round About Town* (Uniformbooks, 2018).

Oliver Bray is Director of Arts at Leeds Beckett University. He is a practising Live Artist and has performed his work widely in international contexts. His current research focuses on practical investigations of constraint in performance and the various implications of a theatrical Oulipo (Ouvroir de Littérature Potentielle or Workshop of Potential Literature). Oliver's well-respected professional practice has toured nationally and internationally to venues and festivals including Sibiu International Theatre Festival, Romania; In between Time, Bristol; and the National Review of Live Art, Glasgow. His performance work seeks always to be genuinely innovative and edgy, while remaining unapologetically inclusive, eminently watchable and often quite a bit funny.

Julia Dobson is professor in French film and performance at the University of Sheffield. Her research across film and performance centres on the construction and representation of alterity. She has published widely on film including work on Kieslowski, first-person documentary, Jacques Audiard and a study of the interactions between gender, genre and auteurism in her book *Negotiating the Auteur* (Manchester University Press, 2012). She is currently working on a series of projects on object-based theatre, including a book *Performing Objects: Puppets and Beyond in Contemporary French Performance* (Liverpool University Press) and a study of adolescence in French cinema.

Charles Forsdick is James Barrow professor of French at the University of Liverpool and Arts and Humanities Research Council theme leadership fellow for 'Translating Cultures'. He has published on travel writing, colonial history, post-colonial literature and the cultures of slavery. He is also a specialist on Haiti and the Haitian Revolution, and has written widely about representations of Toussaint Louverture. His publications include *Victor Segalen and the Aesthetics of Diversity* (Oxford University Press, 2000) and *Travel in Twentieth-Century French and Francophone Cultures* (Oxford University Press, 2005).

Christopher Hall is senior lecturer at Sheffield Hallam University. As well as gaining over 100 broadcast television editing credits, he directed the English-language theatrical premières of Perec's 'The Machine' and *The Raise*, as part of Third Angel (a theatre company).

Amanda Crawley Jackson is a senior lecturer in French and Francophone Studies at the University of Sheffield and faculty director for Impact and External Engagement for Arts and Humanities. Her research focuses on the ways in which space is represented in literature, philosophy and visual arts from the French-speaking world. She has published widely on modern French literature and contemporary art from France and Algeria.

Andrew Leak is professor of French and Francophone Studies at UCL. His research includes three books and numerous articles on Jean-Paul Sartre – in particular on the relationship between his brand of phenomenology and Freudian or post-Freudian psychoanalysis. His current research focuses on literature and politics in Haiti in the contemporary period. But another abiding concern has been the work of Georges Perec. He has published several articles on Perec over the last 25 years and is one of Perec's English translators (*A Man Asleep* [1990] and *Lieux* [2001]). In addition to the above, he has written a short study of the critical theorist Roland Barthes and edited a volume of essays on literary representation of the Holocaust.

Joanne Lee is an artist, writer and publisher of the *Pam Flett Press,* a serial publication essaying everyday life, issue 4 of which focused on actual and conceptual *terrains vagues*. Her research on place has been presented in *Art of the Edgelands*, University of Exeter, and *Species of Spaces: A Transdisciplinary Conference on the Work of Georges Perec*, Teesside University, resulting in an article for the journal *Literary Geographies.* It has also featured in exhibitions including *Green and Pleasant Land?* Harris Museum and Art Gallery, Preston, and *re-turning*, AirSpace Gallery, Stoke-on-Trent. She is senior lecturer in graphic design at Sheffield Hallam University.

Daryl Martin is senior lecturer in sociology at the University of York, where he also co-directs the Centre for Urban Research (CURB). He has teaching and research interests in the areas of architectural theory, cultural geography and urban studies. He has been involved in a series of recent Research Councils UK projects exploring the intersections of architecture, ageing and health. Literature was his first degree and he still draws on literary works to understand contemporary urban cultures and wider questions of place.

David Matless is professor of cultural geography at the University of Nottingham. He is the author of *Landscape and Englishness* (Reaktion Books, 1998, new edition 2016), *In the Nature of Landscape: Cultural Geography on the Norfolk Broads* (Wiley-Blackwell, 2014) and *The Regional Book* (Uniformbooks, 2015).

Anna-Louise Milne lives and writes in the north-east of Paris. She is director of graduate studies and research at the University of London Institute in Paris where she is currently developing the Paris Centre for Migrant Writing and Expression. Notable publications are a book on Jean Paulhan, an edited collection, *May 68. Rethinking France's Last Revolution* (AIAA, 2011) and *The Cambridge Companion to the Literature of Paris* (Cambridge University Press, 2013). Her latest book entitled *75* was published this spring (2019) by Gallimard in the Collection Blanche. It is her first full book in French, an experiment in urban poetics and trans-lingual writing.

Alasdair Pettinger is the editor of *Always Elsewhere: Travels of the Black Atlantic* (Continuum International Publishing Group Ltd, 1998), and has published a number of essays reflecting his (overlapping) interests in travel literature, the cultures of slavery and abolitionism, and representations of Haiti. His latest book is *Frederick Douglass and Scotland, 1846* (Edinburgh University Press, 2018) and he is currently working on a history of the word 'voodoo'. He works as an archivist at the Scottish Music Centre.

Richard Phillips is the author and editor of a number of books on cultural geography, postcolonial criticism, and creative and experimental fieldwork. These books include *Mapping Men and Empire: A Geography of Adventure* (Routledge, 1997), *Sex, Politics and Empire* (Manchester University Press, 2006); *Muslim Spaces of Hope: Geographies of Possibility in Britain and the West* (Zed, 2008); *Liverpool '81: Remembering the Riots* (Liverpool University Press, 2011), *Fieldwork for Human Geography* (Sage, 2012). He is professor of human geography at the University of Sheffield.

Leslie Satin, a choreographer/dancer and dance writer, is on the Arts Faculty of the Gallatin School of New York University. She has taught or been a guest artist at Bard College, Alvin Ailey American Dance Center/ Fordham University, Princeton University, Centro Coreográfico (Brazil), State University of New York, University of Chichester, Hamidrasha (Israel) and elsewhere. Satin co-edited the Performing Autobiography issue of *Women & Performance: A Journal of Feminist Theory*; her performance texts and writing on dance's intersections with space, memory, autobiography, site-based performance, and the work of Georges Perec appear in numerous journals and edited collections.

Derek Schilling is professor of French at Johns Hopkins University. He is the author of *Mémoires du quotidien: les lieux de Perec* (Presses universitaires du Septentrion, 2006), which explores Percc's sociology of everydayness in relation to the rhetoric of the memory place and various site-bound observational practices. His forthcoming study *Banlieues de mémoire: géopoétique du roman de l'entre-deux-guerres* examines the emergence of the Paris suburb in French novels published at the turn of the 1930s, by the likes of Simenon, Céline, Queneau and Dabit.

Douglas Smith is senior lecturer in French and Francophone Studies at University College Dublin, where he teaches literature, cinema and theory. In 2006, he organised the symposium 'Exploring Supermodernity: Marc Augé in Context(s)' (*Irish Journal of French Studies*, 2009) and in 2007 co-organised the international conference 'Defining Space'. Both of these were under the auspices of the Humanities Institute of Ireland. Recent publications include the edited special numbers 'Empire and Culture Now' (*Modern and Contemporary France*, 2010) and 'Revisiting André Bazin' (*Paragraph*, 2013), as well as contributions to *A Companion to Godard* (eds. Tom Conley and T. Jefferson Kline; John Wiley & Sons, 2014) and *Architecture and Culture* (John Wiley & Sons, 2015).

Ian Trowell gained his doctorate at the University of Sheffield School of Architecture in 2018, researching the travelling fair and its relationship to heritage practices. He has published widely on the British fairground, examining sound, noise, music, voice, spatial practices and visual cultures. He also researches and writes on British music subcultures and is a regular contributor to the journal *Punk & Post-Punk*.

Acknowledgements

Richard Phillips is grateful to members of a Georges Perec reading group, which met in Sheffield University and convened a symposium on Georges Perec's Geographies, supported by the University of Sheffield Department of Geography, in which some draft chapters of this book were aired and discussed. Richard particularly wishes to acknowledge Kiera Chapman, Malcolm Tait, Eric Olund and Morag Rose for their conversations and engagement with this project, and others who attended the conference for their comments and suggestions.

Charles Forsdick acknowledges the assistance of the Arts and Humanities Research Council. He was theme leadership fellow for 'Translating Cultures' (AH/N504476/1) during the editing of this collection. The original conference at which the ideas put forward in this volume were explored was supported by 'Translating Cultures'.

Daryl Martin would like to thank Jonathan Meades for his kind permission to reproduce the two images in Chapter 13. He would also like to thank Paul Shields for his assistance in preparing the digital images for inclusion in the chapter.

1

Introduction: Georges Perec's geographies; Perecquian geographies

Richard Phillips, Andrew Leak and Charles Forsdick

Georges Perec, the novelist, film-maker and essayist who experimented with words and textual constraints, and explored throughout his work memory, absence and loss, was also one of the most inventive and original geographical writers of the twentieth century. His writing speaks to a wide range of spatial, urban and architectural interests, both substantive and methodological. Substantively, these themes include cities and streets; homes and apartments; conceptions of space and place; mathematical and textual spaces; imagined, utopian and dystopian spaces; time and the city; landscapes of memory and trauma; consumption and material culture; everyday life, the everyday, the quotidian; ordinary, endotic and 'infra-ordinary' places. Methodologically, too, Perec has much to offer contemporary readers, having proposed precocious methods of urban exploration and observation; classification, enumeration, categorisation and taxonomy; and geographical and ethnographic description. These substantive and methodological threads relate most directly to the strand of Perec's work that he described as 'sociological', but which was sufficiently broad to encompass at the same time social, cultural and geographical interests.

Overlapping and intersecting with his other major concerns – in what he called autobiographical, ludic and narrative writing – Perec's geographical writing has certainly not gone unnoticed. Critical attention to his geographies focuses upon the everyday (through a major study by Michael Sheringham), the city and places (in work by Derek Schilling, Andrew Leak and others), and social and geographical description (developed by, for example, Howard Becker). In this book, we seek to present a more sustained exploration of Georges Perec's geographies, which begins with readings of Perec's geographical writing and follows through to explore the inspiration and direction that this work has given others.

Perec's geographies

Perec remarked in 1979: 'I might have been born, like my close or distant cousins, in Haifa or Baltimore or Vancouver, but one thing alone in this almost limitless range of possibilities was forbidden to me, that of being born in the land of my ancestors, in Poland, in Lubartów, in Pulawy or in Warsaw.'[1] The crux of this geographical paradox is that, had he been born (in 1936) in Poland, he would almost certainly have perished like nearly all of his family who remained there after the Nazi invasion in 1939. In the event, Perec's earliest years were spent in a *quartier* of the tenth arrondissement of Paris which had a large immigrant – especially Jewish – population. But if the 'cradle' of his family, in Poland, was to become a non-space, so too would the street where he spent the first five years of his life: his father, Icek, was killed at the front in 1940 and his mother, Cyrla, was deported and murdered in Auschwitz in 1943. Perec survived but, along with his parents, the memories of the safe space they had shared had disappeared. Henceforth, space itself became an enigma:

> I would like there to exist places that are stable, unmoving, intangible, untouched and almost untouchable, unchanging; places that might be points of departure, of origin [...] Such places don't exist, and it's because they don't exist that space becomes a question [...] Space is a doubt; I have constantly to mark it, to designate it, it's never mine, never given to me, I have to conquer it.[2]

It is as if the existential question which tormented Perec was not 'who am I?', but – to adopt a more spatially oriented formulation – 'where am I?'

The house at 24, rue Vilin still existed when Perec wrote those words in the 1970s. He had visited it every year since 1969, as part of a huge writing project, if only to document its slow disappearance: one year he notes 'No 24, still intact'; the next, little stands between it and the developers' bulldozers: 'Nos 23 and 25 have been gutted. Past No 25, nothing any longer.'[3] Imaginary spaces have the advantage of being 'intangible' and 'untouchable'. Hence Perec's two approaches to space: to record, describe, measure, mark in order to preserve or to create spaces immune to the degradations of time – imaginary spaces. The world comes into being when it is named: 'a simple pretext for a nomenclature'.[4]

Species of Spaces opens with a kind of poem consisting of 38 expressions including the word 'space': open space, living space, lack of space, wasted space, space invaders. But the primordial space is the blank space and, more specifically, the blank space of the sheet of paper waiting to be written on. The first moment of the conquest of space is to trace signs there: only then does it have an up and a down, a left and a right. He recalls his childhood fascination with maps: 'Here is the desert, with its oasis, its wadi and its salt lake, here is the spring and the stream, the mountain torrent, the canal, the confluence, the river, the estuary, the river-mouth, and the Delta.'[5] In his compendious 1978 masterpiece, *Life: A User's Manual*, he imagines a character called Cinoc who worked as a 'word-killer' for Larousse encyclopaedias. His job was to remove outdated and obscure terms. By the time he retired, 'he had wiped dozens of islands, hundreds of cities and rivers, and thousands of townships off the map […] And cohorts of geographers, missionaries, entomologists, Church Fathers, men of letters, generals, Gods & Demons had been swept by his hand into eternal obscurity.'[6] But what he destroys with his left hand, he restores with his right. He takes words he has 'killed' and preserves them in their own lexicographical crypt: 'In ten years he gathered more than eight thousand of them, which contain, obscurely, the traces of the story it has now become almost impossible to hand on.'[7]

The word 'geography' has two complementary meanings for Perec. It denotes an onomastic drive: the naming/writing of space; but it also acknowledges that the spaces we inhabit have *always already* been written upon by countless generations of our ancestors. Seen in this way, it becomes an unfathomable palimpsest: 'a form of writing, a *geography* of which we had forgotten that we ourselves are the authors'.[8] There is a whole area of Perec's activity concerned with the deciphering of the spaces we inhabit, and it is this aspect of his activities that has, perhaps, attracted most interest from practitioners operating outside of the strictly literary sphere. From the early 1970s, he joined his former teacher Jean Duvignaud and the architect and writer Paul Virilio in the creation of a new journal: *Cause Commune* (Common Cause). Its aim was, among other things, 'to undertake an investigation of everyday life at every level, right down to the recesses and basements that are normally ignored'.[9] 'Recesses and basements' could suggest something hidden or buried, but in reality these phenomena are hidden in plain view: 'To question the habitual, but that's just it: we are habituated to it. We don't question it, it doesn't question us, it doesn't seem to pose a problem, we live it without thinking, as if it carried within it neither questions nor answers, as if it weren't the bearer of any information.'[10]

In 1969, Perec embarked on his most sustained geographical project: called simply *Places*. The plan was to visit 12 places in Paris – chosen for their biographical significance – at the rate of one a month over a period of 12 years. Once there, Perec would simply 'describe as flatly as possible' what he saw from his vantage point – normally a café. The text was then sealed in an envelope to be reopened only at the end of the project when all the texts would be collated and recomposed into an ensemble. As well as describing one place each month in situ, Perec also described a second place from memory, consigning this second piece to another envelope. The project was analogous, in some ways to that of Cinoc in that he envisaged it as a 'commemoration of *dead places that ought to survive*'.[11] This way of 'writing the city' has proved highly influential but there was a hidden side to Perec's project that has provided a different vein of inspiration. The idea that his places and his times (e.g. February 1969: rue Vilin [real] and rue de l'Assomption [memory]) should be *arbitrarily* coordinated was anathema to him. He therefore devised a complex mathematical instrument to programme the pairings of 'real' and 'memory' texts according to a principle of non-repetition.

The somewhat obsessive avoidance of the aleatory – existing often in creative tension with the peripatetic drive Perec foregrounds elsewhere – can be ascribed to the 'Oulipian' strain of his artistic sensibility. In 1967, he had joined a group of writers, scholars and mathematicians who called themselves the Oulipo (Ouvroir de Littérature Potentielle or Workshop of Potential Literature). Central to the aesthetic and practice of the Oulipo was the invention and exploitation of various forms of formal constraint as a stimulus to inventivity and artistic production. Who would have thought, for example, that voluntarily depriving yourself of the letter E could result in the creation of an hilarious detective novel of over 300 pages, the subject of which was the disappearance … of the letter E! Constraint – either as a theme or as a method – has found echoes way beyond the Oulipo, in writers and artists as diverse as Paul Auster, Sophie Calle, Christian Boltanski and Gustav Metzger. To return to Perec's *Places*. The constraint in this instance was twofold. First, to write 'as flatly as possible' – which means eliminating the figurative and limiting oneself to the strictly denotative. Second, to be in a certain place, at a certain time every month for the next 12 years! It was that constraint – eroded by the unpredictable intrusion of 'Life' into the 'User's Manual' – that eventually proved impossible to respect. The project petered out sometime in the mid-1970s.

Talking of his work in 1981 – less than a year before his death – Perec made the following suggestive remarks:

> At the end of *Species of Spaces*, you have: Georges Perec, the street, the house, the stairwell, the city, the country, the universe [...][12] And since the space was originally a space of writing, you start from the blank page and, from that moment onwards, once you have started to criss-cross [*sillonner*] space, because when you've done that, you've left traces [*sillons*], the book goes away from you as it tries to expand: like a pebble you throw into a river and which makes circular ripples.[13]

Several of the authors in this volume are situated in the outermost 'ripples', some consciously driven by the 'pebble' itself, others moved implicitly by the energy and the shape of its wave. Their work may be described as Perecquian; their geographical observations and descriptions as 'Perecquian fieldwork'.

Perecquian geographies

Perec's geographical investigations and descriptions have inspired a series of writers, artists and scholars, who have encountered his work in the original and in translation. Their geographies, explored in the second part of this volume, pick up on elements of Perec's geographical methods, in particular his playfulness; his attention to ordinary things and places and his emphasis upon writing as a means of observation and interpretation.[14] These hallmarks of Perecquian geography run through the chapters in Part II of this book, which work with photography, sound art, creative writing, dance, theatre and radio, in each case with inspiration and direction from Perec.

These Perecquian qualities demand a little more explanation at this stage. First, Perec's geographies are fundamentally ludic. His sense of play included structured and rule-bound practices. The former, involving a form of methodological constraint, allowed observations and events to unfold in unique and unrepeatable ways, against an Oulipian backdrop of probability and possibility. Perec's more openly playful writing included parodic taxonomies, spoof indexes and hidden jokes, all of which de-familiarise and interrogate methods of field observation and description, which have otherwise been adopted and practised mechanistically. Second, Perec brought ordinary places – what he called endotic geographies – into view. He cultivated a quality of attention to the ordinary and quotidian, to happenings in and around the streets, Metro stations and cafés of Paris. This meant turning away from spectacular sights and exotic subjects, 'training the gaze' to see flatly, 'slowly, almost stupidly',[15] in order to see ordinary places afresh. Third, Perec's geographical observations and interpretations revolved around writing. His field-writing included descriptions, lists, poems, novels and essays. Cutting across this work was a fundamentally essayistic quality, an exploratory and meandering way of observing and recording place.[16]

A number of authors in this volume engage explicitly and self-consciously with Perec. Others do so implicitly and less consciously. Some of these experimental geographers, explorers, writers and artists began with and were spurred on by readings of Perec, while others discovered him later, finding resonance between his work and their own, and entering into a form of posthumous exchange with his spirit of enquiry. Of course, Perec was not their only influence. For his part, Perec himself shared with and borrowed ideas from others, not only within Oulipo but also with Henri Lefebvre, Roland Barthes, Paul Virilio and others he encountered in 1960s and 1970s Paris, a world evoked so vividly by David Bellos in his wonderfully *emplaced* 1993 biography of Perec. Perecquian geographies, including those represented in the second part of this book, reach beyond Perec and do more than merely mimic his methods and perpetuate his preoccupations. Taking cues and inspiration from Perec, they break new ground.

Perecquian geographies reach, with his readership and influence, across disciplines, fields of creative practice and languages. Accordingly, the chapters that follow demonstrate an element of Perec's work already highlighted, that is his engagement with a range of fields that underpin the dynamics of constraint and experimentation with which Oulipo was (and is) more generally associated. They also explore the ways in which Perec's work has been subject to complex, creative and highly productive conversations and adaptations – often resulting in surprising cross-disciplinary translations of his work – across a range of areas of enquiry and fields of practice.

These shifts, in particular as they pertain to engagement with Perec beyond French-language cultures, often depend on literal translation and the circulation of his texts in languages other than French. Not only has Perec's work been relatively widely translated, but also his literary methods – and those of Oulipo more generally – have lent themselves to a reflection on the nature of translation itself.[17] Perec's key fictional texts are available in English and have attracted the attention of some of the most talented French–English translators of the late twentieth and early twenty-first centuries. *Les Choses* appeared in an English version by Helen Lane in 1967, two years after its original publication, and was re-translated (as *Things: A Story of the Sixties)* by David Bellos in 1990. Bellos has also complemented his definitive biography of Perec – a key vehicle for knowledge of the author in the English-speaking world, although, in a striking counterflow, it has also been translated into French – by translating a number of other works, including *W ou le souvenir d'enfance* (1975) [*W, or The Memory of Childhood* (1988)] and *La Vie mode d'emploi* (1978) [*Life: A User's Manual* (1987)] as well as posthumous texts such as *Le Condottière* (2012), which appeared as *Portrait of a Man Known as Il Condottiere* in 2014. The contributors to this volume draw primarily on translations of Perec's works relating to space, most notably *Espèces d'espaces* (1974), widely available in John Sturrock's 1997 translation for Penguin Books, *Species of Spaces and Other Pieces*, and *Tentative d'épuisement d'un lieu parisien* (1975), rendered into English by Marc Lowenthal in 2010 as *An Attempt at Exhausting a Place in Paris*. Less well known but of equal importance are the four texts from the *Places* project translated by Andrew Leak that formed the focus of an issue of *AA Files* in 2001. This intervention was a significant reminder that translation can filter and limit knowledge in addition to sharing it; the extracts in *AA Files* were notably a revelation to those interested in Perec and spatiality, but who had no access to material in the original French (or to French-language commentary on it, such as Derek Schilling's key *Mémoires du quotidien: les lieux de Perec* (2006), as yet untranslated into English). At the same time, reading Perec in translation compounds the original poetics of constraint underpinning the author's writing, enhanced in this process by the additional challenges often evident in translation itself. These are reflected in the work of the translation-focused equivalent of Oulipo, Outranspo (Ouvroir de Translation Potencial), a group founded in 2012.[18] Perec himself engaged in homophonic or homographic translation and Alison James has studied the interlingually ludic aspects of much Oulipo work.[19]

The translation of *La Disparition* (*A Void*) presents a striking example of the challenges faced by those translating Perec, and a telling response to the question as to whether this is the work of translation, transposition or transcreation.[20] *A Void* (1994), Gilbert Adair's translation or transcreation, follows the spirit of the lipogrammatic original by avoiding the letter 'e'.

To raise these questions is not to posit value judgements as to the relative merits of studying Perec 'in the original' (whatever that means), not least because such a stable version of the writer arguably does not exist. Instead, understanding the function of translation illuminates the creative dynamics of production and reception inherent in the Perecquian text. It also underlines the extent to which the 'Anglophone' Perec largely represented in this volume, constructed through translation, must be understood in relation to the original 'Francophone' version from which it has evolved. These processes of translation extend beyond the linguistic and relate equally to questions of form and cultural reference. They also reflect other processes of interpretation that are exemplified by this collection, as Perec's work has had an increasingly tangible influence translated across a range of academic disciplines and fields of practice.

Such translatability is not surprising because Perec's work – like that of Oulipo more generally – was born at a site of interdisciplinary creativity, drawing most notably on mathematics (one of its founders, François Le Lionnais, was a mathematician and engineer) as an underpinning principle.[21] There is growing practical interest in the pedagogical and theoretical implications of the work of Perec and his peers for the bridging of gaps between the sciences and humanities,[22] and the links between Oulipo and early computing in what might be seen as proto-digital humanities work has also begun to attract attention.[23] It is particularly striking that the work of Oulipo is increasingly celebrated for its precocious commitment to interdisciplinary working. Johnnie Gratton and Michael Sheringham described Perec's 'inter-in-disciplinarity', by which they understood the adoption of a range of practices central to 'disruptive' research: a commitment to the methodological innovation that drives more speculative working, a rejection of fixed disciplinary boundaries, an openness to the contingencies of practice-led approaches.[24] The chapters that follow demonstrate how the *oeuvre* of Georges Perec continues to inspire the crossing of linguistic and disciplinary lines in highly productive ways. Translating this work across a wide range of contexts, fields and practices, the contributors reveal that its potential for geographical innovation is far from being exhausted.

Chapter summaries

As we have explained, this volume begins by exploring 'Perec's geographies' through a series of essays focusing upon the geographies *within* Perec's work (from descriptions of streets to the spaces of his texts). The opening chapter by **Andrew Leak** explores the ways in which, far from serving as an amusing conceit, the map serves a deeper purpose in Perec's work: it represents a space stripped of coordinates, a space which condemns the hapless vessel which ventures into it to endless, aimless drifting. Analogous cartographic spaces are to be found throughout Perec's work, but the focus in this chapter is on two important texts published within two years of each other in the mid-1970s: *W, or The Memory of Childhood* and 'Backtracking'. What emerges from a comparative reading of these texts is that they are fundamentally preoccupied by the experience of (autobiographical) loss – Perec's implausible spaces provoke a loss of bearings, but they might also map, finally, a bearable loss.

Derek Schilling then shows how Perec's texts lead us to ask in what manner place names (toponyms) work to configure diegetic space, and in what specific ways the resulting world may differ, substantively and formally, from non-marked or would-be 'realistic' story worlds. Rather than produce a would-be 'map' plotting Perec's literary peregrinations, the chapter demonstrates how the selection, distribution and quality of place names in Perec's work helps to establish, in each instance, a distinctive *spatial contract* with the reader and interrogates precise relationships that might obtain between toponymy and the imagined topography that results from our encounter with Perec's work.

Julia Dobson's chapter concerns Perec and Queysanne's film *The Man Who Sleeps (Un homme qui dort)*. In it she explores the film's unsettling narrative and uncanny images through the trope of multiple vanishing points – from those of the subject, contained in the narrator's striking instructions of overwhelming indifference, to the filmic insistence on the vanishing points of spatial perspective that recur in the obsessive tracking movements of the mobile camera and the intertextual presence of other images within the apartment. The crisis of the subject in Perec's city is mapped in terms of the embrace and resistance of disappearance.

Perec's writing is often associated with the infra-ordinary, a recovery of the forgotten granular texture of the everyday, but **Douglas Smith** studies the ways in which he was also interested in totalisation, the attempt to produce a comprehensive model of social reality. As a result, his work in fact operates across a wide range of scales, from microscopic description to globe-trotting meta-narrative. The chapter explores how it is this cross-scalar dimension of Perec's writing that represents a challenge to the Gaullist 'politique de la grandeur' of the 1960s and early 1970s. The chapters of *Species of Spaces* apparently propose a hierarchised spatial taxonomy, working outwards from the bounded page to the limitless universe. However, Perec develops his own politics of scale, one based not on the privileging of a particular scale such as the nation-state or the infra-ordinary, but rather on a more fundamental disturbance of the notion of scale itself.

Starting with Perec's early Marxist-leaning contributions to *Partisan*, **Anna-Louise Milne** argues that he turns unfailingly towards language and literature to activate the 'dispersive' or re-signifying potential that will counteract the abstractions of capital and the forms it takes in our lived environments. Conceived as 'a bridge between the world and ourselves', literature finds its force at the surface of signification, but this surface crucially opens up new itineraries through the material world. The chapter explores how this happens with particular reference to how Perec engages with the topographies of terror that spread across the landscape of Nazi Germany and beyond, plotting in this way a continuity between his early essays, focused on post-war literature, and his 'spatial turn' of the early 1970s.

Amanda Crawley Jackson takes as her starting point three case studies from the Perecquian corpus: the imaginary island of W (in *W ou le souvenir d'enfance*); Ellis Island (*Récits d'Ellis Island*); and the Parisian *îlots insalubres* (usually translated as 'unhealthy zones', but more literally, small islands – or islets – of insalubrity) that dominated French planning discourse from the late nineteenth century right through the Fourth Republic. The chapter argues that around these major islands, and through a series of textual and historical allusions, Perec constellates a broader carceral archipelago, made up of dispersed yet interconnected island territories that are located in multiple space-times. It concludes by exploring the ways in which Perec's archipelagic topographies can be seen to speak both to the networks of power that subtend the organisation of the modern world, but also to the ongoing manifestations of the past in the 'colonial present'.

Perec's geographies take different spatial forms: from material spaces such as streets, buildings, rooms and desks to metaphorical and representational spaces such as the stage and the page. The latter come together in **Christopher Hall**'s chapter on Perec's radio plays. Hall reflects upon his own experiences of staging two of Perec's radio plays: 'The Machine' (*Die Maschine*) and *The Raise* (*L'Augmentation*). Presenting these works, he was forced to confront a series of spatial challenges, in particular: interpreting the layout and typesetting of the script, the work as it appears on the page and adapting radio plays to three-dimensional spaces of performance on the stage. This chapter describes experiences of translating Perec from page to stage, reflecting upon the inherent differences, similarities and paradoxes involved in delivering his work to an audience.

This book goes on, in Part II, to explore 'Perecquian geographies' in a range of material and metaphorical forms and through a variety of disciplines, practices and media. This section begins with an exploration of Perecquian soundscapes by **Alasdair Pettinger.** In the texts he published as part of his *Lieux* project, Perec dwells on what he sees rather than what he hears. Given that one of his objectives was to test the limits of conventional empirical description – to record what is generally not noticed or noted – Pettinger notes it is curious that Perec pays so little attention to sound. His chapter reveals the ways in which Perec clearly thought of his work as extending beyond written documents, embracing 'other sorts of description' including the cinematographic and the radiophonic. Pettinger argues that the use of sound – and silence – suggests that Perec's soundscapes are more varied and extensive than they might at first appear. He also explores some of the questions and possibilities opened up by this body of work by examining several Perecquian soundscapes – field recordings or sonic artworks which show the signs of Perec's influence, ranging from the playful to the ethnological.

Oliver Bray explores the generative possibilities of constraint within Perecquian performance through his Oulipian theatrical work, *The Elision of Scaff*. He describes the translation – inherent in theatre work – from differently constrained spaces: from the two-dimensional, words-on-a-page flatness to the three-dimensional space of live performance. The latter, he finds, is a messy landscape, occupied by a most ineffable and unruly inhabitant, the live performer.

The next chapter, by **Leslie Satin**, addresses Perec's ways of understanding and experiencing the world from the perspective of dance. The analysis emerges from the writer's own work as a dance practitioner and scholar. In particular, Satin considers a Perecquian approach to spatial attention within the frame of an embodied spatial *practice*: an ongoing, contingent process joining the spaces of the body, and the sensations through which we experience them, to their external environments: streets, studios, stages, and the people sharing them. As such, Satin explores ways that dance is like and unlike writing – such as Perec's – in terms of being, at once, act and artefact: embodied practices of observation, recollection, reflection and transformation.

David Matless's chapter opens with a series of descriptions of places in Norfolk which formed part of the author's *The Regional Book* (2015). Matless goes on to reflect on the writing of that book and the way in which the work of Georges Perec, among others, shaped its forms of geographical description. Perec's injunction in *Species of Spaces* to 'Force yourself to see more flatly' acts as a motto for the book, in part playing on the very flat landscape of the Norfolk Broads, with which *The Regional Book* is concerned, but also suggesting a virtue in cutting across styles of seeing that claim conventional, hierarchical authority. The chapter considers the context in which *The Regional Book* was produced and the ways in which the work of Perec and others shaped its form.

Daryl Martin reads Georges Perec alongside a writer from outside Perec's immediate sphere – Jonathan Meades – whose work exhibits similar interests in landscape, biography and space. This 'eccentric' comparative reading offers new insights into each of these writers and also into the themes they explored. It emerges that the *oeuvres* of Meades and Perec share significant affinities and techniques for rendering a sense of place: their propensities for lists and classificatory strategies, and their descriptions of landscapes through an intense focus on their material cultures. Substantively, their work makes a persuasive argument for retaining a fictitious approach in apprehending urban environments, in order to puncture the contemporary and historical myths they help to shape.

Perec had a rich and playful relationship with visual material in his novels and essays. **Ian Trowell** argues that photographs and photography have languished on the margins of Perecquian scholarship and practice. His chapter brings them into focus, exploring the place of photography in Perec's writing and in Perecquian fieldwork, and fleshing these out through a Perecquian field project: an investigation of travelling fairgrounds. Trowell presents a symbiotic relationship between Perecquian fieldwork and photography, which encompasses: recording the seen; seeing flatly and self-reflexively; and shifting the field of photography with a Perecquian impetus.

In another experiment in Perecquian photography, **Joanne Lee** uses the camera to 'see more flatly' and explore what Perec and his collaborators in *Cause Commune* called the infra-ordinary. Lee argues that photography is well attuned to seeing flatly because it translates dimensional space into the flat plane of the picture and focuses upon the 'surfaces of the world'. Lee's photo essay explores the 12-minute walk from her home to the tram stop on her daily commute, in what she calls the visual essaying of the surface of a place.

Kevin Boniface's chapter includes scenes from his postal round in Huddersfield, a town in northern England. Boniface brings a Perecquian quality of attention both to his postal round – to ways in which he sees and experiences the streets, paths, houses and flats on his early-morning walk – and to the ways in which he documents these quotidian geographies. In this chapter, Boniface intersperses quotations from Perec's observations of the streets of Paris with his own notes on Huddersfield. Taking Perec's advice – 'Force yourself to write down what is of no interest, what is of most interest, what is most obvious, most common, most colourless' – Boniface finds his eyes opened to things that others have failed to notice: asphalt (see the front cover of this book, which is based on a photograph taken by Boniface on his postal round), Haribo wrappers, footballs, wheelie bins … . Unlearning some of the judgement and discrimination, which structure everyday experiences of place, Boniface shows how it is possible to see the world afresh.

Notes

1. Perec, *Species of Spaces*, 136.
2. Perec, *Species of Spaces*, 91.
3. Perec, *Species of Spaces*, 220–1.
4. Perec, *Species of Spaces*, 13.
5. Perec, *Species of Spaces*, 13.
6. Perec, *Life,* 288.
7. Perec, *Life*, 290.
8. Perec, *Species of Spaces*, 79.
9. Bellos, *Georges Perec*, 492.
10. Perec, *Species of Spaces*, 210.
11. Bellos, *Georges Perec*, 418. Original emphasis.
12. Perec was talking impromptu. A more accurate reflection of the structure of his book would be: Georges Perec, the stairwell, the house, the street, the city …
13. Perec, *Entretiens et conférences*, Volume 2, 204.
14. Phillips, 'Georges Perec's Experimental Fieldwork', 171–91.
15. Perec, *Species of Spaces,* 50.
16. Forsdick, 'De la plume comme des pieds', 45–60.
17. Baillehache, 'L' Oulipo et la traduction moderniste', 279–90; Collombat, 'L'Oulipo du traducteur', 19; and Schilling, 'Translation as Total Social Fact and Scholarly Pursuit', 841–5.
18. Bloomfield, Galvin and Ruiz, 'Acts de fundación de l'Outranspo', 985–92.
19. James, 'Interlingual Oulipo', 864–76.
20. Baillehache, 'Traduire la littérature à contraintes' ('Translating constrained literature: Translation or transposition?'), 892–904.
21. Bellos, 'Mathematics, Poetry, Fiction', 104–18.
22. Despeaux, 'Oulipo', 238–47.
23. Berkman, 'Digital Oulipo'.
24. Gratton and Sheringham, 'Introduction', 1–30.

Bibliography

Baillehache, Jonathan. 'L'Oulipo et la traduction moderniste', *Formules* 16 (2012): 279–90.

Baillehache, Jonathan. 'Traduire la littérature à contraintes: Traduction ou transposition?', *Modern Language Notes* 131, no. 4 (2016): 892–904.

Bellos, David. *Georges Perec: A Life in Words*. London: Harvill, 1993.

Bellos, David. 'Mathematics, Poetry, Fiction: The Adventure of the Oulipo', *BSHM Bulletin: Journal of the British Society for the History of Mathematics* 25, no. 2 (2010): 104–18.

Berkman, Natalie. 'Digital Oulipo: Programming Potential Literature', *DHQ: Digital Humanities Quarterly* 11, no. 3 (2017). Accessed 6 June 2019. http://digitalhumanities.org/dhq/vol/11/3/000325/000325.html

Bloomfield, Camille, Rachel Galvin and Pablo Martín Ruiz. 'Acts de fundación de l'Outranspo', *Modern Language Notes* 131, no. 4 (2016): 985–92.

Collombat, Isabelle. 'L'Oulipo du traducteur', *Semen: Revue de sémio-linguistique des textes et discours* 19 (2005). Accessed 3 May 2019. https://journals.openedition.org/semen/2143.

Despeaux, Sloan Evans. 'Oulipo: Applying Mathematical Constraints to Literature and the Arts in a Mathematics for the Liberal Arts Classroom', *PRIMUS* 25, no. 3 (2015): 238–47.

Forsdick, Charles. 'De la plume comme des pieds: The Essay as a Peripatetic Genre'. In *The Modern Essay in French: Movement, Instability, Performance*, edited by Charles Forsdick and Andrew Stafford, 45–60. Bern: Peter Lang, 2005.

Gratton, Johnnie and Michael Sheringham. 'Introduction: Tracking the Art of the Project: History, Theory, Practice'. In *The Art of the Project: Projects and Experiments in Modern French Culture*, edited by Johnnie Gratton and Michael Sheringham, 1–30. New York: Berghahn Books, 2005.

James, Alison. 'Interlingual Oulipo', *Modern Language Notes* 131, no. 4 (2016): 864–76.

Perec, Georges. *W ou le souvenir d'enfance*. Paris: Denoël, 1975.

Perec, Georges. *Life: A User's Manual*, translated by David Bellos. London: Collins Harvill, 1987.

Perec, Georges. *W, or The Memory of Childhood*, translated by David Bellos. London: Collins Harvill, 1988.

Perec, Georges. *Things: A Story of the Sixties*, translated by David Bellos. London: Collins Harvill, 1990.

Perec, Georges. 'Scene in Italie', translated by Andrew Leak, *AA Files* 45/46 (2001): 34–41.

Perec, Georges. 'Glances at Gaîté', translated by Andrew Leak, *AA Files* 45/46 (2001): 43–53.

Perec, Georges. *Entretiens et conférences, Volume 2: 1979–1981: Édition critique établie par Dominique Bertelli et Mireille Ribière*. Nantes: Joseph K., 2003.

Perec, Georges. *Species of Spaces and Other Pieces*, edited and translated by John Sturrock. London: Penguin Books, 2008 [1997].

Perec, Georges. *A Void*, translated by Gilbert Adair. London: Vintage Books, 2008.

Perec, Georges. *Portrait of a Man Known as Il Condottiere*, translated by David Bellos. Chicago: University of Chicago Press, 2014.

Perec, Georges. *An Attempt at Exhausting a Place in Paris*, translated by Marc Lowenthal. Cambridge, MA: Wakefield Press, 2010.

Phillips, Richard. 'Georges Perec's Experimental Fieldwork: Perecquian Fieldwork', *Social and Cultural Geography* 19, no. 2 (2018): 171–91.

Schilling, Derek. *Mémoires du quotidien: les lieux de Perec*. Villeneuve: Septentrion, 2006.

Schilling, Derek. 'Translation as Total Social Fact and Scholarly Pursuit', *Modern Language Notes* 131, no. 4 (2016): 841–45.

Part I
Perec's geographies

2
The mapping of loss

Andrew Leak

On the first page of Perec's *Species of Spaces* we are presented with nothing, or almost nothing: a square enclosing a blank space and a rubric underneath reading 'Figure 1: Map of the Ocean (Taken from Lewis Carroll's *Hunting of the Snark*)'. But this 'Map of the Ocean' is not accurately quoted from Carroll's famous ballad. Carroll's map is called 'Ocean-Chart' and appears on the second page of 'Fit the Second: The Bellman's Speech'. The text surrounding it reads:

> He had bought a large map representing the sea,
> Without the least vestige of land:
> And the crew were much pleased when they found it to be
> A map they could all understand.
> [...]
> 'Other maps are such shapes, with their islands and capes!
> But we've got our brave Captain to thank'
> (So the crew would protest) 'that he's bought *us* the best—
> A perfect and absolute blank!'[1]

Perec's 'quotation' is inaccurate in at least two respects. First, it omits the nonsensical topographic labels framing the Bellman's map. Second, while Carroll's map is an oblong reproducing the proportions of the page on which it is printed, Perec's is a precisely drawn square. If we assume this was a deliberate choice on Perec's part, what does it signify? What is immediately clear is that it resists *orientation* much more radically than does Carroll's oblong. The square has a top and a bottom, a left and a right, simply by virtue of being represented on the page of a book and provided with a caption, but if one were to hold in one's hand the object represented (a square of blank paper), it would provide no clue as to its orientation: rotated four times through 90 degrees, it remains defiantly identical to itself. Neither would there be anything to indicate its recto and verso.

Perec's 'Map of the Ocean' is, then, much more radically blank than Carroll's 'Ocean-Chart'. For all that, the Bellman's map does not prove any more helpful than Perec's when it comes to the practical business of navigation. The space represented by the Bellman's map, despite its cardinal points, turns out to be a space of bewildering *disorientation*. Or, more precisely, a space of reversal where left becomes right and back becomes front:

> This was charming, no doubt: but they shortly found out
> That the captain they trusted so well
> Had only one notion for crossing the ocean,
> And that was to tinkle his bell.
> He was thoughtful and grave—but the orders he gave
> Were enough to bewilder a crew.
> When he cried, 'Steer to starboard, but keep her head larboard!'
> What on earth was the helmsman to do?
> Then the bowsprit got mixed with the rudder sometimes:
> A thing, as the Bellman remarked,
> That frequently happens in tropical climes,
> When a vessel is, so to speak, 'snarked'.[2]

I should like to appropriate this term, 'snarked', to refer to certain kinds of space commonly encountered in the work of Perec. The most general property of these spaces is that they are resistant to *sens*, in both senses of that word: direction and meaning. To enter such a space is to be condemned to a desperate wandering, returning always to the same point of departure; or, in terms of the search for meaning, to be adrift in a fruitless divagation that never reaches the *terra firma* of certitude. This could take the form of a rhetoric of deferral:

> I write: I write …
> I write: 'I write …'
> I write that I write …
> etc.

Or perhaps the space which captivates the subject located between two facing mirrors.[3]

It should be noted that the problem here is not necessarily an absence of meaning/direction: it could also be an *excess* – which raises the question of whether Perec's 'Map of the Ocean' is a map of nothing or of everything; and a further question: can nothing and everything be functionally identical?

As I said, these paradoxical spaces of reversal are encountered frequently in the work of Georges Perec. In this chapter, I shall examine related occurrences in three works dating from a short period in the 1970s. These texts all arise from the psychoanalysis that Perec undertook with Jean-Bertrand Pontalis from May 1971 to June 1975. *Species of Spaces* was published in 1974 and its composition is indicated as 'Paris 1973–1974'; *W, or The Memory of Childhood* was published in 1975, having been composed 'Paris-Carros-Blévy 1970–1974'; 'Backtracking' was published in the journal *Cause Commune* in 1977. The first two texts, then, emerged from the midst of that psychoanalysis whereas the third brought the perspective of hindsight, even if, as Perec himself remarked, the actual duration of the analysis was not limited by its start and end dates.[4]

I shall begin, appropriately enough, with the account of a shipwreck.

W, or The Memory of Childhood is a composite text: most visibly, it consists of 19 chapters presented in italic type, alternating with 18 chapters in roman type.[5] The italic text begins as a kind of adventure story in the manner of Jules Verne and is divided into two parts. It had already been serialised in the *Quinzaine Littéraire* between October 1969 and August 1970. Perec first began work on the roman font chapters in 1971, set them aside, then picked them up and completed them in 1974. The roman font chapters are an attempted childhood autobiography – albeit one that commences with the unpromising assertion 'I have no childhood memories'.[6] The work of *assemblage* carried out by Perec in 1974 involved 'stitching' the autobiographical chapters into the pre-existing adventure story.[7] The title itself suggests that the memory of childhood is to be found neither in the sparse collection of faulty recollections and transparent phantasies that make up the overtly autobiographical chapters, nor in the italic text, but in their multiple intersections.

The first-person narrator of Part I of the italic text – Gaspard Winckler – is living under a pseudonym given to him by a network providing support to deserters. Out of the blue he is approached by a representative of that network – one Otto Apfelstahl – and persuaded to set off in search of the person whose name, or identity, he had assumed. That person, it transpires, was an eight-year-old child suffering from a deaf-mutism that 'could only be ascribed to some infantile trauma'.[8]

Having tried everything else, his mother decides that a round-the-world trip on a yacht – the *Sylvandre* –[9] might have a therapeutic effect: perhaps 'new horizons, changes of climate and tempo'[10] would set in train a process allowing him to regain his speech and his hearing. But the journey does not go well: 'The voyage, intended to be a cure, progressively loses its *raison d'être*; it becomes increasingly obvious that it is a useless undertaking, but neither is there any point in bringing it to an end.'[11]

It is not that the waters over which the *Sylvandre* yaws and tacks are uncharted, or that the crew do not possess the relevant charts and maps – rather, the maps are inexplicably set aside in favour of a random wandering: 'The boat wanders before the wind, from one shore to another, from port to port [...].'[12] Until one day, off Tierra del Fuego, it is hit by a cyclone and sinks. When the coastguards arrive on the scene, they find only the broken bodies of the crew. But the child Gaspard is not among them: could he, by some miracle, have survived the catastrophe? The adult Winckler is dispatched by Apfelstahl to Tierra del Fuego to search for the lost child whose name he bears, but what map could assist Winckler in his quest?

Empty maps are referred to in the opening chapter of *W*. We assume that the anonymous third-person narrator of Part II of the italic text is indeed the adult Winckler recounting what he found when he went to search for the lost child. He did not find him, but he found instead the unspeakable horror of the Olympian island of W. That place figures on no map: 'For years I sought out traces of my history, looking up maps and directories and piles of archives. I found nothing.'[13] If Winckler found nothing it is not because W did not exist, or had never existed, but because it is by nature *unmappable*: it exists outside of time and space. That much is suggested by the strikingly odd use of tenses at the opening of the first chapter of Part II (the beginning of the description of the island) – tenses which simultaneously assert the existence of that place and undercut that assertion with doubt: 'Far away, at the other end of the earth, there is an island told of. Its name is W.'[14]

The parallels between the meandering would-be therapeutic journey of the *Sylvandre* and a psychoanalytic cure are hopefully clear enough. So, too, the metaphorical dimensions of the story of the adult Gaspard Winckler who sets out to search for the lost child whose name he bears. As Catherine Clément remarks, 'Georges Perec does not say much about his periods in analysis. But *W* is a precise summary [*relevé*] of them.'[15] What this means is not only that the material (memories, fantasies) presented in the roman font chapters of *W* was in all probability the same material that was endlessly rehashed in the course of the analysis, but also that the interpretations of it provided by Perec were probably part of the analytic material as well.

The *content* of that analysis is unknowable – precisely because what was said was heard only by the person for whom it was intended.[16] But we could choose as our point of entry what, by definition, lies at the centre of any psychoanalytic investigation: namely, the relation with the parental couple. In Chapter EIGHT of *W*, Perec recounts a 'pilgrimage' (*pèlerinage*) to his father's grave in Nogent-sur-Seine. Among the mass of conflicting emotions, he feels 'something like a secret serenity connected to the rooting [*ancrage*] in space, to this writing [*encrage*] on the cross, to this death which had at last ceased to be abstract'.[17] This passage connects doubly with the maritime catastrophe of the *Sylvandre*: first, through the textual *suture* of Angus Pilgrim and 'pilgrimage' (*pèlerinage* in French); second, through the use of the maritime term *ancrage* – which is replaced by a more terrestrial metaphor (rooting) in the English translation.

The contrast, a few pages later, between the grave of the father and the disappearance of the mother could not be more stark: 'My mother has no grave.'[18]

The death – or perhaps the possibility of ghostly survival – of the father is controlled and localised: 'As if the discovery of this tiny patch of earth had at last put a boundary around [*clôturait*] that death.'[19] The fact that his father is somewhere prevents him from being everywhere. But no such (en)closure exists regarding the death of the mother. As Catherine Clément reminds us, Perec's mother was not even buried: 'When one knows nothing – not the time, nor the day, nor the place – and only the sky serves as a grave, when there only remain empty places in the eyes of the millions who perished there [i.e. in Auschwitz], then that is disappearance. It is unbearable.'[20]

The mere presence of a name on a cross gives substance to the affirmation 'Your father *is* dead'.[21] But could not the absence of a cross, and the absence of a name give rise to the unspoken fantasy: 'your mother is *not dead*'. (I insist here on the semantic distinction between '*is* not dead' and 'is *not dead*'.)

Chapter EIGHT of *W* effectively maintains the separation between the father and the mother: it reproduces a text on each, written 'more than fifteen years ago'. But the parental couple is reunited at the very end of the chapter in the much-quoted long final paragraph. This comes as Perec reflects on just how unpromising the two texts he has just reproduced are for the purposes of psychoanalysis:

> It would be quite pointless to hunt down my slip [...] Or to comb my sentences for, and obviously locate straight away, soppy little

> echoes of the Oedipus complex, or castration, for all I shall ever find in my very reiteration is the final refraction of a voice that is absent from writing, the scandal of their silence and mine.[22]

The meaning of this appears to be obvious enough until one stops to reflect on precisely what is meant by the word 'silence' in the quoted passage. The voice that is 'absent from writing' can only be his own – as if writing were something one does to *avoid* speaking, or 'giving voice' to. More puzzling is the reference to the 'scandalous' quality of the silences evoked here – the silence of his parents and his own silence. His parents are silent because they cannot speak, but he *is*, apparently, speaking: the verb 'say' (*dire*) is used four times in this paragraph, precisely to mark the contrast with writing (*écrire*). If, then, he is in some sense silent, even as he speaks, why is *his* silence deemed to be 'scandalous'? There are two possible answers to that question, depending on two senses of the noun *scandale*: first, the moral outrage of speaking precisely in order *not* to say; second, the noisy quality of the silence thus produced: the secondary sense of the word *scandale* in French is 'outcry', 'fuss' or 'racket', leading us to the oxymoron of a 'loud silence'.

I shall return to this notion presently, when I come to discuss 'Backtracking' in more detail. For now, we should note that silence figures strongly both at the start and at the end of *W*. In Chapter ONE, the adult Winckler evokes the destruction of the monstrous dystopia he has seen and to which he must now bear witness: 'What my eyes had seen had really happened: the lianas had unseated the foundations, the forest had consumed the houses; sand overran the stadiums, cormorants swooped down in their thousands, and then silence, sudden icy silence.'[23] Near the end of the book, in Chapter THIRTY-THREE, Perec recounts a visit to the cinema in Villard to see a film called *Le grand silence blanc* (The Great White Silence). Rather than a film about the Klondike, huskies and hardy explorers – as his cousin Henri had promised – it turns out to be a biopic of the French Catholic missionary Charles de Foucauld; and the great white desert is not the Arctic but the Sahara. But the film Perec describes is actually called *L'appel du silence* (The Call of Silence), not *Le grand silence blanc*.[24] Leaving aside the reason for this 'mistake', I should like simply to retain the connection established between 'white/blank' and 'silence', and to follow that connection into 'Backtracking'.

The scene of the analysis is the consulting room of the analyst, and that room has at least two important particularities. The first is that – like the 'Ocean-Chart' where we began – it is a *framed* space. Talking of the rituals that surround the analysis ('The same movements, the same gestures were repeated exactly, identically'[25]), he describes their function as 'to put a frame of space and time around that unending discourse of which, in the course of sessions, over months, and years, I was going to try to take possession and in which I was going to seek to recognise myself and to give myself a name'.[26] The second particularity is that what this spatial and temporal framing encloses is, in fact, a *non-place* and a *non-time*. On the face of it, the place where the analysand finds himself is perfectly mappable:

> I was in Paris, in a neighbourhood I knew well, in a street I had even lived in once, a few yards from my favourite bar and several familiar restaurants, and I could have played at working out my longitude, latitude, altitude, and orientation (my head was west by north-west, my feet facing east by south-east).[27]

But the *space of analysis* has no coordinates – neither spatial nor temporal; it is: 'a stationary time in an implausible space'.[28]

The paradox is that for something to *take place* there must first be established, or framed, a non-place and a non-time – as if what takes place can only take place within that frame. Before going any further it is perhaps worth stressing the connection between this 'implausible space' (of analysis) and the place that is discovered by Winckler's quest: the unmapped island of W. Both are 'implausible' because they cannot accommodate the event – if we understand by 'event' a singularity whose occurrence can be plotted against the axes of place and time. But what 'takes place' in analysis cannot even be defined in language:

> For years you think that talking means finding, discovering, understanding, understanding at last, being illuminated by the truth. But it doesn't. When it comes, all you know only is that it has come; it's there, you're talking, you're writing. [...] It happened one day and I knew it had happened. I would like to be able to say I knew straightaway, but that would not be true. There is no tense to express when it was. It took place, it had taken place, it takes place, it will take place. You knew it already, you know it now.[29]

Likewise, W is a 'thing' that *always already* exists. In an early version of the text, the opening of the first chapter of Part II began thus:

> There is rumoured to be, there will be, there is, at the ends of the earth, an island.
> It is called W [...]

> He will arrive there one day. Perhaps he had been searching for it for weeks, months, years, perhaps he has been circumnavigating it without knowing it was there.[30]

We are not told how Winckler arrives at W, or how he returns to tell the tale; likewise, in the psychoanalysis, what was said, and how it was interpreted, is passed over in silence in 'Backtracking'. In both cases, in the beginning was silence, and blankness. A silence that calls for speech and a blankness that invites inscription: 'So I had to speak – writes Perec – that's what I was there for [...] I had to speak, my speech had to fill this empty space.'[31] But the paradox is that the more he speaks, the less he says: 'I needed to talk, and I had a storehouse, an arsenal of stories, problems, questions, associations, fantasies, puns, memories, hypotheses, explanations, theories, frames of reference, and ways of hiding.'[32] The problem lies both with the nature of the speech being produced and with the intention behind it – that is, who it is addressed to. It transpires that his speech is just another way of remaining silent.

The phenomenon is well known in psychoanalytic literature. In his 'Fonction et champ de la parole et du langage en psychanalyse' (Function and Field of Speech and Language in Psychoanalysis), Jacques Lacan had introduced the terms 'empty speech' (*parole vide*) and 'full speech' (*parole pleine*). Empty speech is speech that does not engage the subject,[33] while full speech is consequential, in that, once it is pronounced, the subject is changed. Empty speech adopts the mode of neutral information, whereas full speech can be heard in what is *not* said, or in what is said apparently incidentally: 'What is redundant as far as information is concerned is precisely what plays the part of resonance in speech. For the function of language in speech is not to inform but to evoke.'[34]

Other analysts have rephrased Lacan's now classic distinction in useful ways. André Green, for example, proposes the term 'narrative-recitative discourse' (*discours narratif-récitatif*) as equivalent to Lacan's empty speech: 'The discourse is bent to the necessity of forming a beautiful whole. Such is the function of the narrative-recitative discourse, which binds the elements of the psychic processes in order to erect a screen between the analyst and the patient.'[35] The appearance in an analysis of this kind of seamless, all-embracing discourse that forms a carapace affording no purchase for interpretation, is a possible sign of resistance.

In 'Backtracking', silence is the inevitable corollary of volubility: 'The words that went through my head flew straight into his head and settled deep inside it, building up over the sessions a neat ball of silence as dense as my speech was hollow, as full as my speech was empty.' But actually falling silent was, if anything, even more painful: 'When I tried to be silent and stop myself from getting stuck in feeble regurgitation or in illusions of the intimation of speech, silence immediately became unbearable.'[36]

Another analyst succinctly summed up the paradox: 'To be enormously talkative is just another way of being a deaf-mute.'[37] And this brings us back round, of course, to the deaf-mute child, Gaspard Winckler, taken on a therapeutic cruise by his mother. The 'talkative' patient is mute in that his words are not addressed to anyone: neither to the analyst who is reduced to the role of answering-machine, nor to himself; and deaf because any possibility of exchange – with himself or with the analyst – has been foreclosed

And yet one day, writes Perec, 'The analyst heard what I had to say to him, what for four years he had listened to without hearing, for the simple reason that I hadn't been telling him, because I wasn't telling it to myself.'[38] In order to understand how that might have come about, we must follow a trail that will lead us back to where we started: namely, to the map.

I would suggest that, at a first level, the 'perfect and absolute blank' represents the space of analysis – not the physical space of the analyst's consulting room, but the framed, metaphorical blank wherein the analysand's voice seeks a response that would be more than just an echo. That space, like the one mapped by the Bellman's 'Ocean-Chart' is 'snarked' – it is a chiasmatic space, a space of reversals and inversions, of meandering and of deferral. It is the kind of space where the discourse of the analysand, yawing and tacking on a featureless ocean, can turn around the object of desire 'for weeks, for months, for years', without even knowing it is there.

From a therapeutic point of view, the patient has to accept being genuinely set adrift, severed from his moorings. That involves recognising that one is lost, and suffering the consequent distress (from Latin *di*, 'apart' and *stringere*, 'to tie tightly'). In Green's terms, that means running the risks attendant upon *déliaison* (unbinding); in Perec's, it means allowing language to play, rather than playing with language. This is why Perec describes what 'took place' in his analysis in the following terms: 'Your mouth opens to speak, your pen is open for writing: something shifted, something shifts and makes a mark, the wavy line of ink on paper with its upstrokes and down.'[39]

At a second, related level, the blank map tells us what it looks like to be lost. It is the mindscape of a subject whose libidinal yearnings have no object to orient them. In a recent essay, the psychoanalyst Adam Phillips wrote this about maps:

> The map tells us that we are already lost; we have maps in the first place because we don't know where there is to get to, and we don't know how to get there. Or, to make the problem rather more domestic, more familiar: if we have been lucky enough to escape the catastrophes of history, we do not need a map to find our parents.[40]

Bearing those remarks in mind, I shall conclude by considering the case of Bartlebooth – the central character of Perec's 1978 masterpiece *Life: A User's Manual*.

Bartlebooth plans to occupy what he imagines will be the last 50 years of his life producing precisely nothing – 'a perfect and absolute blank'. Initially, this project involves painting 500 watercolours of 500 sea-ports scattered across the globe.[41] His itinerary is prepared by his factotum, Smautf, and it involves the gathering of maps: 'The ports were chosen more or less at random by Bartlebooth, who thumbed through atlases, geography books, travellers' tales, and tourist brochures and ticked off the places that appealed to him. Smautf then studied how to get there and find accommodation.'[42] The time allotted for the paintings is 20 years – 20 years, as it happens of global conflict: 1935–55. Yet, if one were to draw a map of Bartlebooth's itinerary, it would bear no trace of the 'catastrophes of history': 'Historical and political circumstances – the Second World War and all the regional conflicts before and after 1939 and 1945 [...] had virtually no influence on their travels.'[43]

Serendipity is a feature of life but not of fiction: to better understand the significance of Bartlebooth's good fortune, we need to look elsewhere in Perec's *oeuvre*. In the first autobiographical chapter of *W, or The Memory of Childhood*, Perec alleges a more or less total blank of prolonged infantile amnesia: '"I have no childhood memories": [...] It was nobody's business to press me on this question. It was not a set topic on my syllabus. I was excused: a different history, History with a capital H, had answered the question in my stead: the war, the camps.'[44] When one knows that Perec's father had been killed at the front and that his mother had been murdered in Auschwitz, that formula – 'the war, the camps' – translates quite simply as: 'the father, the mother'.

Viewed in this way, the map of Bartlebooth's peregrinations is a map that bears no trace of the father and the mother. Or rather, it is a map of their absence.

Bartlebooth's dilatory, meandering itinerary that so uncannily enabled him to circumnavigate the catastrophes of History eventually leads him 'home' – even if he has to die in order to reach there. The puzzle he is attempting to solve when he dies depicts 'a little port in the Dardanelles at the mouth of the river the Ancient Greeks called the Maiandros, the Meander'.[45] In Greek mythology, Maiandros was one of the sons of Oceanus (the 'father of everything') and Tethys (a Titan daughter of Uranus and Gaia). In reaching the ocean, Maiandros is finally reunited with his parents. His tortuous itinerary may have delayed his homecoming, but he must finally return to the parental couple.

Unlike his parents, Perec did escape (at least directly) the catastrophes of History, but not intact. Unlike them, he survived, but his whole work was a means of transforming a catastrophic loss of bearings into a bearable loss – about finding a way to live rather than merely survive.

Notes

1. Carroll, *The Annotated Hunting of the Snark,* 27.
2. Carroll, *The Annotated Hunting of the Snark*, 29.
3. Perec, *Species of Spaces*, 9. The figure of opposing mirrors appears elsewhere in Perec: in the film he made with Bernard Queysanne in 1973 of his 1967 novel *A Man Asleep*, for example, or in 'The Scene of a Flight', 106–7.
4. Perec, 'Backtracking', 52.
5. The alternation is not perfect: there is a roman font chapter 'missing' between chapters XI and XII, or ELEVEN and TWELVE in the English translation.
6. Perec, *W*, 6.
7. Magné, 'Les sutures dans *W ou le souvenir d'enfance*'. These *sutures* are deliberate echoes between the italic and roman texts.
8. Perec, *W*, 23. Perec gives the name Gaspard Winckler to two other characters in his work: the forger who is the protagonist and first-person narrator of his first completed novel, *Le Condottiere*; and the puzzle-maker of *Life*.
9. The name of the yacht, as well as being borrowed from Raymond Roussel, is an example of 'suture', being a composite of the names of Perec's parents: Cécile and André.
10. Perec, *W*, 23.
11. Perec, *W*, 24.
12. Perec, *W*, 24.
13. Perec, *W*, 3.
14. Perec, *W*, 65. The nuances of the original French are hard to render: 'Il y aurait, là-bas, à l'autre bout du monde, une île. Elle s'appelle W.' Perec, *W ou le souvenir d'enfance*, 89.
15. Clément, 'Auschwitz ou la disparition', 16. My translation.
16. And that despite the fact that Perec's analyst discussed his 'case', albeit using pseudonyms, in no fewer than eight texts. See Burgelin, *Les parties de dominos chez Monsieur Lefèvre*, 95–128.
17. Perec, *W*, 38.
18. Perec, *W*, 41.
19. Perec, *W*, 38.
20. Clément, 'Auschwitz', 90. My translation.
21. Perec, *W*, 38. Original emphasis.
22. Perec, *W*, 42.
23. Perec, *W*, 4.
24. Bellos, 'Les "erreurs historiques"', 21–46.

25. Perec, 'Backtracking', 54.
26. Perec, 'Backtracking', 54–5.
27. Perec, 'Backtracking', 53.
28. Perec, 'Backtracking', 52.
29. Perec, 'Backtracking', 51.
30. Quoted in Lejeune, *La mémoire et l'oblique*, 109. The 'weeks, months, years' bring to mind the 'two or three times a week for four years' during which Perec immersed himself in the 'implausible space' of analysis.
31. Perec, 'Backtracking', 49.
32. Perec, 'Backtracking', 56.
33. 'But beneath the ephemeral flashes of verbal collisions [...] my voice encountered only its own emptiness. It did not engage with the faint echo of my own past or with the clouded turbulence of my affrontable enemies.' Perec, 'Backtracking', 49.
34. Lacan, 'Fonction et champ de la parole et du langage en psychanalyse', 247.
35. Green, *Narcissisme de vie,* 67. My translation.
36. Perec, 'Backtracking', 58. The parallels with Green are striking: 'Silence plays a symmetrical role [to volubility]. Thus, one could say that discourse and silence each perform in their own way the same task. A heavy, thick silence produces a feeling of opacity and impenetrability. Seamless.' Green, *Narcissisme de vie*, 67. My translation. The similarities are perhaps not coincidental. Green's article was originally published in Pontalis's *Nouvelle Revue de Psychanalyse* in 1976 – the year before 'Backtracking'. We know that Perec and his circle read the *NRP*. Indeed, he even published a piece in it (No. 16, 1977). That same issue contained articles by André Green and Catherine Clément, and was jointly edited by two of Perec's previous analysts: Michel de M'Uzan and Pontalis himself.
37. Viderman, 'Le temps du silence', 216.
38. Perec, 'Backtracking', 61.
39. Perec, 'Backtracking', 51. The original reads 'quelque chose de plein et de *délié*'. Perec, *Penser/Classer*, 62. My emphasis.
40. Phillips, *On Balance*, 162. I would like to thank Jessica Dubow for bringing this essay to my attention.
41. It would be more accurate to say 500 perfect and absolute blanks: once painted, the watercolours are made into jigsaw puzzles that Bartlebooth would take 20 years reconstructing, after which they are separated from their support, returned to their place of origin, and washed clean in the sea.
42. Perec, *Life*, 52.
43. Perec, *Life*, 55.
44. Perec, *W*, 6.
45. Perec, *Life*, 493.

Filmography

The Man Who Sleeps/Un homme qui dort (France, 1974, Queysanne)

Bibliography

Bellos, David. *Georges Perec: A Life in Words*. London: Harvill, 1993.

Bellos, David. 'Les "erreurs historiques" dans *W ou le souvenir d'enfance* à la lumière du manuscrit de Stockholm', *Etudes Romanes* 46 (2000): 21–46.

Burgelin, Claude. *Les parties de dominos chez Monsieur Lefèvre: Perec avec Freud, Perec contre Freud*. Strasbourg: Circé, 1996.

Carroll, Lewis. *The Annotated Hunting of the Snark*, edited by Martin Gardner. New York: W.W. Norton and Company, 2006.

Clément, Catherine. 'Auschwitz, ou la disparition', *L'Arc* 76 (1979): 87–90.

Green, André. *Narcissisme de vie, narcissisme de mort*. Paris: Éditions de Minuit, 1983.
Lacan, Jacques. 'Fonction et champ de la parole et du langage en psychanalyse'. In *Écrits I*, 111–208. Paris: Éditions du Seuil, 1966.
Lejeune, Philippe. *La mémoire et l'oblique: Georges Perec autobiographe*. Paris: P.O.L., 1991.
Magné, Bernard. 'Les sutures dans *W ou le souvenir d'enfance*', *Textuel* 21 (1988): 39–55.
Perec, Georges. *W ou le souvenir d'enfance*. Paris: Denoël, 1975.
Perec, Georges. *Espèces d'espaces*. Paris: Éditions Galilée, 1985.
Perec, Georges. *Life: A User's Manual*, translated by David Bellos. London: Collins Harvill, 1987.
Perec, Georges. *W, or The Memory of Childhood*, translated by David Bellos. London: Collins Harvill, 1988.
Perec, Georges. *Species of Spaces and Other Pieces*, edited and translated by John Sturrock. London: Penguin Books, 2008.
Perec, Georges. 'The Scene of a Flight'. In *Species of Spaces and Other Pieces*, edited and translated by John Sturrock, 103–12. London: Penguin Books, 2008.
Perec, Georges. 'Backtracking'. In *Thoughts of Sorts*, translated by David Bellos, 49–61. Boston: David R. Godine, 2009.
Perec, Georges. *Things: A Story of the Sixties, with A Man Asleep*, translated by David Bellos and Andrew Leak. London: Vintage Books, 2011.
Phillips, Adam. *On Balance*. London: Hamish Hamilton, 2010.
Viderman, Serge. 'Le temps du silence', *Nouvelle Revue de Psychanalyse* 20 (1979): 215–32.

3
'Entre Frence et Engleterre': Toponyms and the poetics of reference in Perec's fiction

Derek Schilling

> From Palais-Royal to Saint-Germain-des-Prés, from Champ-de-Mars to the Champs-Elysées, from the Luxembourg Gardens to Montparnasse, from Ile Saint-Louis to the Marais, from Place des Ternes to Place de l'Opéra, from the Madeleine to the Monceau Gardens, the whole of Paris was a perpetual temptation.[1]

Placed at the crossroads of linguistics and geography, the place name ranks among those elements that writers of fiction can ill do without. Whether borrowed from existing nomenclatures or forged anew, toponyms authenticate story events by anchoring them in a world that is knowable to the extent that it can be named. In a manner akin to the names of historical figures, events and institutions, of trademarked products or the titles of artworks, these linguistic markers bolster the 'referential illusion' that was the great love affair of the nineteenth century, a legacy that modernist and post-modernist writers never liquidated in full. Indeed, even that most experimentally minded and adventurous of fictions, that of French polymath Georges Perec (1936–82) who is our focus here, turns on the capacity of toponyms to render a story world legible relative to an accepted world of reference. Perec's unfailingly playful fiction prompts us to ask 'What's in a (place) name?' and what insights might a poetics attentive to the toponym as referential anchor and site of reverie bring to our understanding of the workings of literary language?

Toponyms exert an unusually strong mimetic pull upon readers. As scholar of literary onomastics Yves Baudelle has written, 'remove all the toponyms from a novel, and one sees that it's easier to conceive of a story lacking any character names than a narrative that is completely delocalised.'[2] The logic of fiction all but requires that story events *take place*; some manner of localisation seems a condition for the success of the imaginative transaction that is storytelling. Chief among the native powers of the place name is its resolute economy. Unlike the extended passages of description which Philippe Hamon associates with discursive 'luxury,' grammatical subordination and coordination,[3] the toponym is a free-standing sign capable of instantiating a set of story existents far more extensive than the 'dot on the map' to which it is conventionally tethered.[4] A constellation of place names can activate, via synecdoche, a complex topographical *Gestalt* that lends the diegetic world specific ideological and historico-cultural content.

To this first function of referential anchoring is conjoined a second. As a verbal signifier the toponym carries associated meanings: 'Names themselves have a content inseparable from the qualities of their syllables and from the free associations in which they participate,' writes Gilles Deleuze in his noted essay on Proust.[5] Its morphology, phonemes or letters make it poetic in the strong sense: it speaks *as a name*. It fosters onomastic reverie, cutting through strata of etymology and phonology now foreign, now familiar. This expressive potential is particularly acute when no real-world referent exists, as in the case of Orsenna and Farghestan in Julien Gracq's *The Opposing Shore* (1951) or of S. Thala, T. Beach and U. Bridge in Marguerite Duras' *The Ravishing of Lol V. Stein* (1964). In this respect, place names in narrative fiction are facts of language firstly, and geographical markers secondarily. Seeming to resist Saul Kripke's[6] notion of the proper name as a 'rigid designator', that is, the proper name as purely referential and non-descriptive, they stir Cratylian longings for a truly proper name that would evoke properties intrinsic to its object; this is a contradistinction to Hermogenes' competing thesis of language as local convention.[7]

These referential and poetic functions are but two sides of the same linguistic coin. In practice, reading flits between comparisons of textual data with what geopoetician Audrey Camus calls the 'zero world (the world at the origin of the signpost)'[8] and explorations of the place name's resonance as a verbal signifier. The toponym speaks of and for the world from the standpoint of language; insofar as it is a name, it must name something, which can never be more than an absent presence.

In the wake of Franco Moretti's *Atlas of the European Novel* (1994/1998) and Bertrand Westphal's *Geocriticism: Real and Fictional Spaces* (2014), literary comparatists have begun to recognise the hybrid, dynamic character of the geographies adumbrated by fiction. The impetus isn't simply to 'map' the territories projected by literary texts[9] but also to discern what is peculiar, ontologically speaking, to literary spatiality. Rather than survey intimate landscapes that connect an author's style and personal themes to lived sites, critics look to post-classical theories of narrative and to the pragmatics of reading to ask how fictional worlds come about and how they cohere. Does the diegetic world adhere to the implicit laws of the zero-world we inhabit, or does it present improbable fault lines, overlaps, inversions, substitutions, condensations or displacements? To what extent is spatial reference gradated rather than absolute, given that most fictions include both attested place names and invented ones? What roles do toponyms play in the *spatial contract* that authors implicitly enter into with readers? Are place names in a given text evenly distributed or concentrated in pockets? Are they allogenic or autochtonous with respect to the language of composition (or of translation)? What scalar values are favoured in apprehending the component parts of the fictional world? Do the places named lay out a path followed by one or more characters or is their role to provide context or backdrop? What axiology do they represent, whether correlated to a social class or (imagined) community? To sum up, to what extent is localisation undecidable, despite our best attempts at 'mapping' textual sites on paper or, as is increasingly the case, on a computer screen?[10] All these questions speak to Pierre Bayard's 'paradoxical' invitation in *Comment parler des lieux où l'on n'a pas été?* to 'reflect on the relationship literature holds with the world it depicts, in particular with the places it contains',[11] as well as to Westphal's plea in *Geocriticism* that we 'prob[e] the human spaces that the mimetic arts arrange through, and in, texts, the image, and the cultural interactions related to them'.[12] In short, it's not about making pilgrimage to writers' haunts, however rewarding such pursuits may prove.

* * *

Georges Perec's fiction begs a targeted study of place names for three reasons. The first is its extraordinary variety. From one book to another, formal and generic variation brings about distinct approaches to the French language, to arresting effect.[13] Like other parts of speech in the Perecquian lexicon, the toponym floats between the ideal of descriptive neutrality – a 'writing degree zero' that finds its analogon in the itemised list – and an unbridled inventiveness born of Oulipian constraint. The range of its possible uses and contexts is hence considerable.

A second reason is quantitative. Perec's prose is saturated with proper names of persons and places, sometimes to the point of (knowing) unreadability. Take Chapter XXII in *Life: A User's Manual* (1987). Here, in the entry hall, passing reference to a 'sepia-tint photograph of a man in a black cloak'[14] triggers a 15-page 'novel' on the forgers who entrap the collector of *unica*, or one-of-a-kind treasures, James Sherwood. In 1896, Sherwood purchased a precious Venetian Quarli of the famed *Vita brevis Helenae*, only to finds between its leaves a 'fastidious and minute' handwritten inventory of relics of Christ's Passion and their respective conservation sites:

> [...] the fragments of the Holy Cross at St Peter's, Rome, at St Sophia, at Worms, at Clairvaux, at Chapelle-Lauzin, at the Hospice of the Incurables at Baugé, at St Thomas's, Birmingham, etc.; the Nails at the Abbey of Saint-Denis, at Naples Cathedral, at S Felice at Syracuse, at SS Apostoli in Venise, at the Church of Saint-Sernin, Toulouse; the spear with which Longinus pierced the Lord's breast at S Paulo fuori le Mura, at S Giovanni in Laterano, at Nuremberg, and at the Sainte-Chapelle in Paris; the chalice, in Jerusalem; the Three Dice used by the soldiers to gamble for Christ's Tunic, at Sophia Cathedral; the Sponge Soaked in Vinegar and Gall at S Giovanni in Laterano, at S Maria-di-Trastevero, at S Maria Maggiora, at Saint Mark's, at S Silvestro-in-capite, and at the Sainte-Chapelle in Paris; the Thorns of the Crown at St Taurin's, Evreux, Châteaumeillant, Orléans, Beaugency, and at Notre-Dame in Reims, at Abbeville, Saint-Benoît-sur-Loire, Vézelay, Palermo, Colmar, Montauban, Vienna, and Padua; St Lawrence's Vase at S Lorenzo in Genoa, Veronica's Veil (the *vera icon*) at S Silvestro in Rome; the Holy Shroud, in Rome, Jerusalem, Turin, Cadouin in the Périgord, Carcassonne, Mainz, Parma, Prague, Bayonne, York, Paris, Ayrshire, etc.[15]

Enumeration, which Perec, like Rabelais and Verne, considered to be a source of 'ineffable joys,'[16] can also be deadly: what relics, in which dioceses has the closing 'etc.' spared us, indeed? Rather than refer to sites implicated in the novel's diegesis, place names here become figures of discourse, ciphers of the encyclopaedic vocation of Perec's 600-page 'novels' itself. Yet this show of pseudo-erudition is, simultaneously, a pretext to ham it up. (In his crafty translation that routinely re-italicises Perec's gallicised place names, e.g. 'S Maria Maggiora' for 'Sainte-Marie-Majeure', David Bellos dispels any hint of uncertainty by adding to the closing sequence of 'Parma, Prague, Bayonne, York, Paris', the tell-tale 'Ayrshire'.)

Many passages in Perec's work exhibit such onomastic density. Yet density is equally important where place names are less numerous: take the lipograms *La Disparition* (1969; English translation *A Void,* 1994) and *Les Revenentes* (1972; English translation *The Exeter Text: Jewels, Secrets, Sex*, 1996), in which the letter-based constraint enacts a geographical excision.

Third, toponyms betray the worldly purview of this writer of French who refused to be pigeonholed as a 'French writer', and who, his dwelling habits aside, rejected Parisiocentrism in favour of heterogeneous spaces, places and tongues. From Poland to Tunisia and from Yugoslavia to Australia, from Azincourt to Zanzibar, an openness towards the nameable world underwrites themes of travel, displacement, exile, migration and accent, pointing toward the restrained lyricism of *Récits d'Ellis Island* (with Robert Bober, 1980), as well as to the unfinished *53 Days* with its colonial themes and settings.

In the selective exploration to follow, I shall examine the rapport between toponymy and reference in three of Perec's books, one of which (*Les Choses*) was written well before the writer began to engage with explicit formal constraints. The two others are very much indebted to his activities with the Oulipo (Ouvroir de Littérature Potentielle or Workshop of Potential Literature). The works are discussed in order not of their publication history but in accordance with increasing levels of onomastic saturation. From the novella *Les Revenentes* (1972), whose founding constraint outlaws on principle the majority of locales on planet Earth, we move backwards in time to the début novel *Les Choses* (1965), where toponyms function as cultural signs unevenly freighted with connotation. Lastly, in *Life: A User's Manual* (1987), we will see how ekphrasis and nested storytelling allow this literary summa to incorporate myriad places the world over without ever leaving rue Simon-Crubellier, an imaginary address in Paris's seventeenth *arrondissement* which the author entrusts to readers as a form of collective property. This triple foray into Perec's fiction lays bare the deep connection between naming and the ability to instantiate a world.

I. Gone Missing

> Ils sont partis trois ans, ils ont couru trois ans, bravant tourbillons, ouragans ou typhons, du Labrador aux Fidji, du Cap Horn à l'Alaska, d'Hawaii au Kamtchatka.[17]

> Away four springs, abroad four springs, braving whirlwind, whirlpool and typhoon, from Labrador to Fiji, from Jamaica to Alaska, from Hawaii to Kamchatka.[18]

> Mehmet ben Berek prétend défendre les Berbères ? Les benqes de Berne et de Genève, et de Gènes, et de Dresde, et de Brème et de Denver, et même de Metz, le démentent expressément […][19]
>
> When Mehmet ben Berek tells them he yet defends the Berbers, the check-tellers between here 'n' Berne, Genève, Leeds, Dresden, Brème, even Metz'll then decree the reverse […][20]

Sentence after sentence, Perec's long-form lipograms *La Disparition* and *Les Revenentes* expose the innermost workings of literary mimesis to undercut the possibility of referencing the object world in its integrity. No longer can the writer choose at will places from the would-be universal atlas: only a small number of locales obey the privative (and generative) alphabetical constraint. This truncation of the tellable world puts the writer in a difficult spot. Either he may select natively lipogrammatical elements (e.g. 'Berne', 'Gènes' and 'Dresde') or alter spellings slightly to meet the spec. (e.g. 'Besse-en-Chendesse', 'Engleterre', 'Espègne'[21]); or he must forge place names anew, to the potential detriment of textual verisimilitude. Faced with this alternative, Perec unsurprisingly opts for what Jacques Jouet calls 'le respect de […] règles sévères (respect de préférence extrême)',[22] an extreme respect for the adopted rules. To forge names outright is to admit defeat, in that the real world proffers many so excellent solutions.

The lipogram not only excludes some place names while authorising others; it requires that allowable names conform to French syntax. Hence, some names of countries or islands may follow a preposition but may not serve as grammatical subject ('du Labrador aux Fidji' in *La Disparition*), while for others ('Le Kef', 'Le Yémen' in *Les Revenentes*) the inverse holds true. Prepositions in *Les Revenentes* are initially limited to 'from' (*de*), 'towards' (*vers*) and 'in' (*en*, for feminine countries, as in 'en Grèce et en Perse'[23]); to this battery of prepositions that indicate provenance, direction and location in the original French, Perec adds *dens* (a homophonic workaround for *dans*), further enriching the text's expressivity.

As befits *The Exeter Text*, Ian Monk's peerless rendering of *Les Revenentes*, Franco-English bilingualism helps Perec skirt more than one obstacle. Here is the novella's opener, and it's a gem, in whichever version you choose to read it:

> Telle des chèvres en détresse, sept Mercédès-Benz vertes, les fenêtres crêpées de reps grège, descendent lentement West End Street et prennent sénestrement Temple Street vers les vertes

venelles semées de hêtres et de frênes près desqelles se dresse, svelte et empesé en même temps, l'Evêché d'Exeter.[24]

Deep Dentelle screened, the seven green Mercedes Benzes resembled pestered sheep. They descended West End Street, swerved left, entered Temple Street then swept between the green vennels' beeches, elms 'n' elders. These trees enkernelled Exeter See's svelte, yet nevertheless erect steeples.[25]

The uninitiated may wonder whether the quite plausible West End Street and Temple Street grace maps of the town of Exeter.[26] Determining their localisation is nonetheless of secondary importance: from the start, the narrator sets up a spatial contract that is anti-realist (we never, ever, see seven green Mercedes descend Exeter's well-swept streets). Strategically, Perec draws on the generic English noun 'street' to imbue his monovocalic French with a phantom phoneme otherwise barred from the text. Adoption of the double 'ee' to express the sound [i] aligns with the last of three rules stipulated in the book's front matter: 'Various distortions will be gradually accepted as the text progresses.'[27] We thus find later references in Perec's original French to 'des bergères Chesterfeeld' and to 'Derek's Reseedence'.[28] But 'street' also prompts the author to reimagine Exeter circa 1970:

Needle Street ! Le repère 'freek' d'Exeter. C'est près de l'Evêché, entre Ethelbert Crescent et Temple Street. Le centre de cette kermesse hébétée ? Qelqes réverbères et qelqes frènes étêtés encerclent le Keetchener éqestre, en très belle brèche verte, de Werner Ebersweld ; des bencs près desquels s'étend cette plèbe désespérée qe bercent éphémèrement, telles ces légendères 'fées vertes' de Verlène, ces népenthès des temps récents : l'herbe, le bétel, l'éther, l'élesdé, le speed, etc ...[29]

Needle Street, Exeter's hep set's den, ley neer the See, between Ethelbert Crescent 'n' Temple Street. The street's excesses were centred where the few breeze-swept elms encercled Werner Ebersweld's resplendent green-pebbled 'Keetchener's Steed'. Here, desprette dregs slept between the benches; when newer nepenthes (beer, reefers, ether, LSD, speed, etc) sent them frenzeed, they resembled Verlène's legenderee 'Green Feys'.[30]

Following this satire of tripped-out longhaired 'freeks' hypnotised by 'les chents des Beetles'[31] is an outrageous neo-Sadean parody of ecclesiastical orgies in the Exeter See. *Les Revenentes* is Perec's sex & drugs text par excellence.

These creative appropriations have direct effects upon the diegetic world: they instantiate an in-between space that is culturally and linguistically 'entre Frence et Engleterre'.[32] Insofar as the novella's geography is determined by the language of expression, then, it often fails to meet key expectations, especially where extension and scale are concerned. To be sure, given toponyms can still reference attested places of the zero-world: so 'Ellesmère' refers to Ellesmere (Shropshire) even as it poetically evokes women figures generally (*elles*) and the mother in particular (*mère*). But *Les Revenentes*' full set of place names, many of which depart from the known world, is no longer isotopic with the zero-world. Diegetic space presents rifts, tears and holes; each manifest element is surrounded by uncanny absences, the available reference points forming a discontinuous array: 'le désert, c'est des verstes et des verstes de sécheresses. Errence sens trève : Le Kef, Meknes, Zemzem, Le Yémen'[33] ('The desert steppes were mere creekless versts, endless extents: Kef, Meknes, Zemzem, Yemen'[34]). Here, a string of Arabo-Berber toponyms sends us from Tunisia to Morocco, to Saudi Arabia[35] and finally dispatches us to Yemen, with nary an interval in between. And where ordinary language would permit nested scalar designations as in *Species of Spaces* – Sheffield, South Yorkshire, the North, England, the British Isles, Europe, etc. – letter-based constraints make such shifts from city to region and from region to nation most problematic.

Paradoxically, this curtailment of lexicon heightens readability: in *Les Revenentes* the same place names recur, chief among them the made-to-order 'Exeter' and the tailored 'Engleterre'. By contrast, the plurivocalic *La Disparition* gives broader territorial coverage, though in reality the narrative in its strange nomadism is no less inimical to verisimilitude than is *Les Revenentes*. In both cases diegetic space is made starkly unfamiliar: deterritorialised in and through language. Entire segments of the known world are crossed out – no London and no Paris in *Les Revenentes*, no more than Sheffield, Leeds or Liverpool in *La Disparition*! Action transpires in that eminently Perecquian utopia of a circumscribed alphabet at once severed and severe.

II. From rhetorical commonplace to social geography

Contrasted with these Oulipian texts, the début novel of 1965 *Les Choses* reads like a bravado exercise in style by a budding writer indebted to Flaubert. In this 'story of the sixties', repeated actions take precedence over singular events. The imperfect dominates all other verb tenses so as to create what I have called, in *Mémoires du quotidien: Les lieux de Perec*, 'sociology effects' correlated to a class and to a generational subset. In this critical compilation of the 'rhetorical loci of market fascination', as Perec once described his novel,[36] place names appear as signs in Deleuze's sense, namely, as part of a 'temporal apprenticeship, not of an abstract knowledge'.[37] The simple fact of living in, visiting or knowing by reputation such and such a place distinguishes protagonists Jérôme and Sylvie from their peers, or rather associates them with an aspirational subset of Parisians from their generation. Toponyms designate less plot points in the personal trajectory of Perec's model couple, than a set of values forming a semi-exclusive cultural horizon.

The novel's first part describes the Parisian geography of consumer desire from the standpoint of two twenty-somethings who can't bear the thought of leaving the French capital. Their cramped quarters correspond to their objective status: neither rich nor poor, 'they had only what they deserved to have'.[38] Even as they dream of more spacious lodgings and quality furniture to match, they struggle to reconcile their dreams of a comfortable lifestyle and the exigencies of daily life as low-level market researchers. The calm Jardin des Plantes neighbourhood may have its charms, but countless seductions lure them elsewhere within the French capital: 'From Palais-Royal to Saint-Germain-des-Prés, from Champ-de-Mars to the Champs-Elysées, from the Luxembourg Gardens to Montparnasse, from Ile Saint-Louis to the Marais, from Place des Ternes to Place de l'Opéra, from the Madeleine to the Monceau Gardens, the whole of Paris was a perpetual temptation.'[39] Each place name becomes an invitation, incantation or promise. As Jérôme and Sylvie's tastes develop, faraway locales beckon: they consider 'the alleged pleasures of lightning visits to New York or to London'.[40] Short on funds, they must make do with treasures from the Saint-Ouen flea market and budget entertainments, as this passage replete with ternary groupings suggests:

> They discovered the smart little restaurants near Gobelins, Ternes, Saint-Sulpice, the empty bars where, on weekend trips away from Paris you can enjoy whispering, long walks in the woods in autumn, in Rambouillet, Vaux, and Compiègne, the almost perfect pleasures proffered in every place to the ear, to the eye and to the palate.[41]

The plural pronoun 'ils' used liberally in the text favours slippage between Jérôme and Sylvie and their well-nigh indistinguishable group of friends, none of whom is named. Corollary to this absence of proper names of persons is a textual surfeit of toponyms. Geography seems to speak in the place of the anonymous Parisian couples who live in the same districts and haunt the same watering holes:

> Their flats, flatlets, lofts, two-roomed conversions in dilapidated houses, in selected neighbourhoods – Palais-Royal, Contrescarpe, Saint-Germain, Luxembourg, Montparnasse – were very similar.[42]
>
> They were habitués of 'Harry's New York Bar', denizens of Rue Daunou, frequenters of the cafés in Palais-Royal, of 'Le Balzar', 'Le Lipp', and a few other bars.[43]

The paradox is that these destinations of distinction serve to homogenise further this limited social set. In compiling the names of posh districts, *Les Choses* describes a situated Parisian imaginary in which toponyms become generational commonplaces.

Perec's insistence on habit and the patterns of daily life means that rarely do place names appear singly. Concentrated in packets of three or four, they authorise a double reading: an internal one, from the perspective of characters who invest each name with desire; and an external reading, from the standpoint of the narrator who underscores the contradiction between the couple's dreams and meagre means. Thus, the expression 'a short trip [*petit voyage*] to Bruges, Antwerp or Basel'[44] at once betrays the class prerogatives of quality tourism and exposes the cliché behind the well-worn myth, in Roland Barthes' sense, of the 'petit voyage artistique'.[45]

The novel's second – Tunisian – half sports a very different tone which critics have linked to the absence of objects to stoke consumerist desire. The description of the Sfax neighbourhood where Jérôme and Sylvie take a flat is cold and precise:

> The port and the European quarter of Sfax had been destroyed during the war, and the city now consisted of about thirty streets set at right angles to each other. The two main streets were Avenue Bourguiba, running from the station to the Central Market, near where they lived, and Avenue Hedi-Chaker, which ran from the port to the Arab quarter. The city centre was the intersection of these two streets.[46]

If the narrator distinguishes between the European neighbourhoods and the 'ancient, beautiful, fortified'[47] Arab city, few other evaluative judgments are forthcoming. Place names are for the protagonists empty, largely meaningless signs, absent of colour and redolent of death:

> All around, on the quayside, on the ramparts, it was dead: the huge sand-strewn esplanade in front of Sfax's hideous cathedral encircled by dwarf palms, Boulevard de Picville, lined by waste plots and two-storey maisonettes, Rue Mangolte, Rue Fezzani, Rue Abd-el-Kader-Zghal were bare, straight and sand-swept.[48]

In the post-protectorate era of Maghrebi independence, markers of colonisation persist alongside signs of advancing Arabisation; for Anne Roche, Perec's description of desert-like Sfax with its autochtonous place names 'describes a double alienation: the alienation of the colonised, and the different alienation of the colonisers who only see what is in front of their eyes'.[49] Among the couple's shortcomings is an inability to understand the spaces around them. Disillusioned with Sfax, they criss-cross Tunisia in search of a remedy for their boredom. In recounting these travels the text favours enumeration: once uttered, place names seem to exhaust their referents, leaving nothing behind. The promise of discovery inherent in each foreign place name founders on the baleful reality of blank sites:

> They saw Gabes, Tuzer, Nefta, Gafsa and Metlaoui ; the ruins of Sbeitla, Kasserine and Thelepte ; they passed through dead towns with names which had previously sounded to their ears like magic : Mahares, Moulares, Matmata, Medenin.[50]

The couple's onomastic reverie is short-lived; meant to fill an existential void, these visits prove sterile. When Jérôme and Sylvie discover the house of their dreams at Hammamet, another life in Tunisia seems possible: 'At La Marsa, or Sidibou Säid, or El Manza, they would have had a fine detached house, a big garden.'[51] But again, as the sentence's ternary rhythm suggests, such projects are to remain unrealised. No concrete project seems possible in the colonial space. It's no accident, then, that during the couple's return journey to France via Tunis, narrative discourse incorporates the *topoi* of tourist bureau pamphlets and travel guidebooks:

> Sakietes-Zit, El Djem and its amphitheatre, Msaken the city of brigands, Susa and its overpopulated sea-front, Enfidaville and its huge olive plantations, Bir bou Rekba and its coffee shops, fruit and ceramics, Grombalia, Potinville and its vine-covered hills, Hammam Lif, then a stretch of motorway, industrial suburbs, soap factories, cement works: Tunis.[52]

Perec's irony-laden epilogue lets on that the couple's sentimental education, like that of Flaubert's Frédéric Moreau and his chum Deslauriers, has led nowhere: 'They will see Paris again, and it will be all that life can afford. They will saunter by the banks of the Seine, in the gardens of the Palais-Royal, in the side-streets of Saint-Germain.'[53]

Les Choses upholds basic referential functions in that place names correlate to sites in the zero-world that one can readily find in an atlas or city map. Readers should not, for all that, assume that the narrative conforms to a 'realist' literary mode as Kristin Ross does in her study of the twinned processes of French decolonisation and modernisation, *Fast Cars, Clean Bodies*.[54] If toponyms in *Les Choses* tether the diegesis to the zero-world, narrative discourse ceaselessly converts places into signs, much like the luxury objects that Perec's couple covet. Consequently, the connotations that place names bear for these upwardly mobile provincials-turned-Parisians take precedence over cartographic localisation. Just as Jérôme and Sylvie form a model couple, so too do place names in *Les Choses* function as commonplaces in period-specific topography of elusive happiness, one suffused with post-colonial melancholy.

III. A world of names

Of the several hundred places named in *Life: A User's Manual*,[55] the first to appear is the quite fictive yet eminently plausible rue Simon-Crubellier. Before mentioning by name a single occupant of the apartment building (Bartlebooth, Winckler, Valène ...), the narrator specifies the site of narrative construction: 'Yes, it will begin here, between the third and fourth storey at 11 rue Simon-Crubellier.'[56] This would-be Parisian street is authenticated by the actually existing city block it cuts in two: according to a drawing held by the businesswoman who climbs the stairwell in Chapter I, it lies 'roughly halfway along Rue Simon-Crubellier, which cuts at an angle across the quadrilateral formed by Rue Médéric, Rue Jadin, Rue de Chazelles, and Rue Léon Jost, in the Plaine Monceau district of the XVIIth arrondissement of Paris'.[57] Some 500 pages later, we learn that from 1875 the land was developed by its owners Samuel Simon and Norbert Crubellier: whence the hyphenated street name which inextricably conjoins, in an autobiographical key, Jewish and French identities.

Chronologically, the stories comprising *Life: A User's Manual* span one and a half centuries.[58] Outside the epilogue, however, narration turns on the evening of 23 June 1975, at the moment Percival Bartlebooth expires at his desk, his puzzle left unfinished. This temporal suspension and the exclusive focus in present-tense descriptive passages on the building's interiors means that the diegetic world beyond rue Simon-Crubellier appears principally through retrospection, as a function of stories told about occupants past and present. The surroundings of the apartment building and adjacent neighbourhoods are barely sketched out: Gaspard Winckler often walks in the Parc Monceau and the Marigny Gardens; widow Madame Albin takes the 84 bus then the train from the Gare d'Orsay to reach the Juvisy-sur-Orge cemetery; Mme Lafuente shops for her employer Véra de Beaumont in rue de Chazelles.[59]

And yet, by virtue of the stories it compiles, this book concerned with a single (fictive) address would contain the whole of the world. In recounting the lives of collectors, artists and world travellers, the narrator routinely signals places of birth. Born in Russia, Véra Orlova transited through Vienna and Amsterdam before reaching Paris; Olivia Rorschash was born in Sydney, and Mademoiselle Crespi outside Ajaccio.[60] Endpoints are mentioned too: the Jewish resistance fighter Mme Appenzzell was killed in June 1944 near Vassieux-en-Vercors.[61] Entire careers are summarised as a function of places: Mme Moreau, who spent her active life 'between her factories in Paris and Romainville, her offices in Avenue de la Grande Armée, and this luxury flat',[62] left Paris and its suburbs whenever she could for her parents' farm at Saint-Mouezy.[63] The polymath Carel Van Loorens, a naturalised Dutchman, skipped from one European city to another doing everything under the sun: 'setting up in Lahore a cannon foundry, founding in Shiraz a veterinary school, teaching physiology at Bologna, mathematics at Halle, and astronomy at Barcelona'.[64]

In its diversity of provenance the toponym bespeaks Perec's taste for tales of high adventure. Take the story of Henri Fresnel, a charlatan who crosses Africa and South America before beginning his *rags to riches* American dream as Grace Twinkler's cook in New York's Bowery,[65] or the Trévins sisters Marie-Thérèse and Odile who criss-cross the globe in their cabaret dancing act:

> the *Crazy Sisters* could be seen at the Paris *Lido*, at *Cavalier's* in Stockholm, at *Naughties* in Milan, at the Las Vegas *B and A*, and at *Pension Macadam* in Tangiers, the Beirut *Star*, the *Ambassadors* in London, the *Bras d'or* in Acapulco, the Berlin *Nirvana*, at *Monkey Jungle* in Miami, at *Twelve Tones* in Newport and *Caribbean's* in Barbados [...].[66]

And how could we forget the voyage undertaken from 1935 to 1955 by Bartlebooth with his assistant Smautf to document, in watercolours, 500 maritime ports? Among the seaports noted by the narrator are 'the little harbor of Muckanagherderdauhaulia, not far from Costelloe, in Ireland's Camus Bay, and the even tinier port of U in the Caroline Islands,'[67] namely, the two coastal localities in the world sporting what would appear to be the longest and shortest names.

Names are ripe for the 'ineffable joys' of enumeration. Ekphrastic description of a map of France and its colonies associates two orders of names, those of famous men and their corresponding places of birth:

> Marseilles (Thiers), Dijon (Bossuet), Rouen (Géricault), Ajaccio (Napoleon I), Grenoble (Bayard), Bordeaux (Montesquieu), Pau (Henri IV), Albi (La Pérouse), Chartres (Marceau), Besançon (Victor Hugo), Paris (Béranger), Mâcon (Lamartine), Dunkirk (Jean Bart), Montpellier (Cambacérès), Bourges (Jacques Cœur), Caen (Auber), Agen (Bernard Palissy), Clermont-Ferrand (Vercingétorix), La Ferté-Milon (Racine) and Lyons (Jacquart).[68]

Elsewhere, perhaps a nod to Proust's reveries on the 'nom du pays', the text reproduces all the 'exotic and mysterious names' printed on the face of a wireless: 'Hilversum, Sottens, Allouis, Vatican, Kerguélen, Monte Ceneri, Bergen, Tromsö, Bari, Tangiers, Falun, Horby, Beromünster, Puzzoli, Muscat, Amara.'[69]

In addition to potted biographies and ekphrastic passages, two stories in particular foreground the materiality of toponyms. Chapter LXXX, 'Bartlebooth, 3', chronicles a fin-de-siècle row between two geographers who each claim to have established the earliest name bestowed upon the American continent. Do the deteriorated letters 'TE RA COI B I A' found on a globe of 1503 designate TERRA COLUMBIA or rather TERRA CONSOBRINIA?[70] The story of the luxury hotel group Marvel Houses International is likewise a matter of conjoined letters. Its directors chose the sites of 24 hotel complexes based not on perceived market advantage or ease of access, but on a quasi-Oulipian constraint fusing together the names of parent companies MARVEL HOUSES INCORPORATED and INTERNATIONAL HOSTELLERIE.[71] Though astute, the acrostic does not prove a good business strategy.

Whatever their status in the zero-world of reference, the hundreds of places indexed in *Life: A User's Manual* are secondary with respect to rue Simon-Crubellier, sole theatre of present action. The text foretells the destruction of the city block itself, a reminder of the urban renovation that swept through Paris in the 1970s. Like the 500 watercolours that Bartlebooth paints, only to have them destroyed once each puzzle has been reassembled, the narrator notes that 'the same fever which around eighteen fifty brought these buildings out of the ground from Batignolles to Clichy, from Ménilmontant to Butte-aux-Cailles, from Balard to Pré-Saint-Gervais, will henceforth strive for their destruction'.[72] The building and its pictorial representation in Serge Valène's unfinished canvas are imagined from the standpoint of absence and effacement. Not unlike the noted legend of Greek poet Simonedes of Ceos that tied the genesis of artificial memory (*ars memoriae*) to the spectacle of destruction, the site is converted into a veritable memory palace comprising individual *loci* or rhetorical places in which to lodge specific images.

Ultimately, in this incomparable collection of words and things that is *Life: A User's Manual*, a reversal occurs in our understanding of what makes a place a place. It's not through attempts at sheer saturation or exhaustion that we might come to decipher the world in its totality: countless places will always escape this accounting, only to be displaced by others. What Perec's extraordinary 'novels' of 1978 make visible, rather, notably through its use of chapter titles based on character names, is a world in which names for places are inseparable from the names of those persons who have made these sites their own, by the simple fact of dwelling there. In the necessarily utopian language of Perec's literary fiction, 'Beaumont', 'Dinteville', 'Berger' and 'Bartlebooth' become place names in and of themselves, so many designations serving to particularise and to invest with meaning the collective habitat that is 11 rue Simon-Crubellier. Across its 99 chapters Perec's masterwork thus gradually transforms the private (or privative) and singular, into collective goods: into common places, in the best sense of the term. This transformation both fulfils and extends Perec's abiding promise to found the real anew in and through the creative literary act and to retrieve from the clutches of history spaces neglected, forgotten or otherwise overlooked. A world so renamed is a world remade.

Notes

1. Perec, *Things*, 27–8.
2. Baudelle, 'Noms de pays ou pays de noms: toponymie et référence dans les récits de fiction', 56. My translation.
3. Hamon, *Introduction à l'analyse du descriptif*, 47.
4. Barthes, *S/Z*, 95.
5. Deleuze, *Proust and Signs*, 108.
6. Kripke, *Naming and Necessity*.
7. Genette, *Mimologics*, 11–40.
8. Camus, 'Espèces d'espaces: vers une typologie des lieux fictionnels', 34.
9. Engberg-Pedersen, *Literature and Cartography*.

10. Schilling, 'On and Off the Map', 215–28.
11. Bayard, *Comment parler des lieux où l'on n'a pas été*, 15. My translation.
12. Westphal, *Geocriticism*, 6.
13. Montémont and Reggiani, *Georges Perec artisan de la langue*.
14. Perec, *Life*, 81.
15. Perec, *Life*, 84–5.
16. Perec, 'Think/Classify,' *Species of Spaces*, 194.
17. Perec, *La Disparition*, 85.
18. Perec, *A Void*, 69.
19. Perec, *Les Revenentes*, 32.
20. Perec, *The Exeter Text*, 67.
21. Perec, *Les Revenentes*, 46 and 73.
22. Jouet, 'Les sept règles de Perec', 17.
23. Perec, *Les Revenentes*, 23.
24. Perec, *Les Revenentes*, 13.
25. Perec, *The Exeter Text*, 59.
26. Exeter's present-day nomenclature includes a 'Temple Road' as well as a 'West Street', minus the 'End'; needless to say, Perec did not avail himself of the ready-made 'Regent Street'.
27. Perec, *The Exeter Text*, 55.
28. Perec, *Les Revenentes*, 73 and 74.
29. Perec, *Les Revenentes*, 67.
30. Perec, *The Exeter Text*, 82–3.
31. Perec, *Les Revenentes*, 68.
32. Perec, *Les Revenentes*, 45.
33. Perec, *Les Revenentes*, 27.
34. Perec, *The Exeter Text*, 64.
35. Zemzem is a sacred well at Mecca.
36. Perec, 'Pouvoirs et limites du romancier français contemporain', 37.
37. Deleuze, *Proust and Signs*, 4.
38. Perec, *Things*, 27.
39. Perec, *Things*, 27–8.
40. Perec, *Things*, 31.
41. Perec, *Things*, 42.
42. Perec, *Things*, 45.
43. Perec, *Things*, 52.
44. Perec, *Things*, 53.
45. Schilling, *Mémoires du quotidien*, 77–86.
46. Perec, *Things*, 105.
47. Perec, *Things*, 106.
48. Perec, *Things*, 110.
49. Roche, 'Perec et le monde arabe', 161. My translation.
50. Perec, *Things*, 114.
51. Perec, *Things*, 120.
52. Perec, *Things*, 122.
53. Perec, *Things*, 123.
54. Ross, *Fast Cars, Clean Bodies*, 123–56.
55. Perec, *Life*, 505–63.
56. Perec, *Life*, 4.
57. Perec, *Life*, 4.
58. Perec, *Life*, 625–32.
59. Perec, *Life*, 29, 211 and 452.
60. Perec, *Life*, 19, 380 and 406.
61. Perec, *Life*, 112.
62. Perec, *Life*, 96.
63. Perec, *Life*, 130. This ranks among the many programmed borrowings laid out in the novel's 'cahier des charges': see Perec, 'Emprunts à Queneau', *Les Amis de Valentin Bru*, 13–14.
64. Perec, *Life*, 371.
65. Perec, *Life*, 258.
66. Perec, *Life*, 449.

67. Perec, *Life*, 52.
68. Perec, *Life*, 198–9.
69. Perec, *Life*, 471.
70. Perec, *Life*, 385 and 387.
71. Perec, *Life*, 425.
72. Perec, *Life*, 130.

Filmography

Récits d'Ellis Island (Paris, 1980, Bober and Perec)

Bibliography

Barthes, Roland. *S/Z*, translated by Richard Miller. New York: Hill and Wang, 1974.

Bayard, Pierre. *Comment parler des lieux où l'on n'a pas été?* Paris: Éditions de Minuit, 2012.

Camus, Audrey and Rachel Bouvet, eds. *Topographies romanesques*. Rennes: Presses universitaires de Rennes, 2011.

Deleuze, Gilles. *Proust and Signs*, translated by Richard Howard. New York: George Braziller, 1972.

Duras, Marguerite. *The Ravishing of Lol V. Stein*, translated by Richard Seaver. New York: Grove Press, 1966.

Engberg-Pedersen, Anders, ed. *Literature and Cartography: Theories, Histories, Genres*. Cambridge, MA: MIT Press, 2017.

Genette, Gérard. *Mimologics*, translated by Thaïs E. Morgan. Lincoln: University of Nebraska Press, 1994.

Gracq, Julien. *The Opposing Shore*, translated by Richard Howard. New York: Columbia University Press, 1986.

Hamon, Philippe. *Introduction à l'analyse du descriptif*. Paris: Hachette, 1981.

Jouet, Jacques. 'Les sept règles de Perec'. In *Cahiers Georges Perec 4: Mélanges*, 15–17. Paris: Éditions du Limon, 1990.

Kripke, Saul. *Naming and Necessity*. Cambridge: Harvard University Press, 1980.

Montémont, Véronique and Christelle Reggiani, eds. *Georges Perec artisan de la langue*. Lyon: Presses universitaires de Lyon, 2012.

Moretti, Franco. *Atlas of the European Novel, 1800-1900*. London: Verso, 1998.

Perec, Georges. *La Disparition*. Paris: Denoël, 1969.

Perec, Georges. *Les Revenentes*. Paris: Julliard, 1972.

Perec, Georges. *Life: A User's Manual*, translated by David Bellos. Boston: David R. Godine, 1987.

Perec, Georges. *Things: A Story of the Sixties*, translated by David Bellos. London: Collins Harvill, 1990.

Perec, Georges. *53 Days*, edited by Harry Mathews and Jacques Roubaud, translated by David Bellos. London: Harvill, 1992.

Perec, Georges. *Species of Spaces and Other Pieces*, edited and translated by John Sturrock. London: Penguin Books, 1997.

Ribière, Mireille, ed. *Parcours Perec: Colloque de Londres, mars 1988*. Lyon: Presses universitaires de Lyon, 1990.

Ross, Kristin. *Fast Cars, Clean Bodies: Decolonization and the Reordering of French Culture*. Cambridge, MA: MIT Press, 1995.

Schilling, Derek. *Mémoires du quotidien: Les lieux de Perec*. Villeneuve d'Ascq: Presses universitaires du Septentrion, 2006.

Schilling, Derek. 'On and Off the Map: Literary Narrative as Critique of Cartographic Reason'. In *Literary Cartographies: Spatiality, Representation, and Narrative*, edited by Robert T. Tally Jr., 215–28. New York: Palgrave Macmillan, 2014.

Westphal, Bertrand. *Geocriticism: Real and Fictional Spaces*, translated by Robert T. Tally Jr. New York: Palgrave Macmillan, 2011.

4

Vanishing points: Shifting perspectives on *The Man Who Sleeps / Un homme qui dort*

Julia Dobson

To live is to pass from one space to another [...][1]

Georges Perec and Bernard Queysanne's astonishing film *The Man Who Sleeps* (*Un homme qui dort*) won the Prix Jean Vigo in 1974 yet remains a relatively neglected filmic text, often approached through its written predecessor, first published in French in 1967.[2] Indeed, the film was difficult to access for many years and risked a vanishing of its own before a restored version was released on DVD in 2007. This chapter seeks to address this imbalance and to assert new perspectives on the film which, through attention to the filmic construction of meaning and a re-siting of the film in relation to filmic intertexts and conventions, challenges critical conflation with the written text and asserts Perec's cinematic sensibilities. Perec's film script (the 'texte intégral inédit du film'), included with the film's DVD release in 2007, is a heavily edited version of the 1967 text. The film's uncanny negotiations of both the subject and the city spaces suggest that Paris, here an oneiric empty city, is the mute central character, desperately seeking indifference. The work projects a suspended subject awaiting a new connection to time and space. This chapter will explore the film's unsettling narrative, uncanny images and soundscapes through the trope of multiple vanishings. These range from those of the dwindling subject, constrained and repurposed by the narrator's instructions, to the strikingly deserted cityscapes which evoke the disappeared, and to the filmic insistence on the vanishing points of one-point perspective that recur throughout the film. *The Man Who Sleeps* is thus mapped in terms of the presence, construction and contestation of different vanishings and re-mapped in relation to the specifics of film.

Film / text: asserting Perec's cinema

The film equivalent of Oulipo's (Ouvroir de Littérature Potentielle or Workshop of Potential Literature) experimental literary adventures, OUCINEPO (later OUCIPO; Ouvroir de Cinématographie Potentielle), founded by François le Lionnais in 1974, seems to have remained largely inactive. Perec's own engagement with film, however, extended across roles as critic, scriptwriter and (co)director. His partner, Catherine Binet, whom he met in 1974, was a fiction and documentary film-maker. He published film reviews over two decades, wrote a dozen scripts, from the dialogue for *Série noire* (Corneau, 1979) to commentary for an anthology of amateur films on the everyday (*La Vie filmée des français*, produced by FR3 in 1975). After his co-direction of *The Man Who Sleeps*, Perec went on to adapt and direct his *Les lieux d'une fugue* (1978) and worked with Robert Bober on the haunting documentary *Ellis Island Revisited* (1980) – in the latter case the film preceded the written text. Queysanne noted their shared love of Jerry Lewis, Billy Wilder and classic melodrama, and their preferred French auteurs as Franju, Grémillon and Resnais.[3] Perec's characters in *Things* mock Resnais' work, but this might be seen as an ironic comment on the protagonists' carefully contrived tastes and displays of cultural capital, rather than the formal qualities of the film.[4] Queysanne's remark that *The Man Who Sleeps* bears no resemblance to any of his and Perec's favourites will be challenged later in this chapter.

Perec's dismissal of the film industry as 'entirely dominated by market ideology which [...] functions in 99 per cent of cases as a reductive constraint'[5] is no indicator of his engagement with the potential of film form and language. In a reversal of the common perception of film, in the context of adaptation and in broader cultural hierarchies of form, as attempting to illustrate an earlier written narrative or formal model, Perec asserts that: 'The novel, books are a form which are necessarily informed by work in cinematography [...] in *Life: A User's Manual* for example I know that there is a way of writing which is almost like a travelling shot [...] I think this comes from a cinematic sensibility [...]'[6] Perec's insistence on intermedial practice, his focus on the interactions of different media and arts *within* cinema, thus bears witness variously to his engagement with cinematic form, to the implications of this for further consideration of his written *oeuvre* and to the importance of not approaching the film *The Man Who Sleeps* as a simple adaptation of the written text.

It is important both to mind the gap between the publication of Perec's written text (1967) and his co-direction of *The Man Who Sleeps* (1973–4) and to avoid conflating the different written and filmic texts which risk transposing Perec as author of the literary work to Perec as sole 'auteur' of the film – a creative practice described by co-director Bernard Queysanne as an emphatically joint venture.[7] The contribution of the film-making team must also be considered because main actor Jacques Spiesser, cinematographer Bernard Zitzermann, editor Andrée Davanture and sound engineer Jean-Pierre Ruh were all engaged in the wider filmic practice. All had connections with the work of the Left Bank group (Varda, Marker, Resnais, Rouch) and their interest in innovation in documentary work as well as in questions of the representation of memory, history and the everyday. Queysanne also made two documentaries on Perec in 1999.[8] After an unsuccessful start influenced by the neo-realist *Il Posto* (Ermanno Olmi, 1961) and its focus on the alienating language and spaces of corporate employment, they rejected the use of dialogue and reinstated a heavily edited version of Perec's text to be delivered in voice-over.[9] From the book's structure, based on alternation between action and reflection, they retained only the 'action' sections for the film. The edited text was then not used as a guide during filming – but resurfaced as structuring reference in the editing process. Queysanne described the film as 'three different works, image, text, sound, which form a story, a story which creates emotion.'[10] Perec's knowing pitch for a 'a feature film when there is only one character, no story, no events, no dialogue, but only a text read by a voice-over'[11] may seem to frame his proposal in terms of lack, yet such constraints function as triggers for creativity in Perec's filmic work as in his written texts.[12]

The Man Who Sleeps is set in Paris, and focuses on a student (played by Jacques Spiesser) who, without motivation, fails to attend an exam and develops a practice of indifference to the world around him. He stops studying, refuses social contact and excludes choice and taste to assert a 'neutral' existence.[13] Evoking a depressive state, the claustrophobic scenes set in his tiny *chambre de bonne*, in which he is rarely seen sleeping, alternate with poetic scenes of walking around Paris which remain ambiguously sited between material mobility and imaginary itineraries. A sense of withdrawal and paranoia builds until he rejects indifference as radical practice and reconnects with city and self. There is no dialogue but rather a voice-over commentary in which a female voice addresses the student as 'you' (using the familiar *tu* form in the French). The black and white images are accompanied by a menacing score, commissioned from Ensemble 010 (Philippe Drogoz and Eugénie Kuffer).

The vanishing subject

The central protagonist's quest to withdraw from the social, from memory, from markers of choice and pleasure to assert an everyday practice of indifference can be read as a depressive state (with potential autobiographical origins).[14] Subjectivity is already undermined by formal means in both written and filmic texts in that the character remains nameless – is an unremarkable 'a man ...' in the French title rather than 'the man' and is seemingly defined by an action or state that he rarely fulfills.[15] This weak designation is challenged by his apparent insomnia thus suggesting a status that is more dormant than '*dormant*'.

The text's striking use of narration in the second person singular addresses the protagonist directly as you (*tu*) and allows him no response. The linguistic resonances between the character's silence and the text's form of address will not have escaped Perec as the French '*il s'est tu*' (he stopped speaking) also suggests '"he" is "you"' ('"il"' c'est "tu"'). This mode of address is signaled in the novel's epigram from Kafka and aligned with further strategic uses of voice-over in Perec and Bober's *Ellis Island Revisited* (1980), which is delivered in a historically and emotionally charged 'we' form.[16] The impact of narrative voice in the film is, of course, that of a spoken voice and any potential ambiguity of its status as internal monologue is undone by the choice of female voices. The defamiliarisation caused by Ludmila Mikaël's voice in the original pales in comparison with Shelley Duval's English version with strong Texan accent and trademark disconnected style.[17] The combination of the use of the present tense and the voice-over's asynchronous nature further obscures a subjective ordering of the spatio-temporal scapes of city or film. The common markers of the subject are placed under risk of erasure by the voice-over's form and content[18] and by the protagonist's association with a restricted space, yet he remains constantly visible on screen. Indeed, the use of mid-shot or close-up asserts his dominance of the too-small bed and apartment, evoking Perec's descriptions of the uninhabitable in *Species of Spaces* (which he was writing while filming) but refutes that text's view of the bed as site par excellence of imagination.[19] A reflective space for the spectator is created through the rupture between script, sound and image and the use of asynchronous sound. At the same time, however, the protagonist's subjectivity, conventionally posited via the filmic point of view, is elided as the camera, independently positioned in both stasis and movement, asserts his position as but one relative element in the composition of the frame. Recurring close-ups on the infra-ordinary objects designated repeatedly in the voice-over – the plastic bowl, books read and unread[20] – suggest diverse sites of meaning informed further by the familiar Perecquian trope in which the presence of significant numbers in his work carry traces of unspeakable loss in the text, for example the date of his mother's disappearance.[21] Annelies Schulte Nordholt draws on Claude Burgelin's analysis[22] to trace intertextual links with Perec's other works and to suggest that the written text, *A Man Asleep*, attempts to gain access to the suffering of the murdered parents via representation of the apartment space as cell and that its enforced occupation serves further as metaphor for the process of psychoanalysis with the 'neighbour' as analyst.[23] Support for such readings is less evident in the film as the repeated close-ups of the protagonist's reflection in the cracked mirror and the pattern of alternating scenes between domestic and city spaces foreground rather the protagonist's fragmented interiority and general dislocation from the world.[24]

The filmic construction of the apartment adds pictures not described in the written texts. These pictures serve as visual *mises-en-abyme* of central themes of the film and recall Godard's strategies of inserting visual intertexts in domestic settings that encourage reflection on representation itself.[25] The book on the protagonist's lap is switched from the political sociology of Perec's 1967 written text, Aron's *Eighteen Lectures on Industrial Society,* to Lefebvre's *Everyday Life in the Modern World,* a contextual and conceptual update and ironic comment on the protagonist's (in)capacity for revolutionary practice.[26] The placing of Escher's *Relativity* on the apartment wall suggests not a labyrinthine incarceration but a hermetic vision of time and space not measurable in linear progression. Several shots of the protagonist are dominated by the emphatic positioning of Magritte's *Not to be reproduced* (1937) set above his bed, which provokes a sense of malaise in its rupture with expectations of the returned image in the mirror, anxieties around seeing (as subject) and being seen (as object) and questions of the limits of representation (see Figure 4.1).

The filmic response to the presence of these images is to assert its cinematic capacity to represent actual and virtual dimensions. This is achieved through the insertion of the special effect that produces visual infinite regress of the protagonist and thus extends the impact of the Magritte image (see Figure 4.2). It also serves to prefigure Perec's recurrent use of the one-point perspective that dominates the compositions of external landscapes in *The Man Who Sleeps*. The one-point perspective is

Figure 4.1 Visual intertextualities – the protagonist in his domestic space in *The Man Who Sleeps*. © La vie est belle editions

Figure 4.2 Infinite regress: an example of the creation of non-realist space in *The Man Who Sleeps*. © La vie est belle editions

a highly artificial construction of an image, used first in drawing to create the impression of three-dimensional space, in which all visual lines in the image appear to converge on a single point in the centre of the horizon (known as the vanishing point).

Cityscapes, the disappeared and vanishing points

Paula Klein describes the topographies of Perec's novel as constructing places of indifference,[27] yet in the filmic text, although the protagonist's gaze is described as only drifting over objects and images,[28] the filming of these spaces cannot but construct meaning through position, movement and sound. The potential for creative rules in the protagonist's itineraries that was present in the novel is largely cut from the French voice-over. The voice-over's emphatic use of the verb 'traîner', suggesting sluggish navigation of space and time, ensures he manifests neither the desiring gaze of the *flâneur* nor the serious play of the Situationist *dérive*. However, this sticky movement contrasts with the oneiric, sweeping travelling shots, which construct a slow, smooth movement – one which suggests both an independent point of view and an eerie phantom presence.

The film's representation of external spaces, whether a deserted classroom[29] or empty cityscape, creates a strangely timeless, spatial uncanny in which sites are seemingly chosen for their lack of signals of modernity and further defamiliarised through the use of black and white coupled with the emphatically non-realist, slow, formal movements of an independently mobile camera often across deserted spaces.[30] The apparently vanished inhabitants fill the screen with their absence, evoking Perecquian tropes of loss (including specifically that of his mother, as a disappearance rather than a death) as an emphatically visible void.[31] Unfortunately, there is not room in this chapter to map the real spaces filmed against places noted in the text that provide autobiographical sites,[32] intertextual links[33] and historical traces.[34]

Filmic conventions of the use of the travelling shot construct it as a visual signal of narrative progression (left to right) or regression (right to left) that – if a central protagonist is within the frame – builds spectatorial identification with the character and their projected narrative, future or past. The cityscapes of *The Man Who Sleeps*, however, are dominated by travelling shots, which feature the camera moving forwards rather than horizontally across the screen. This shot – with its evocation, through the apparently fixed frame, of the still image – undermines the association of movement with a linear temporality. These smooth, eerie travelling shots of country roads, embankments and empty streets are not, however, still images and, while not associated with narrative progression or regression, they invite the spectator to enter the filmic space through a movement that communicates duration and projection of time as the camera moves towards a fixed point. Thus, the film language, through these travelling shots, provides a visual counterpoint to the voice-over's description of the protagonist's attempts to forget, to suspend time, to be 'the nameless master of the world, he on whom history has no grip'.[35] The advancing or retreating travelling sequences are usually followed in the film by a shot which responds directly to it. These sequences present the same landscape – empty roads and embankments – but feature a static camera centred on the protagonist who walks towards the camera, positioned within the converging lines of the one-point perspective but some way from the vanishing point. At first, the spectator anticipates radical spatial rupture in that the protagonist may break the fourth wall of the film by walking past the camera, by subjecting us to his direct gaze or even by speaking to us. None of these ruptures occurs, however, as the protagonist stops before reaching the camera position and looks beyond us with an anxious, distracted look that is contained within narrative parameters. The dynamic built up in these paired sequences thus moves between the travelling shots' dread-filled projection of an inevitable but unrepresentable future and a seeming return and witnessing of inevitable horror at an inescapable distance. The independent camera position reinforces the protagonist's inability to escape this spatio-temporal constraint set within a superficially open landscape. While the protagonist attempts to suspend his relationship with linear time(s) and space(s), as evident in the never-ending present tense of the voice-over and his practices of routine indifference, the construction of these travelling shots suggests a sinister subjective temporality – a channel, which traps both him and us in an empty, endless, claustrophobic durationality.

The simultaneous disruption of linearity and construction of subjective time are further supported by the use of asynchronous sounds in which noises associated with the apartment are often heard when the image is of external spaces. The emphatic use of the commissioned *musique concrète* of Ensemble 010, whose atonal refrains create sounds in slow motion and indecipherable syllables, provides a striking match with the slow rhythms of the camera movement.

In *The Man Who Sleeps*, the menacing nature of these sequences is reinforced by the use of striking one-point perspective and central vanishing points at which receding parallel lines appear to converge, creating a focal site which organises all around it (see Figures 4.3 and 4.4).[36]

Figure 4.3 The imposing use of the vanishing point in *The Man Who Sleeps*. © La vie est belle editions

Figure 4.4 Constructing a visual malaise: the haunted empty streets of *The Man Who Sleeps*. © La vie est belle editions

The visual imposition of a geometric conception of space, which projects an abstracted and impossible position of universal control and mastery, constructs suspense, apprehension and a visual malaise.

Filmic 'impli-citations'

The written text of *A Man Asleep* is constructed almost entirely from dense, unacknowledged citational networks, including Proust (the title), Kafka (the epigraph), Melville, Michaux, Butor, Joyce and Dante to create a strangely familiar voice.[37] Perec's 'impli-citations'[38] create a textual uncanny that might be seen to suggest the vanishing point of the text and the (under)mining of the construction of authorial presence itself were it not for the paradoxical model asserted throughout Perec's *oeuvre* of a creative agency asserted via textual experiment and constraint. In asserting the cinematic qualities of *The Man Who Sleeps*, we must also pursue the visual 'impli-citations' which populate its filmic construction of time and space. The filmic 'impli-citations' I want to propose here are those of Resnais and Kubrick.

The Man Who Sleeps may seem to belong to a different era than Kubrick's *oeuvre*, yet Perec wrote a review of *A Clockwork Orange* (1971), which he described as a representation of the symbolic violence of capitalism,[39] and he wanted Kubrick and Kazan to co-direct a film of his *W, or The Memory of Childhood* (1975).[40] The construction of Kubrickian dread relies upon his signature use of the one-point perspective and central vanishing point, which creates an oppressive sense of unease. This permeates Kubrick's films from the too-perfect interiors of the space station in *2001: A Space Odyssey* (1968), which provide superficial counterpoints to the collapse of time, to the menacing landscapes of *A Clockwork Orange* and the gardens and hotel corridors of *The Shining* (1980) whose extreme symmetries seem to invite violent disorder.

A line of influence can be traced from Kubrick back to Alain Resnais, suggesting the impact of *Last Year at Marienbad* (1961) on *2001: A Space Odyssey*. Resnais' formal experimentation throughout the 1950s and 1960s foregrounds the radical disruptions of narrative time and space, wrought by traumas personal and historical, to navigate the ethical, aesthetic and political dynamics of representing memory and trauma. Resnais' use of contrapuntal editing, asynchronous sound and image, an independently mobile camera, smooth sinister tracking and panning shots, use of voice-over and detached delivery of dialogue creates a spectacular formal severity which, through formal distanciation, enhances emotional and ethical impact. Queysanne notes their repeated viewing of *Hiroshima mon amour* (1959) before filming, and reveals Perec's refusal to cut references to it from the voice-over narration.[41] The use of one-point perspective, asserted through a centrally situated vanishing point, punctuates Resnais' cinema of the 50s and 60s – from the silent hospital corridors of hidden trauma in *Hiroshima mon amour* to the oppressive formal gardens and labyrinthine corridors of the chateau in *Last Year in Marienbad*. *Hiroshima mon amour*'s use of a disembodied voice for Lui's challenges to Elle's access to trauma – 'you [*tu*] saw nothing at Hiroshima' – also prefigure Perec's choice of address (his novel text was written after Resnais' film was released). The cinematographer of *The Man Who Sleeps*, Bernard Zitzermann, had worked on *Far from Vietnam* (1967) with members of the Left Bank group (Varda, Resnais, Marker and Godard) who were at the forefront of the construction of political meaning through film form (in addition to film content), including interrogations of the ethics and aesthetics of representing memory and trauma in cinema.[42] Indeed, Zitzermann, Spiesser and Ruh all also worked on Resnais' *Stavisky* in 1974.

While this discussion of Resnais' work has focused on two later films, the work partially obscured by these references is of course the 'cinéma concentrationnaire' of *Night and Fog* (1955),[43] in which smooth travelling shots move above the abandoned rail tracks towards the extermination camps, bearing witness through film language to a vanishing point that defeats direct representation but is projected nonetheless.[44] The film script of *The Man Who Sleeps* has a short section title, 'Destruction', in which an apocalyptic vision emerges, described thus: 'Now you have run out of hiding places. You are afraid. You are waiting for everything to stop, the rain, the hours, the stream of traffic, life, people, the world [...] waiting for the fire without flames to consume the stairs [...] waiting for the rust and mist to invade the city.'[45] In the voice-over, the sounds of this annihilation in the French '*rouille et brume*' (rust and mist) clearly evoke the term '*nuit et brouillard*', the name given to the Nazi decree which ordered the 'disappearing' of innumerable people.[46] In an interview on the written text of *A Man Asleep*, Perec describes the protagonist's existence as being 'entre parenthèses', as suspended, as put aside.[47] The protagonist's attempts to 'bracket out' the unsaid, the losses, the deprivations and suffering of others that haunt him, assert a textual vanishing point, and containment of them reinforces the parameters of the screen image, drawing our eye towards an inevitable imminence – textual, visual and filmic vanishing points leading to horizons of unrepresentable loss.

Figure 4.5 The surveillance camera evokes the question of bearing (visual) witness for both film and spectator in *The Man Who Sleeps*. © La vie est belle editions

As the protagonist becomes increasingly distressed (signalled by the film text's section headings of 'Anxiety', 'The Monsters' and 'Destruction') so the voice-over describes an increasing loss of agency and control over space and time, presenting him as a lab rat in an abandoned experiment and a messenger carrying a letter with no address.[48] Yet, except for two lingering shots of early surveillance cameras (see Figure 4.5), the filmic representation of the navigation of space does not change.

Escaping the vanishing point

As the narrator recounts the failure of the radical practice of indifference – 'indifference has not made you different'[49] – so the protagonist's return to a different mapping of the city space and the self is asserted by a radical shift in the film's construction of space. The repeated visual trope of the protagonist walking towards the camera down the middle of an empty road with converging lines of perspective begins (suggested by the lines of parked cars), yet this time there is no vanishing point on screen and the one-point perspective is shattered as he turns to the left, almost leaving the frame, and walks into a populated Belleville street clearly marked as rue du Transvaal (*not* the place Clichy of the narration). The final sequences of the film feature a magical coincidence as Queysanne's substitution of Belleville for Clichy and the final panorama across Paris includes Perec's childhood home in rue Vilin. The camera moves smoothly away from the protagonist and pans across apartment windows, trees and rooftops, creating a layered texture of complex, inhabited spaces that are not ordered by the sinister geometries of the one-point perspective nor by any trace of an abstract mastery of space. The filmic device of the lap dissolve (in which an image fades in as another fades out) evokes a sense of time as constructed through the layering of images and suggests memories emerging from within each other in non-linear relations. As the narrator instructs him to 'stop speaking like a man dreaming and look', an extensive panning shot (540°) takes in a misty panorama with the (barely visible) Eiffel tower before returning to the streetscape just as the protagonist walks away down a dark flight of steps and into a street where the camera does not follow him. The temporal integration asserted by the voice-over – 'you are no longer the anonymous master of the world, he on whom history had no grip [...]' – is joined by the visual and spatial re-integration of the protagonist into the social fabric of the city beyond the claustrophobic parameters of both the apartment and the one-point perspective. He escapes the gaze of the camera and the frame of the screen.[50] The camera pans again to settle on the same shot of the cityscape that opens the film (see Figure 4.6), suggesting not a cyclical narrative but rather an ambiguous sense of the narrative's duration and a continuing everyday reality.

In the narrator's 'everything begins again, everything begins, everything continues', the striking similarity between the French '*tout*' (everything) and '*tu*' (you) resonate to suggest that the self also begins again. In dismissing his attempt to experience a living death (*vivre au point mort*),[51] thus referencing the containments and deprivations of absent others, the protagonist is seemingly reintegrated into linear, historic time and social space.

The quotation from Perec with which this chapter begins – 'To live is to pass from one space to another [...]'[52] – suggests an alignment between life and the capacity to negotiate space successfully, constructing a spatial agency achieved through progression, transposition and integration. The film's ending suggests that to live, therefore, entails escaping the constraints of the one-point perspective and the vanishing point whose dual functions project both an anxious, illusory mastery of time and

Figure 4.6 Everything begins again. The opening and closing shot of *The Man Who Sleeps*. © La vie est belle editions

space and an over-determined channel of temporal movement and spatial perception.

This chapter's mapping of *The Man Who Sleeps* reveals Perec's engagement with the specificities of the construction of meaning through film language and identifies the ways in which the film works across textual, filmic, intertextual and intermedial spaces to articulate a complex series of vanishings and absences. In doing so it creates a new network of connections for the film and other written text(s). Perec and Queysanne's *The Man Who Sleeps* is a film in dialogue with Perec's *oeuvre* and with its central thematic and formal concerns, but also with the capacity of film language and filmic practice to manipulate and disrupt the representation and perception of time and space. Deleuze, in a discussion of Resnais' *Last Year at Marienbad* among other films, describes: 'a simultaneity of a present of past, a present of present and a present of future, which makes time frightening and inexplicable'.[53] Cinema's capacity to render time and thought visible, asserted in Deleuze's analysis of the time-image, provides a rich medium through which Perec and Queysanne worked with their innovative film collaborators to construct cinema not (only) 'as a factory for making ghosts',[54] but as a spatio-temporal site of representation in which memory, absence and life can be reconfigured.

Notes

1. Perec, *Species of Spaces*, 6.
2. The title *A Man Asleep* signals the English translation of Perec's written text and I use the commonly cited translation *The Man Who Sleeps* for the title of the film.
3. Queysanne, 'Afterword', in *Un homme qui dort*, 46.
4. 'Last Year in Marienbad' is described by them as 'a load of crap'. Perec, *Things*, 56.
5. Perec, *Entretiens et Conférences*, 151. My translation.
6. Perec and Corneau, 'A propos du film *Série noire*'. My translation.
7. 'We co-directed, co-wrote but also co-edited, co-mixed, co-promoted. [...] All decisions, all choices were to be made jointly.' Perec and Queysanne, 'Afterword', in *Un homme qui dort*, 46. My translation.
8. Perec and Queysanne, *Lire-traduire* and *Propos amicaux à propos d'espèces d'espaces*, 2007.
9. Perec and Queysanne, 'Afterword', in *Un homme qui dort*, 47.
10. Perec and Queysanne, 'Afterword', in *Un homme qui dort*, 49. My translation.
11. Perec, *Entretiens et Conférences, Volume I, 1965–1978*, 151. My translation.
12. It was produced by Pierre Neurisse, whose company Dovidis supported radical film-making and funded Marker's *Le Fond de l'air est rouge* (1977).
13. 'You're not going to say on four, eight, or twelve ruled pages what you know, what you think, what you know you should think about alienation, the working class, life and leisure, about the working class, modernity or leisure, about the white-collar worker or automation, about our ability to know other people, about Marx versus Tocqueville [...] You won't get your degree, you'll never begin your advanced studies. You won't study any more.' Perec and Queysanne, *Un homme qui dort*, 9. My translation.
14. Lejeune discovered an earlier version of the project entitled 'Auto-portraits'. Lejeune, *La mémoire et l'oblique*, 29.
15. He is neither a Romantic sleeper (*dormeur*) nor a sinister Sleeper.
16. The epigram functions ambiguously here in its instruction to 'you' (and us) to stay 'absolutely silent and solitary' at home and to wait for the world to reveal itself.
17. Okiishi, 'On Georges Perec's *Un homme qui dort*'.
18. 'Something has broken. You no longer feel supported: something that had comforted you until now, warmed your heart, the feeling of existence, the impression of being connected, of immersion in the world, starts to break down.' Perec and Queysanne, *Un homme qui dort*, 10. My translation.
19. Perec, *Species of Spaces*, 16, and 'the skimped, the airless, the small, the mean, the shrunken, the very precisely calculated', 89.
20. The key objects also appear in *Species of Spaces*. 'When does somewhere become truly yours? Is it when you've put your three pairs of socks to soak in a pink plastic bowl?' Perec, *Species of Spaces,* 24.
21. See Bellos, *Georges Perec*, and Schulte Nordholt, *Perec, Modiano, Raczymov*.
22. Burgelin, 'Perec et la cruauté', 33.
23. Schulte Nordholt, *Perec, Modiano, Raczymov*, 68.
24. This recalls the central visual trope of Godard's *Le Petit Soldat* (1963) (reprised in Claire Denis' *Beau travail*) of covering / revealing the protagonist's face before a mirror to reveal fixation with the gap between interiority and external reality.
25. The incongruous tourist posters for Tunisia reference the film's co-production by Tunisian state film company, SATPEC, via Perec's friend Noureddine Mechri.
26. *La vie quotidienne dans le monde moderne* was first published in 1968.
27. Klein, 'Surmonter le sommeil'.
28. Perec and Queysanne, *Un homme qui dort*, 11 and 24.
29. The empty classroom seen in the film was that of Paul Virilio.
30. They also avoided using easily datable cars or clothing. Perec and Queysanne's 'Afterword', in *Un homme qui dort*, 47.
31. Perec's father died at the front in 1940 and his mother disappeared in Auschwitz in 1943. See Burgelin, 'Perec et la cruauté', 33.
32. For such mappings, see Bellos, *Georges Perec*, 347 and 362–3.

33. Perec worked simultaneously on two projects because some of the spaces filmed for *The Man Who Sleeps* are those that he needed to revisit as part of his highly structured, ongoing *Lieux* project. Bellos, *Georges Perec*, 524.
34. Schulte Nordholt notes the Gestapo addresses of quai des Orfèvres, place Beauvais and the mention of 'the wearers of invisible stars'. *Perec. Modiano, Raczymov*, 85.
35. Perec and Queysanne, *Un homme qui dort*, 25. My translation.
36. The French term 'ligne de fuite' also triggers Deleuzian trajectories of escape from linearity but his usage should not be conflated here with the visual construction of the image.
37. Andrews, 'Puzzles and Lists'.
38. The neologism 'impli-citation' was coined by Bernard Magné in his 'Quelques problèmes de l'énonciation en régime fictionnel'.
39. Perec, 'L'orange est proche', 1–2.
40. Bellos, *Georges Perec*, 660.
41. Perec kept 'the queues that form every two hours in front of the seven cinemas of the rue Champollion' for its echo of the 'seven branches of the estuary above the river Ota' from *Hiroshima mon amour*. Queysanne, 'Afterword', in *Un homme qui dort*, 48. My translation.
42. Zitzermann provided the same tone to Perec's *Les lieux d'une fugue* (1978).
43. See Pollock and Silverman, *Concentrationary Cinema*.
44. The voice-over in *Night and Fog* also reminds us that 'any small country lane could lead to a camp'.
45. Perec and Queysanne, *Un homme qui dort*, 35. My translation.
46. This 'brume' is positioned prominently at the start of Perec's *W, or The Memory of Childhood*, published in 1975 in the epigraph from Queneau 'that mindless mist where shadows swirl, how could I pierce it?' Perec, *W*, 2.
47. Perec, 'à propos de *Un homme qui dort*'. My translation.
48. Perec and Queysanne, *Un homme qui dort*, 24. My translation. Schulte Nordholt links the references to rats as evoking the common representation in Nazi propaganda of the Jew as rat. *Perec, Modiano, Raczymov*, 54.
49. Perec and Queysanne, *Un homme qui dort*, 37. My translation.
50. Perec and Queysanne, *Un homme qui dort*, 38. My translation.
51. Description on cover of DVD release 2007.
52. Perec, *Species of Spaces*, 6.
53. Deleuze, *Cinema 2*, 98.
54. Cocteau, *The Art of Cinema*, 131.

Filmography

2001: A Space Odyssey (UK, 1968, Kubrick)
A Clockwork Orange (UK, 1971, Kubrick)
Ellis Island Revisited: Tales of Vagrancy and Hope/Récits d'Ellis Island: histoires d'errance et d'espoir (France, 1980, Bober)
Far from Vietnam / Loin du Vietnam (France, 1967, Ivens, Klein, Lelouch, Varda, Godard, Marker, Resnais)
Hiroshima mon amour (France, 1959, Resnais)
Il Posto (Italy, 1961, Olmi)
Last Year at Marienbad / L'Année dernière à Marienbad (France, 1961, Resnais)
Les lieux d'une fugue (France, 1978, Perec)
Night and Fog / Nuit et Brouillard (France, 1955, Resnais)
Série noire (France, 1979, Corneau)
Stavisky (France, 1974, Resnais)
The Man Who Sleeps / Un homme qui dort (France, 1974, Queysanne)
The Shining (UK, 1980, Kubrick)

Bibliography

Andrews, Chris. 'Puzzles and Lists: Georges Perec's *Un homme qui dort*', *Modern Language Notes* 111, no. 4 (1996): 775–96.

Bellos, David. *Georges Perec: Une vie dans les mots*. Paris: Éditions du Seuil, 1994.

Burgelin, Claude. 'Perec et la cruauté'. In *Cahiers Georges Perec 1: Colloque de Cerisy (juillet 1984)*, 31–52. Paris: P.O.L., 1985.

Cocteau, Jean. *The Art of Cinema*, translated by Robin Buss. London: Marion Boyars, 2001.

Deleuze, Gilles. *Cinema 2: The Time-Image*, translated by Hugh Tomlinson and Robert Galeta. London: Athlone Press, 1989.

Klein, Paula. 'Surmonter le sommeil, espérer contre toute attente: Un homme qui dort et l'exploration des "lieux" de l'indifférence', *Fabula LHT: Littérature histoire théorie* 15 (2015). Accessed 4 May 2019. http://www.fabula.org/lht/15/klein.html.

Lejeune, Philippe. *La mémoire et l'oblique: Georges Perec autobiographe*. Paris: P.O.L., 1991.

Magné, Bernard. 'Quelques problèmes de l'énonciation en régime fictionnel: L'exemple de *La vie mode d'emploi*'. In *Perecollages 1981–1988*, 61–98. Toulouse: Presses universitaires du Mirail-Toulouse, 1989.

Molteni, Patrizia. 'Perec's Painterly Eye', *Review of Contemporary Fiction* 29, no. 1 (2009): 210–23.

Okiishi, Ken. 'On Georges Perec's *Un homme qui dort*', *Bidoun* 14 (2008). Accessed 4 May 2019. https://bidoun.org/articles/the-archive.

Penz, François. *Cinematic Aided Design: An Everyday Life Approach to Architecture*. London: Routledge, 2017.

Perec, Georges. 'Georges Perec à propos de *Un homme qui dort*', *Lectures pour tous*, 3 May 1967. Video. Accessed 9 May 2019. http://www.ina.fr/video/I08261871.

Perec, Georges. 'L'orange est proche', *Cause commune* 3 (1972): 1–2.

Perec, Georges. *Species of Spaces and Other Pieces*, edited and translated by John Sturrock. London: Penguin Books, 1997.

Perec, Georges. *Entretiens et conférences, Volume 1: 1965–1978*. Nantes: Joseph K., 2003.

Perec, Georges. *Things: A Story of the Sixties, with A Man Asleep*, translated by David Bellos and Andrew Leak. London: Vintage Books, 2011.

Perec, Georges. *W, or The Memory of Childhood*, translated by David Bellos. London: Vintage Books, 2011.

Perec, Georges and Alain Corneau. 'Georges Perec et Alain Corneau à propos du film *Série noire*', *Ciné regards*, France Régions 3, 8 April 1979. Video. Accessed 9 May 2019. http://www.ina.fr/video/I00005540/georges-perec-et-alain-corneau-a-propos-du-film-serie-noire-video.html.

Perec, Georges and Bernard Queysanne. 'Entretien avec Perec et Queysanne', *Cinéma* 189 (1974): 47–51.

Perec, Georges and Bernard Queysanne. *Un homme qui dort*. DVD. Paris: La vie est belle éditions, 2007.

Perec, Georges and Bernard Queysanne. *Un homme qui dort: Texte intégral inédit du film*. Included with DVD release. Paris: La vie est belle éditions, 2007.

Pollock, Griselda and Max Silverman, eds. *Concentrationary Cinema: Aesthetics as Political Resistance in Alain Resnais's Night and Fog (1955)*. New York: Berghahn Books, 2011.

Queysanne, Bernard. 'Lire-traduire Georges Perec (1999)'. Included in DVD release of *Un homme qui dort*. Paris: La vie est belle éditions, 2007.

Queysanne, Bernard. 'Propos amicaux à propos d'espèces d'espaces (1999)'. Included in DVD release of *Un homme qui dort*. Paris: La vie est belle éditions, 2007.

Saxton, Libby. 'Holocaust Writing and Film'. In *The Cambridge History of French Literature*, edited by William Burgwinkle, Nicholas Hammond and Emma Wilson, 671–79. Cambridge: Cambridge University Press, 2011.

Schulte Nordholt, Annelies. 'Georges Perec: Topographies parisiennes du flâneur', *RELIEF: Revue électronique de littérature française* 2, no. 1 (2008): 66–86.

Schulte Nordholt, Annelies. *Perec, Modiano, Raczymov: La génération d'après et la mémoire de la Shoah*. Amsterdam: Rodopi, 2008.

Van Montfrans, Manet. *Georges Perec: La contrainte du réel*. Amsterdam: Rodopi, 1999.

Villeneuve, Lisa. 'The Urban Experience of Placelessness: Perceptual Rhythms in Georges Perec's *Un homme qui dort*'. *In Rhythms: Essays in French Literature, Thought and Culture*, edited by Elizabeth Lindley and Laura McMahon, 171–86. Bern: Peter Lang, 2008.

Wagstaff, Peter. 'The Dark Side of Utopia: Word, Image, and Memory in Georges Perec's *Récits d'Ellis Island: Histoires d'errance et d'espoir*'. In *The Seeing Century: Film, Vision, and Identity*, edited by Wendy Everett, 36–48. Amsterdam: Rodopi, 2000.

Yvan, Frédéric. 'L'extase du vide de *Un homme qui dort* à *Espèces d'espaces* de Georges Perec', *Savoirs et clinique* 1, no. 8 (2007): 143–53. Accessed 4 May 2019. https://www.cairn.info/revue-savoirs-et-cliniques-2007-1-page-143.htm.

5

Species of Spaces and the politics of scale: Perec, Gaullism and geography after Lefebvre

Douglas Smith

In certain respects, 1974 marks the apogee of Gaullism. It is the year in which some of its most ambitious infrastructural projects, such as the Paris ring road and Roissy airport, were completed. But, in other ways, the same year represents the end of Gaullism, with the death of Georges Pompidou, de Gaulle's successor and political heir, and the election to the presidency of Valéry Giscard d'Estaing, a liberal with a taste for conservation rather than modernisation and a preference for private enterprise rather than state intervention. If in 1974 Gaullism found itself politically outflanked on the Right, it was also the object of sustained intellectual critique from the Left, exemplified by the publication of two significant works that engaged with the spatial planning undertaken by the Gaullist regime since 1958: *Species of Spaces* by Georges Perec and *The Production of Space* by Henri Lefebvre.[1]

In spite of generational differences, Lefebvre and Perec were acquainted both personally and professionally. As a young man completing his military service, Perec entered Lefebvre's social and intellectual circle in the late 1950s and was employed by him as a research assistant in the early 1960s.[2] They shared intellectual and political interests in the organisation of everyday life and spatial planning. In the immediate post-war period, Lefebvre had pioneered the study of the everyday in the early volumes of his *Critique of Everyday Life* before engaging critically with urban and spatial planning in the late 1960s and early 1970s.[3] Lefebvre's work was underpinned by a Hegelian humanist critique of the alienation that in his view permeated the minutiae of life in developed capitalist society and by a countervailing commitment to an ideal of wholeness or totality understood as both a social goal (the full realisation of human potential freed from the constraints of capitalism) and an intellectual ambition (the global analysis of socio-economic relations offered by the Marxist tradition). Perec, however, was sceptical of all totalising projects, which he viewed as controlling and oppressive rather than liberating. So, in spite of their shared interests, he and Lefebvre adopted significantly different approaches to the subject of space in their respective publications of 1974.

Lefebvre's *The Production of Space* was an ambitious attempt by an academic sociologist to develop a new model for the understanding of space within a capitalist economy. It represented the culmination of six years of intensive research devoted to the relations between space, politics and economics, a period that encompassed not only the writing of multiple books and articles but also the founding of the journal *Espace et politique* in 1970.[4] Lefebvre's work on space had a significant impact on French critical urbanism in the 1970s and it would go on to exert a strong influence on anglophone Marxist human geography from the 1980s, as figures such as David Harvey and Neil Smith proceeded to tease out many of the implications of his ideas.[5]

In contrast, Perec's *Species of Spaces* was a much more modest work by a creative writer committed to an ironic and quizzical investigation of the spaces of everyday life. It combined a microscopic attention to detail with a quirky project of spatial classification. In the process, Perec's work proposed a vision of space that opened up new critical perspectives on Gaullism but also laid the basis for questioning some of the assumptions shared by Lefebvre and the geographers working within the framework he established. The particular focus of this chapter will be the relationship of Perec's work to Gaullist spatial planning and the 'politics of scale' model developed by Neil Smith and others. The discussion opens with Perec's work, proceeds to explore some aspects of Gaullist planning before finally considering how both might be understood in terms of the notion of scale as developed within what might be called a Lefebvrian human geography. Essentially, the main points of the argument are as follows: first, in spite of his emphasis on the microscopic aspects of everyday life, Perec is concerned with the large-scale as well as the small-scale; second, in spite of its enthusiasm for macro-planning, Gaullism is concerned with the small-scale as well as the large-scale; and third, both Perec and Gaullism engage in what geographers have called 'scale-jumping' or 'scale-bending', with the twist that Perec ends by bending the very notion of scale itself out of shape.

Perec: The micro and the macro

In 1972, Perec collaborated with Jean Duvignaud and Paul Virilio to found the journal *Cause commune,* whose aim was to explore the unexamined dimensions of everyday life in post-1968 France.[6] The following year, with this shared project in mind, Perec invented the concept of the 'infra-ordinary' to describe the object of his writing practice.[7] The infra-ordinary stood in contrast to both the extra-ordinary, the spectacular events that command our attention, and the ordinary, the familiar events of which we remain minimally aware, designating instead the microscopic texture of the everyday that we completely overlook. In his essay 'Approaches to What?', Perec outlined one of the guiding questions of his work as follows: 'How should we take account of, question, describe what happens every day and recurs every day: the banal, the quotidian, the obvious, the common, the ordinary, the infra-ordinary, the background noise, the habitual?'[8] Perec's notion of the infra-ordinary clearly built on the work of previous analysts of the everyday, notably Henri Lefebvre, who more or less invented the field in 1947, and Roland Barthes, whose *Mythologies* of 1957[9] pioneered the exploration of how thoroughly ideology permeated daily life. Like the work of Lefebvre and Barthes, Perec's emphasis on the infra-ordinary had political implications, operating on two levels. First, it represented a rehabilitation of the small-scale in an era of the grandiose, and, second, it offered considerable scope for a contestation of the ground-level effects of governmental planning.

Given his early awareness of the work of Georg Lukács and Jean-Paul Sartre, however, Perec was interested not just in the details of everyday life but also in attempts to produce more comprehensive models of social reality. So, in many of his texts, the macroscopic accompanies the microscopic. This is most visible perhaps in his longest single work, *Life: A User's Manual/La Vie mode d'emploi* (1978), a plural novel (subtitled *romans* or 'fictions') whose multiple micro-narratives nest within an overarching plotline.[10] Another form of totalisation emerges in the many taxonomies that recur across his writing, apparently aspiring to complete coverage of the diverse manifestations of a given phenomenon: Perec's work is full of lists. Far from being simple inventories, however, Perec's lists are deeply ambivalent, haunted by the twin impulses of totalisation and deliberate omission: 'In every enumeration there are two contradictory temptations. The first is to list *everything*, the second is to forget something. The first would like to close off the question once and for all, the second to leave it open.'[11] As this suggests, while Perec's works frequently describe or undertake apparently encyclopaedic projects, they also often seek to debunk or sabotage their claim to exhaustivity. Even if the comprehensive nature of such projects is called into question, however, the initial aspiration to provide a total account of a given field persists. Overall, rather than focusing exclusively on the infinitesimal, Perec's work operates across a wide range of scales, including the macroscopic. It is arguably through this range, and not in any exclusive focus on the infra-ordinary, that Perec seeks to challenge the Gaullist administration of space.

Gaullism and spatial planning

One of the chief goals of Gaullist spatial planning in the 1960s and 1970s was the state-sponsored modernisation of national infrastructure with a view to promoting economic growth and international competitiveness, thereby enhancing the prestige of France on a global level. From 1963, planning strategy was developed and overseen at national level by a dedicated body chaired by the Prime Minister, Georges Pompidou: the *Délégation interministérielle à l'aménagement du territoire et à l'action régionale* (DATAR). If the level of government intervention was often regional (the construction of a motorway or a power station), the intended aim was national and international. Spatial planning or territorial development (*aménagement du territoire*) was envisaged as a key instrument of the 'politique de la grandeur' pursued by de Gaulle.

Often translated into English as 'politics of greatness' or – retaining the French partially as a loan-word – 'politics of grandeur', de Gaulle's policy aimed to re-establish the diminished international prestige of France in the wake of the Second World War.[12] This involved a transition from what the historian Michel Winock has called an 'extensive' to an 'intensive' form of nationalism, the transformation of France from an overstretched late imperial power to a modern nation-state with a technologically advanced economy driven by consumer demand.[13] If decolonisation and a concentration on the domestic economy might have seemed a withdrawal from the world stage, such moves were accompanied on the level of foreign and defence policy by a strong reassertion of French independence in relation to the Cold War superpowers of the US and the USSR. In effect, both domestically and internationally, de Gaulle was challenging existing hierarchies of scale in order to enhance the image of France. His policies re-scaled both the internal space of the nation (through infrastructural development) and the external space of international relations (through an insistence on the continued relevance of the self-determining nation-state in an era of superpowers and satellites). In both instances, the importance of smaller units is reasserted against larger entities, as infrastructure links the local to the national and diplomacy amplifies the national to the global. In this context, it is useful to remember that the French 'grandeur' may be translated not only as 'greatness' or 'grandeur' but also as 'size' and 'scale'. In fact, the best translation for de Gaulle's 'politique de la grandeur' might well be 'politics of scale'. That de Gaulle himself was aware of this scalar aspect of his policy is clear from a speech of 1961: 'The ruler [*décimètre*] that measured the tiny advances of the past is now unusable [...] France is devoting itself to an immense undertaking [...] becoming before our eyes a great industrial power, that is to say, a great power full stop.'[14]

The politics of scale: Lefebvre and after

The basic premise of Lefebvre's *The Production of Space* is that space is a social product that is also a means of production and so can be used to generate capital accumulation through rent and development.[15] Far from being conceived as a passive container, space is actually a dynamic participant in multiple processes of exchange.[16] As a result, all space is necessarily layered (*feuilleté*) or composed of different scales.[17] The modern nation-state attempts to control its territory and its economy by intervening across a wide range of scales through development planning, but it cannot entirely control either local conditions or the global flow of capitalism.[18] According to Lefebvre, these multiple spatial processes can only be effectively analysed through a multi-scalar approach that is attentive to the different levels at which they function: 'Space's hegemony does not operate solely on the "micro" level [...]; nor does it apply only on the "macro" level [...] its effects may be observed on all planes and in all the interconnections between them.'[19]

Lefebvre explicitly understood his model of space as a critical intervention in the political debates around spatial planning in France, and the political implications of his discussion of scale would be taken up and extended by anglophone Marxist human geographers in the 1980s and 1990s. For Neil Smith, scale is the 'primary means by which geographical difference is organized'.[20] This means that scale is not just a geographical category but a key stake in political debates and conflicts. Political units or formations such as nation-states attempt to manage potential threats to their territorial identity by defining and managing different levels of analysis, decision and intervention. The result is what Smith calls a 'politics of scale'. The kind of threats to which a politics of scale attempts to respond may be internal (class-based social unrest or region-based secession movements) or external (the decisions of multinational corporations or supranational bodies).[21] One of the most significant threats to territorially defined entities such as nation-states is that posed by the effects of the time-space compression caused by the global operations of the capitalist economy.

As David Harvey has outlined, time-space compression is produced by the drive to increase the accumulation of capital by reducing its turnover time as far as possible, an imperative that leads to an acceleration of processes of production, distribution and consumption and the consequent 'shrinking' of physical space through the development of a global market for labour and commodities served by ever-advancing communications and transport technologies.[22] In order to manage the stresses produced by time-space compression, nation-states often have recourse to a spatial fix, a provisional solution that involves the exploitation or manipulation of space.[23] Historically, one classic way of generating a spatial fix has been to create overseas markets for surplus labour or capital through colonial expansion. Another form taken by the spatial fix is the elaboration of a politics of scale (as, for example, in the implementation of regional development programmes designed to compensate for the delocalisation or offshoring of industrial production).

The Gaullist programme of the 1960s clearly sought a spatial fix through a politics of scale. De Gaulle's domestic policy aimed at making the French economy more competitive by creating bigger internal markets and encouraging larger units of mechanised agricultural production and high-tech industrial output. At the same time, as we have seen, his foreign policy was designed to assert the importance of the nation-state in relation to multinational power blocs. In both instances, de Gaulle was engaging in 'scale-bending' or 'scale-jumping', that is, challenging relative notions of size in order to secure political advantage by pursuing, in Neil Smith's words, 'the concrete *production and reproduction of geographical scale* as a political strategy of resistance'.[24]

According to Smith, however, such manipulation of scale is 'double-edged', which means that scale-bending is not the sole preserve of instituted political authority and may indeed be directed against the state in turn.[25] On the political Left, de Gaulle's policies were widely perceived as colluding with capitalism rather than seeking to contain and manage it in the interests of the national community (as Gaullist ideology would have it). So Gaullist scale-bending was met with oppositional scale-bending. The street demonstrations and occupations of universities, cultural institutions and factories of May 1968 represented perhaps the most visible form of oppositional 'scale-bending', reasserting the space of everyday life against that of the nation-state. Other instances would follow, such as the campaign against the extension of the army base on the Larzac plateau, from 1971 on, a campaign that defended the space of pastoral agriculture against the expansion of the militarised nation-state and quickly escalated from a regional development dispute to a major national issue.[26] If Gaullism sought to further its ends by jumping scales from the infra-ordinary to the geopolitical, so too did its opponents.

Scale-bending in Perec: taxonomy and heterotopia

One significant focus of intellectual opposition to Gaullism was, as mentioned earlier, Perec's journal *Cause commune*. When fellow-founder Paul Virilio was invited by the publisher Galilée to edit a new series of books entitled 'L'Espace critique' (Critical Space), he promptly commissioned Perec to write *Species of Spaces*. Published at the end of a 16-year period of Gaullist hegemony, Perec's book represents perhaps the clearest instance of his practice of oppositional scale-bending.

The title of *Species of Spaces* seems to invoke the authority and example of the eighteenth-century Swedish naturalist Carl Linnaeus and his pioneering work on the classification of flora and fauna. A first glance at the table of contents apparently confirms that the book proposes an orderly taxonomy of different kinds of space, working upwards from the bounded confines of the printed page to the limitless extent of the universe, through the intermediate levels of bed, bedroom, apartment, building, street, quarter, town and so forth. This progression resembles the 'nested hierarchy' of scales sometimes evoked by human geographers as a way of conceptualising how different levels of space are articulated with one another.[27] However, upon further examination, Perec's commitment to a hierarchical taxonomy appears less clear-cut. First of all, in terms of overall organisation, the book begins by stressing the proliferating multiplicity of spaces in the modern world: 'There isn't one space [...], there's a whole lot of small bits of space.'[28] The book's conclusion ultimately emphasises the uncertainties that arise from contemplating such spaces: 'Space is a doubt'.[29] In both instances, *Species of Spaces* is bounded by an elusive heterogeneity rather than a stable system of distinctions. Further, some of the intervening sections of the text, far from devoting themselves to a single type or level of space, move frequently between different spaces and scales, as, for example, in the section devoted ostensibly to the apartment, where Perec digresses to discuss the idea of living in an airport.[30] Other sections deny the possibility of offering even a preliminary definition of their declared subject, such as the chapter devoted to 'The Town'.[31] Finally, the book as a whole does not in fact build towards a discussion of the all-encompassing space of an open universe (as the table of contents suggests); rather, the last specific space mentioned in the book is the uninhabitable space of a Nazi extermination camp, exemplified by the appalling incongruity of the landscape-gardening requirements of Auschwitz.[32] In the process, the neatness of an enclosed flowerbed is aligned with a genocidal desire for order. Throughout, then, the book seems to call into question the very idea of a tidy taxonomy of space, and this is borne out by the only passage that actually refers to Linnaeus.

The reference itself is characteristically oblique and takes the form of an anecdote located in the Parisian street named in honour of the Swedish naturalist, the rue Linné in the fifth arrondissement, adjacent to the Jardin des Plantes and the Natural History Museum.[33] Perec recounts seeing a blind man and woman walking along the street with the aid of flexible white canes, as the older woman adeptly explains to her younger companion the nature of the different items of street furniture they encounter. Perec might seem here to be associating scientific taxonomy with blindness, in which case the setting of the anecdote is ironic, and none too subtle. However, elsewhere in the book, Perec describes space as a predominantly visual construct, which is then necessarily limited by the human field of vision and becomes in turn an obstacle to that vision: 'Space is what arrests our gaze, what our sight stumbles over: the obstacles, bricks, an angle, a vanishing point.'[34] In this context, space and vision are antithetical, and blindness would paradoxically allow us to escape a constraining optical relationship to space. In fact, what is most striking about the rue Linné anecdote is how skilfully the visually impaired couple navigate the street. The blind woman in particular comes to represent an alternative mode of relating to space, a form of exploration and orientation that seems to embody one of Perec's opening remarks on the human relationship to space: 'To live is to pass from one space to another, while doing your very best not to bump yourself.'[35] That this goal is achieved through the mediation of a flexible prosthesis suggests a further parallel with Perec's writing practice, where the pen functions as an equivalent to the woman's white cane, both understood as indirect means of knowing and negotiating the everyday. If the street name rue Linné proposes an alignment between urban topography and scientific taxonomy, Perec's anecdote about the blind couple suggests how the visual emphasis of spatial knowledge, including the taxonomic tabulation of data, is itself a kind of metaphorical blindness to which actual blindness offers an alternative and more insightful way of engaging with the world.

Rather than proposing a neat taxonomic hierarchy of different kinds of space, then, *Species of Spaces* expresses a deep scepticism about the possibility of spatial classification. It does so by engaging in almost constant scale-jumping, challenging the distinctions it appears to propose and sliding across dimensions in a disconcerting way. As Perec says at one point, his project is one of 'playing with [units of] measurements [*jouer avec les mesures*]'.[36] In fact, Perec's space is not a stable defined space at all but rather a space that defies classification. The opening of the book suggests as much, with its juxtaposition of an empty box with a list of 52 types of space (or 51 if the word *espace* is itself excluded) whose sequence seems very loosely associative and certainly not descriptive of the contents to follow.[37] The relatively brief and arbitrary nature of this list suggests that it follows neither of the temptations of enumeration identified by Perec in 'Think/Classify': it neither aspires to totality nor sabotages itself through deliberate omission. In fact, it seems much closer to a third type of list, identified in *Life: A User's Manual*: one that contains an 'odd item' (*intrus*), something that does not belong.[38] In this instance, however, the problem is not that of a single incongruous item, but of a list that seems to consist almost exclusively of things that do not belong together, in spite of sharing the same lexical term (*espace*).

One of the best-known literary examples of heterogeneous listing is Jorge Luis Borges's 'John Wilkins' Analytical Language' (1942), a text to which Perec refers in 'Think/Classify'.[39] Counterintuitively, Perec suggests that Borges's egregious classifications are not as fantastic as they might appear, since similarly miscellaneous items and categories frequently occur in state regulations and statutes: 'An almost equally mind-boggling enumeration might be extracted simply enough from government documents that could hardly be more official.'[40] For Perec, the language of government is capable of the same random range and diversity as literary fantasy. Perhaps this is just as well, since the desire for orderly enumeration of a closed taxonomy represents in Perec's view a dispiritingly utopian project: 'All utopias are depressing because they leave no room for change, for difference, for the "miscellaneous".'[41] As a result, Perec's own approach to the classification of space is not utopian but heterotopian, in the sense first given to the term by Michel Foucault in his celebrated discussion of the Borges text in the *The Order of Things*. According to Foucault, a heterotopia is an other place whose otherness is predicated on the overflowing heterogeneity of what it ostensibly contains.[42] Since the heterotopia offers no common space within which to unify its disparate contents, it is itself strictly speaking an impossibility: 'What is impossible is not the propinquity of the things listed, but the very site on which their propinquity would be possible.'[43] In Foucault's terms, the heterotopia does away with the table, understood both as a flat horizontal surface that allows the arrangement of miscellaneous objects upon it and as a classificatory grid that organises data.[44] In his subsequent lecture 'Of Other Spaces' (1967), Foucault would go on to demonstrate how heterotopic the notion of heterotopia itself could be, proposing an almost endlessly proliferating set of different examples of heterotopian space, to the point where the specificity and explanatory power of the notion begins to evaporate.[45] Foucault's inventory of heterotopias includes such different spaces as gardens, cemeteries, asylums, brothels, prisons, theatres, cinemas, museums, libraries, funfairs, holiday camps, schools, barracks, saunas, motels, colonies and ships, and ultimately gives the impression that almost anywhere can be a heterotopia. So the point of the heterotopia is not to propose an alternative category of space but to explode the notion of spatial classification by postulating a space that is both impossible and (more or less) all-encompassing. Perec's *Species of Spaces* is a similarly heterotopic exercise, undoing the claims of scientific taxonomy in the interests of a more modest exploration of diverse multi-scalar spaces.

Conclusion: spaces, species and currencies

In response to Gaullism, Perec develops his own politics of scale. If in certain respects this appears to involve the consistent privileging of the microscopic and infra-ordinary, the reality is somewhat different. Faced with the full spectrum of Gaullist spatial planning, which runs from road repairs through regional development to international relations, Perec exploits an equally wide range of scales. However, in Perec's work, the result is not the assertion of a new scale, as with Gaullism, whose ultimate standard of measurement was the nation-state, but rather a disturbance of the notion of scale itself. *Species of Spaces* is a heterotopic work, one that bends scale to such an extent that it challenges the notion of a single stable space within which scale could be meaningful. The model of space as nested hierarchy is contested through the multiplication of heterogeneous spaces that operate simultaneously at different scales.

As such, Perec's work challenges not only the strategy adopted by the Gaullist administration of space but also some of the assumptions behind the analysis of scale undertaken by Lefebvre and the anglophone human geographers who elaborated on his ideas. For the latter, space as a social product may be multi-layered and contradictory but it is ultimately a single entity whose unity is assured by an all-encompassing capitalist system. In these terms, space is understood as a medium for the circulation and accumulation of capital, a commodity elevated to the status of a universal equivalent that allows the exchange of other more heterogeneous goods and services. Thus envisaged, space is a kind of money, a single currency into which everything else can be converted. The risk of full-spectrum multi-scalar analysis is then that it threatens to reduce the diversity of existing spaces to a closed list of items defined by a common denominator. In this process of homogenisation, classification is the first step towards the isolation of shared features that allows for reciprocal conversion.

In the title of his book, Perec acknowledges that spaces may be 'currencies' as well as 'species' (both are possible translations of *espèces*), but they are above all plural, that is, multiple and heterogeneous and, in Perec's view, unsuited either to assume the function of a universal equivalent or to undergo easy conversion into one. If we pursue the parallel economic and ecological resonances of the term *espèces*, it is clear that to refuse to convert multiple spaces into a single currency is also to protect their survival and diversity as distinct species. The reason behind Perec's departure from Linnaeus emerges: in his view, a classification table is a conversion table in the making. In a context where classification threatens to turn multiple spaces into endangered species, Perec opts for a deliberately scrambled and incomplete taxonomy as the most effective guarantee against their extinction.

Notes

1. Perec, *Species of Spaces*, 1–91, and Lefebvre, *The Production of Space*.
2. Bellos, *Georges Perec*, 192–3 and 236–7, and Sheringham, *Everyday Life*, 250–1.
3. The *Critique de la vie quotidienne* had a protracted publishing history: the first edition of volume one appeared in 1947 and was then re-edited in 1958 with a substantial new foreword (*Critique de la vie quotidienne I: Introduction*), followed by volume two in 1961 (*Critique de la vie quotidienne II: Fondements d'une sociologie de la quotidienneté*), and finally volume three in 1981 (*Critique de la vie quotidienne III: De la modernité au modernisme (Pour une métaphysique du quotidien)*). The *Critique* was only fully translated into English in the 2000s: volumes one and two translated by John Moore in 1992 and 2002 respectively (*Critique of Everyday Life 1: Introduction; Critique of Everyday Life 2: Foundations for a Sociology of the Everyday*), and volume three by Gregory Elliott in 2008 (*Critique of Everyday Life 3: From Modernity to Modernism (Towards a Metaphilosophy of Daily Life)*).
4. Hess, 'Henri Lefebvre et la pensée de l'espace', 5–16.

5. On the importance of Lefebvre for Marxist human geography in the anglophone world, see Soja, *Postmodern Geographies*, 41–2. *The Production of Space* was translated into English in 1991, and quickly became a key work in the so-called 'spatial turn' in the social sciences, but it is worth noting that figures such as Harvey, Smith and Soja were reading Lefebvre in French well before this. On some of the complexities of the history of the translation of Lefebvre's work into English, see Merrifield, *Henri Lefebvre*, 100–3.
6. Bellos, *Georges Perec*, 491–2, and Sheringham, *Everyday Life*, 249–50.
7. Bellos, *Georges Perec*, 523.
8. Perec, 'Approaches to What?', in *Species of Spaces*, 206.
9. Barthes, *Mythologies*.
10. Perec, *Life*.
11. Perec, 'Think/Classify', in *Species of Spaces*, 194.
12. Cerny, *The Politics of Grandeur*.
13. Winock, *Chronique des années soixante*, 41.
14. de Gaulle, 'Allocution radiodiffusée et télévisée prononcée au Palais de l'Élysée, le 12 juillet 1961', 327–9. My translation.
15. Lefebvre, *The Production of Space*, 26.
16. Lefebvre, *The Production of Space*, 93–4.
17. Lefebvre, *The Production of Space*, 86.
18. Lefebvre, *The Production of Space*, 378–9.
19. Lefebvre, *The Production of Space*, 412.
20. Smith, 'Geography, Difference and the Politics of Scale', 60.
21. Smith, 'Homeless/Global', 99–100.
22. Harvey, *The Condition of Postmodernity*, 284–307.
23. Harvey, *The Urban Experience*, 34.
24. Smith, 'Homeless/Global', 90.
25. Smith, 'Homeless/Global', 114.
26. Lebovics, *Bringing the Empire Back Home*, 13–57.
27. Smith, 'Geography, Difference and the Politics of Scale', 73.
28. Perec, *Species of Spaces*, 5–6.
29. Perec, *Species of Spaces*, 91.
30. Perec, *Species of Spaces*, 26–7.
31. Perec, *Species of Spaces*, 60.
32. Perec, *Species of Spaces*, 90.
33. Perec, *Species of Spaces*, 49.
34. Perec, *Species of Spaces*, 81.
35. Perec, *Species of Spaces*, 6.
36. Perec, *Species of Spaces*, 84. Translation slightly modified by addition of material in square brackets.
37. Perec, *Species of Spaces*, 2–3. The translated list differs considerably from the original, substituting 38 entries for Perec's 52, and only 13 of these could really be described as translations, as opposed to freely inspired 'equivalents'.
38. Perec, *Life*, 416.
39. Borges, 'John Wilkins' Analytical Language', 192–3.
40. Perec, 'Think/Classify', *Species of Spaces*, 192.
41. Perec, 'Think/Classify', *Species of Spaces*, 187.
42. Foucault, *The Order of Things*, ix.
43. Foucault, *The Order of Things*, xviii.
44. Foucault, *The Order of Things*, xviii–xix.
45. Foucault, 'Of Other Spaces', 350–6.

Bibliography

Barthes, Roland. *Mythologies*. Paris: Seuil, 1957.
Bellos, David. *Georges Perec: A Life in Words*. London: Harvill, 1995.

Borges, Jorge Luis. 'John Wilkins' Analytical Language'. In *The Total Library: Non-Fiction 1922–1986*, edited by Eliot Weinberger; translated by Esther Allen, Suzanne Jill Levine and Eliot Weinberger, 229–32. London: Allen Lane, 1999.

Cerny, Philip G. *The Politics of Grandeur: Ideological Aspects of de Gaulle's Foreign Policy*. Cambridge: Cambridge University Press, 1980.

De Gaulle, Charles. 'Allocution radiodiffusée et télévisée prononcée au Palais de l'Élysée, le 12 juillet 1961'. In *Discours et messages III: Avec le renouveau (mai 1958–juillet 1962)*, 327–29. Paris: Plon, 1970.

Foucault, Michel. 'Of Other Spaces: Utopias and Heterotopias'. In *Rethinking Architecture: A Reader in Cultural Theory*, edited by Neil Leach, 350–56. London: Routledge, 1997.

Foucault, Michel. *The Order of Things: An Archaeology of the Human Sciences*. London: Routledge, 2002.

Harvey, David. *The Urban Experience*. Oxford: Blackwell, 1989.

Harvey, David. *The Condition of Postmodernity: An Enquiry into the Origins of Cultural Change*. Oxford: Blackwell, 1991.

Hess, Rémi. 'Henri Lefebvre et la pensée de l'espace'. In *La production de l'espace*, by Henri Lefebvre, 4th ed., v–xvi. Paris: Anthropos, 2000.

Lebovics, Herman. *Bringing the Empire Back Home: France in the Global Age*. Durham, NC: Duke University Press, 2004.

Lefebvre, Henri. *Critique de la vie quotidienne I: Introduction*. Paris: L'Arche, 1958.

Lefebvre, Henri. *Critique de la vie quotidienne II: Fondements d'une sociologie de la quotidienneté*. Paris: L'Arche, 1961.

Lefebvre, Henri. *Critique de la vie quotidienne III: De la modernité au modernisme (Pour une métaphilosophie du quotidien)*. Paris: L'Arche, 1981.

Lefebvre, Henri. *The Production of Space*, translated by Donald Nicholson-Smith. Oxford: Blackwell, 1991.

Lefebvre, Henri. *Critique of Everyday Life, Volume 1: Introduction*, translated by John Moore. London: Verso, 1992.

Lefebvre, Henri. *Critique of Everyday Life, Volume 2: Foundations for a Sociology of the Everyday*, translated by John Moore. London: Verso, 2002.

Lefebvre, Henri. *Critique of Everyday Life, Volume 3: From Modernity to Modernism (Towards a Metaphilosophy of Daily Life)*, translated by Gregory Elliott. London: Verso, 2008.

Merrifield, Andy. *Henri Lefebvre: A Critical Introduction*. New York: Routledge, 2006.

Perec, Georges. *Species of Spaces and Other Pieces*, edited and translated by John Sturrock. London: Penguin Books, 1997.

Perec, Georges. *Life: A User's Manual: Fictions*, translated by David Bellos. London: Vintage Books, 2008.

Sheringham, Michael. *Everyday Life: Theories and Practices from Surrealism to the Present*. Oxford: Oxford University Press, 2006.

Smith, Neil. 'Geography, Difference and the Politics of Scale'. In *Postmodernism and the Social Sciences*, edited by Joe Doherty, Elspeth Graham and Mo Malek, 57–79. London: Macmillan, 1992.

Smith, Neil. 'Homeless/Global: Scaling Places'. In *Mapping the Futures: Local Cultures, Global Change*, edited by Jon Bird, Barry Curtis, Tim Putnam, George Robertson and Lisa Tickner, 87–119. London: Routledge, 1993.

Soja, Edward W. *Postmodern Geographies: The Reassertion of Space in Critical Social Theory*. London: Verso, 1989.

Winock, Michel. *Chronique des années soixante*. Paris: Éditions du Seuil, 1987.

6
Accumulation versus dispersion: Perec and 'his' diaspora

Anna-Louise Milne

What sort of opposition is the apparent antinomy of this chapter's title? Are accumulation and dispersion two rival choices? At key junctures in Perec's writing he does suggest this to be the case, as I will show. Do they stand in a temporal relation, dispersion logically following a process of accumulation? And if so, do they inform our understanding of the chronology that organises the elaboration of Perec's complex corpus? To address these questions requires a consideration of the writerly dynamics – from gathering and listing to scattering or disrupting – operating at once within Perec's texts and between them. The following discussion will focus particularly on *Species of Spaces* (1974), both as a text that is organised with explicit compositional patterning that brings accumulation and scattering into play, and as a marker of a historical and personal moment when it may be useful to consider whether we can observe something like a turn or a (re)dispersal. At stake in the second of these considerations is the claim that Perec's work reveals an early phase marked by political militancy and a later phase more preoccupied with memory, both personal and cultural. I will question that chronology by plotting a persistent strain through Perec's corpus that is best designated as the 'realist' strain in his writing.

'Realism' is the notion Perec himself foregrounded, but it evidently came to him freighted with a lot of accessory baggage and continues to occupy a space in critical discourse that is difficult to delimit.[1] This volume's focus on questions of geography offers a tangential angle of approach, ostensibly leading away from a terrain in which realism sits in relation to modernism or, closer to the idiom of Perec's own parameters, within a constellation defined by 'committed literature' or the 'nouveau roman' of the post-war decades. The following chapter will return to these parameters and this period, but it will do so guided by a series of spatial figurations drawn from Perec's work. Accumulation and dispersion will underpin two of these, between which the third is more prominently spatial, enabling us to get closer to the terms of geography. This third term is what I will refer to as 'the cusp', that being one possible translation of 'la crête'. Reading along the 'crête', as it appears explicitly and compositionally in Perec's writing will enable this chapter to move towards a conclusion that maps how 'diaspora' emerges in his work against the patternings of its textuality.

The process of accumulation is perhaps most famously associated with an effort to 'exhaust' a place, in effect place Saint-Sulpice between the hours of 10.30am and 1.55pm on 18 October 1974, just after the publication of *Species of Spaces*. This 'attempt to exhaust' drew on the 'practical exercises' announced in *Species of Spaces* in the section entitled 'The Street' where the aim of the experiment was to miss nothing.[2] The totality of the site was to be re-ordered as an exhaustive inventory in an effort to be alive to the smallest feature of the space, an ambition he had already enjoined his reader to adopt in the 1973 piece in *Cause commune*, 'Approaches to What?': 'Describe your street. Describe another street. Compare. Make an inventory of your pockets, of your bag. Ask yourself about the provenance, the use, what will become of each of the objects you take out. Question your tea spoons.'[3] This process would go on to underpin his own attachment to the 'infra-ordinary' and from there to infuse the broad development of sociological and literary interest in the 'everyday', making the textual proliferation prompted by inventory perhaps Perec's most fruitful legacy to date.[4]

Sounding through this accumulative drive, though, is the tauter strain of loss and fragmentation, which Perecquian scholarship has gradually drawn out with growing attention to how the annihilation of Perec's closest family echoes in the gaps within the texts.[5] Extending this critical effort more recently, Alexandre Gefen has placed Perec's work at the very outset of what he defines as 'a comprehensive re-configuration of the literary field'.[6] For Gefen, the impulse to accumulate that emerges so paradigmatically in Perec is underpinned by the desire, or need, to repair the tear or neglect inflicted upon the world by history. He suggests that this newly therapeutic function ascribed to literature breaks with the long attachment in French writing to the autonomy or intransitivity of the literary text. It operates through attention to the spaces and conditions of those ground down by various forms of crisis endured during times of war, but also in the longer dilemmas of a country recurrently and stubbornly mired in economic recession and inequality.[7] He locates Perec's specific contribution to this attention in the impulse 'to join up spaces that may exist on maps and through satellite imagery, but which remain invisible' – invisible because neglected or positively rejected. Foregrounding *Species of Spaces*, he quotes the final lines of the section on 'The World' in which, with characteristic but perhaps deceptive directness, Perec suggests that attention to 'insignificant' happenings can open up the 'the rediscovery [*retrouvaille*] of a meaning, the perceiving that the earth is a form of writing [*une écriture terrestre*], a *geography* of which we had forgotten that we ourselves are the authors'.[8]

This statement is the most explicit claim Perec makes to being the author of (a) geography, a claim which is equally a projection towards his readers, whom he constitutes in the same move as authors of geographies. It defines a point of contact running between terrestrial crust and the graphic extrapolation of writing, in which dispersion and accumulation operate in dynamic relation, as we can note with the emphasis on the 're-discovery' of meaning, which implies a circling round of loss and recovery as opposed to a linear vector of transformation. Moreover, it reduces the distance between materiality and writerly elaboration – or any putative separation between subject and world – to nil while it also reconvenes the position of authorship. This 'geography' is thus a complex space of writing, and it is from within this complex convergence that the figure of the cusp can help us observe in order to understand better what is at stake in this singular literary project.

A cusp is a drawing towards a point or an apex, a culmination from within a field that also knows gentler or more scattered inclines. It implies accent or intensity, and can have interruptive effect, but will also be dispersed when perceived from within a continuous or larger series. In their dynamic interaction 'cusp' and 'dispersion' announce a more disruptive relation to social groupings compared with the implied structure of concentric inclusion that goes from page to world, as in *Species of Spaces*, or a flatly accumulative drive. Their pairing thus invites, as I will show, a sceptical stance with regard to the reparative project that Gefen claims for literature in the twenty-first century. Their strong spatial resonance owes a lot, of course, to the ways in which social space was coming to be conceptualised in the key post-1968 years. But their interest, I hope to show, lies in what we might call a 'staying power', or a holding relative to the sweep that is commonly held to ensue from 1974 when, in France, the Trente Glorieuses (1945–74) of post-war economic growth came to an end and the effects of the oil crisis sent shock waves across the developed world, closing down some of the aspirations and actions that had converged in May '68 or, in some cases, forcing them into more radical configuration.

This broad historical context tends to position the interest in 'the everyday' or the 'infra-ordinary' as a reaction emerging out of May '68, a 'turn' away from the divisive politics of revolution towards a more modest focus, the hallmark of which is its claim to empirical carefulness and local inclusiveness. Both of these dispositions echo in the explicitly therapeutic function underscored by Gefen.[9] By tracing the dynamics of accumulation and dispersion and using them to focus on the salience of the cusp, the aim here will be to zoom in on alternative spatial incitements present in Perec's writings and to read the geography of *Species of Spaces*, circa 1974, as poised between his writings from the early 1960s and the later moment of 1978, which thereby displaces both the metaphorics of a 'turn', on the one hand, and the appeal of accumulation, on the other.[10]

Avenues to What?

The lines from the section 'The World' in *Species of Spaces* that announce 'a geography', quoted partially above, express an explicit distancing from a process of accumulation, if we read them in full. 'Accumulation' is the word they use for the mere process of consigning things (Sturrock has chosen 'acquisitiveness') that offers no hope or is 'désespérante' ('despairing' in Sturrock's translation). Following a list of apparently random fragments from 'the world', Perec cautions that these do not derive their significance from the fact of our latching on to them, holding them out or up in their infra-ordinary plenitude, but rather from the reflexive 're-discovery' of a meaning, as already stressed above. Moreover the 'geography' he calls for is italicised and follows the notion of an 'écriture terrestre' or 'earthly writing'. This invites us to approach this 'geo-graphy' very literally, as a 'graphos' of the world. Perec's tone here is ponderous, even cautionary. It asks us to slow down to address the question of what sort of 'graph-ing' of the world this announces and how it relates to a sense of 'familiarity' such as is also intimated in the idea of a 'retrouvaille' or a 're-connecting'.

In contrast, the way he expresses his leaning towards 'dispersion' in *Species of Spaces* is provocative and playful: 'Why not set a higher value on dispersal?' ('Pourquoi ne pas privilégier la dispersion?') he writes, towards the end of the section on 'The Neighbourhood' ('le quartier'), earlier in the book.[11] What follows is a tongue-in-cheek dismissal of the appeal of neighbourhood attachments and a projected lifestyle distributed in individual rooms across Paris: 'I'd go and sleep in Denfert, I'd write in the Place Voltaire, I'd listen to music in the Place Clichy, I'd make love at the Poterne des Peupliers' ('J'irais dormir à Denfert, j'écrirais place Voltaire, j'écouterais de la musique place Clichy, je ferais l'amour à la Poterne des Peupliers ... ').[12] The allusive quality of these place names is gently humorous (and largely lost in translation) and leads towards an absurdist tirade against ghettoisation, or putting 'all Jews in the rue des Rosiers', the heart of the Jewish quarter in the Marais, 'all the students in the Latin Quarter, all the publishers in Saint-Sulpice, all the doctors in Harley Street, all the blacks in Haarlem?'[13] Perec's choice of the original Dutch spelling of Haarlem is of a piece with his spoof on the idea that there is something to be valued in the emergence of a defining characteristic to a particular area, a sort of spatial identity. 'Chinatown' for example. And with its anachronistic preciosity, it speaks back to the colloquial elision of the subject and verb at the beginning of this section that sets up 'the neighbourhood' as a vaguely oppressive self-evidence: 'D'you live in the neighbourhood? You from round here? Moved neighbourhoods, have you? You're in what neighbourhood now?' ('T'habites dans le quartier? T'es du quartier? T'as changé de quartier? T'es dans quel quartier?') The 'neighbourhood' means the sort of familiarity that authorises, not just the 'tutoiement', but the insistent button-holing of the 't' form. With its brusqueness it leaves no space to dodge an interrogation, and in this respect it operates with a decisiveness that also characterises the fact that 'le quartier' is a formal administrative entity, the 'little bit of city' attached to a given police station, as Perec reminds us with a telling ellipsis at the end of this same paragraph, and not in its strict delimitations the result of historical, architectural or social factors.[14]

Perec is sceptical about togetherness, especially about togetherness founded on a version of the everyday underpinned by a neighbourhood: 'always go to the same butcher's, leave your parcels at the *épicerie*, open an account at the ironmonger's'.[15] This would only ever be 'putting a mawkish face on necessity' ('un aménagement douceâtre de la nécessité') or a way of 'sugar-coating market relations'.[16] He would be less opposed to the collective practice of street theatre, or of music, and he does not close down the idea of there being other means of binding people together – 'making demands on them, making them fight' ('une exigence ou un combat') – but there is little to suggest in this text that he sees these demands operating within the frame of the neighbourhood. It is significant to note how far in this regard he is from Michel de Certeau's famous discussion of the *quartier* which emerged from the long-haul project, which began in the same year of 1974 and was finally published in 1980 as the opening section of the second volume of *The Practice of Everyday Life*.[17] For de Certeau the *quartier* is precisely the stage where the individual can 'privatise' public space, appropriating the structures of the city, inserting him or herself into the interstices left unobserved by the surveillance apparatus of the State through such actions as imaginative re-signification of street names, or the poetisation of banal episodes like daily frequenting of the same butchers. For de Certeau these 'surreptitious creativities' constitute 'a second' or 'poetic' geography which lies over the ostensible geography of urban planning and administration.[18] It is not clear, however, that Perec's geography has this secondary quality. If he is dismissive of the idea that the *quartier* can be the frame of social change – a 'fight' or 'une exigence' – it is because his horizon remains a heuristic that will transform the very patterns of the world, not just what the world can signify in a given individual's everyday poetics.

This much is indicated in the way in which he brings forward the notion of 'aménagement' in his description of neighbourhood processes. Where de Certeau mobilises the discourse of ap-propriation, insisting on the individual subject's capacity to 'capture' his or her space through poetic or narrative investment, Perec redirects one of the most prominent words of urban development at the time towards surface measures that merely disguise structural forces. 'Aménagement' is deceptive. This is crucial for Perec and for the period. It was against the massive acceleration in this sort of instrumentalised urban planning, encapsulated particularly in the famous 'schéma directeur d'aménagement et d'urbanisme', a hugely significant set of guidelines for urban and regional planning introduced in 1965, that the nebulae of critical thinking and architecture clustering around Henri Lefebvre developed. These nebulae produced a multitude of forms of expression, including Paul Virilio's developing collection L'Espace critique of which *Species of Spaces* was the second volume published. When Perec defines neighbourhood practices as 'un *aménagement* douceâtre de la nécessité', this context is uppermost.

The word 'aménagement' returns in the section 'The Uninhabitable', which itself is part of the more fragmented closing section 'Space' at the end of the volume. In one and a half pages, Perec compiles all the dominant forms of contemporary oppression in the built environment, from barbed wire fences to the 'fake' shine of 'head offices', then moves his text towards much more 'infra-ordinary' forms of private accumulation such as they were (and still are) expressed by property developers: 'fashionable studio flats in leafy surroundings', 'luxurious designer conversion', culminating in the associated imperative to police one another: 'you are asked to give your name after 10pm' ('On est prié de dire son nom après dix heures du soir': the mildness of this has a cruel irony in our world of intensified finger-printing and optical recognition). Then the text shifts abruptly to a reproduced circular issued by the chief of the Waffen SS central building office at Auschwitz. It concerns the 'aménagement' (translated as 'embellishment') of the perimeter around the crematoriums I and II, which were to be planted up with a 'green border' composed of trees detailed in the letter. This 'green border' will sugar-coat – 'enrober' – the catastrophically efficient though still rudimentary industrialisation of massacre that occurred in Auschwitz. The operation of town planning towards social improvement ('aménagement') and systematic and unsparing persecution are held together, closing off for Perec any possibility of imagining a space or spatial transformation as a preserve for the subject. 'To live is to pass from one space to another', as he writes at the outset of the book, and many of these spaces are inherently 'uninhabitable', whatever their ostensible guise.[19] *Species of Spaces* ends after the quoted extract from the Waffen SS directive with the recognition that there are no 'stable spaces', that space is always 'a doubt', not a starting point or an objective, leaving writing – 'a mark or a few signs' – as the only mechanism Perec envisages to combat the violence that can also take the 'mawkish face' of 'aménagement douceâtre'.

There is, then, despite Perec's intense attention to particular configurations of space, a fundamental non-differentiation of spaces at work here. As Dominique Rabaté has discussed, and contrary to attempts to route Perec's work back to particular locations, notably the rue Vilin, there is no Combray, such as there was for Proust, to anchor the Perecquian subject, no 'room' that would offer a matrix for memory. Rooms are instead relatively anonymous, and Rabaté insists on the difference between the Proustian quest to produce the singular subject as bearer of unalienable memories and Perec's effort to give voice to a subject who is barely individualised.[20] This claim finds an echo that will be important to us in the minimally anonymised account that the psychoanalyst J. B. Pontalis gives of his four years of analysis with Georges Perec, referred to as Pierre G. in the text *L'amour des commencements*. Pontalis describes his patient's tendency to describe rooms with fetishistic detail, then adds 'listening to this endless enumeration that tried to lose nothing, provoked a poignant sense of absence in me. Pierre's rooms: the more I saw them filled with objects, the more they seemed empty to me; the more he detailed the topography, the greater the desert appeared; the more the map was filled with names, the less it spoke out loud.'[21]

This, of course, contradicts Perec's own account of what he is engaged in doing, not just in *Species of Spaces*, but in a range of projects from 1969 onwards, including his famous *Lieux*, in which he undertook to return to 12 sites for 12 years, as well as his attempt to exhaust place Saint-Sulpice. In the section on 'The Bedroom', Perec remarks on the 'self-evidence' of Proust's influence on his undertaking, suggesting that 'the space of the bedroom' operates for him as a 'Proustian madeleine': this project 'is of course invoked by this; all it is is nothing more than a rigorous extension of paragraphs 6 and 7 of the first chapter of the first part (*Combray*) of the first volume (*Du côté de chez Swann*) of *A la recherche du temps perdu*'.[22] But for all this effort to home in on a foundational moment in Proust's text, it is clear from Perec's own writing that there is no one bedroom to anchor his experience. The foundation, if such there is, is in a textual impulse (from Proust), not an embedded space. 'The' bedroom is an abstract concept, despite all the detail Perec claims he can supply, and the text reveals this all too well as it slips away from the 'je' to a 'vous' – 'As from when does somewhere become truly yours' ('A partir de quand un lieu devient-il vraiment vôtre') – and then an 'on' ('one' in English): 'Is it when you've ('quand on a …') put your three pairs of socks to soak in a pink plastic bowl'.[23] The plastic basin is hovering somewhere between a possible fact of Perec's life and the banal likelihood that the sort of basin that anyone would buy to soak their socks in would be pink, or light blue, or yellow … . This paragraph is asking precisely de Certeau's question of how to appropriate a given place but, contrary to the author of *The Practice of the Everyday Life*, it suggests that one simply does not appropriate spaces. Not in any lasting way. And what matters in Perec's writing is less how the subject emerges through the mesh of the text than the articulation of a porous or transpersonal subjectivity in which his readers may change the colour of the bowl without reconfiguring beyond recognition the experience in question.[24]

This brings us back to the collective expression of authorship with which Perec ended 'The World' when he foregrounded the notion of 'a geography'. 'We' are the authors of this terrestrial writing, he posits. And the section 'The Uninhabitable' demonstrates what this might mean. There is no attempt to singularise the succession of denominations or qualifications of space. The discourse is 'clichéd', deposited on the page in such a way that, at best, the accumulation of forms of 'unliveability' produces despair, until this accumulation starts to veer towards re-signification when Perec begins to pick out the forms of alienation with a finer grained lens: 'unbeatable view, double exposure, trees, beams, character'.[25] The language starts to bristle as if it were itself taking on renewed 'concreteness', as Perec writes in 'The World', building gradually, from term to term, through a series of unstated mediations which bind these coordinates together and us, as readers, to them too, until we reach that impersonal but coercive statement 'you are asked to give your name after 10pm'. This, I would like to suggest, produces a form of 'cusp' in the writing, a stasis or skip in the beat, after which follows the written circular from SS-Obersturmbannführer Höss to Sturmbannführer Bishoff. The relation between the 'green border' they are planning around the Auschwitz crematoriums and the forms of urban re-conditioning that real estate promoters like to foreground do not collapse into one another as terms in exactly the same series, but neither can they be held apart as if the Nazi circular were a 'fragment of history that had unfolded somewhere beyond us', as Perec had written of Robert Antelme's work, which we will presently discuss.[26] This circular is part of a system, part of the 'evidence' of the camps with their proclivities for planted borders, which is there but has not been 'seen' or read as part of the 'geo-graphy' of the 'aménagement' that is also erecting its forms in the newly developed neighbourhoods of the 1970s.[27]

When the reader turns the page marked only by the word 'Space', the notion of authoring a 'geography' is still resounding powerfully from the end of the previous section 'The World', which closes the concatenation of specific 'volumes' with its emphatic statement about our authorship of 'a geography'. The eye can thus easily slide over the text on the left-hand page, eager to follow the 'we/nous' that connects us as authors to us as observers in the opening line of the more disparate 'Space' section. The typeface of the block of quoted text inserted on the left-hand page is notably smaller, not italicised as other long quotations are, and it comes after an ellipsis. This has the effect of positioning it as a continuation of another strand that we must have missed. It is perhaps the moment where this extraordinary compendium of writerly resourcefulness creates the biggest lurch, breaking with the apparently smooth and inclusive transitions that run from 'page' to 'world'.[28] The compositional work is subtle, as it is in the 'prière d'insérer' or loose-leaf addition included at the outset of *Espèces d'Espaces* in another disruption of the steadiness of the finished text. It pays, however, to slow our momentum and look a little closely at this dense 'aside'. It is a quotation from Italo Calvino's *Cosmicomics* and it concerns the signage of the world: the eyes in the peacock's tail feathers, the vein of limestone in basalt, the crest ('crête') of sand in a desert … . These signs are fully 'of the world' and Calvino's thought is that they may or may not be significant. In other words, they may or may not be part of the world 'on purpose' or merely 'fallen there by chance', like the badly formed leg on a letter 'R' in an evening newspaper.[29] This example jumps out with its Perecquian significance, an anticipation of the complex interplay between the legs of the X, V and W that runs through *W, or The Memory of Childhood*.[30] It prompts me to pinpoint this 'hidden' quotation as a rival impulse to the Proustian madeleine held so insistently to the fore in the 'bedroom' section. And it also draws out into full salience the figure of the 'cusp' or 'crête', where the matter of the world is pushed into an apparent line of demarcation, a trace on the landscape that is eminently graphic and asks to be read, but may mean nothing and merely disperse with the next sandstorm.[31]

The 'cusp' of 1974–5

It was in 1975 that *W, or The Memory of Childhood* finally found its print form as *W ou le souvenir d'enfance* after what Philippe Lejeune has called the 'double catastrophe' that had previously broken Perec's effort to produce this distressing – for both writer and reader – work.[32] And also in June 1975 that Perec drew a close to the analysis with Pontalis conducted since 1971, a date he then gave to Bartlebooth's death in *Life: A User's Manual* (23 June 1975). It was also at this point that he abandoned his *Lieux* project, after six years. His friend Harry Mathews writes in *Le Verger* that he remembers how, in the first dinner they had together after he had ended his analysis, Perec told him that now, when he goes down the road to post a letter, he knows that he is going down the road to post a letter.[33] This moment might be hugely significant, or it might not. In the next section of this chapter, we will plot along this 'cusp' in Perec's life and thinking, approaching it as an 'avenue' of potentially particular salience, when different impulses appear to converge in a pattern that makes sense for our heuristic endeavour of giving expression to what Perecquian geography might be. But to do so means to resist establishing it as a 'turn' or redirection as such. Perhaps nothing new happens here. Perhaps it is not an avenue *to* something. My claim is rather that the spread of Perec's immensely complex system of writings finds a particular clarity when read according to experiences of interruptive intensity. To see this more sharply, we have to come back to Perec's critical conception of 'realist literature'.

The reference to realism is there at the beginning for Perec, and it will still be there as a claim or 'revendication' at the end, so any suggestion that there is a land shift or 'turn' *circa* 1974 has to be read against that constancy. Initially, in 1959, Perec adopts something of the manifesto posture common to the period with 'Pour une littérature réaliste' ('For a realist literature'), followed by 'Engagement ou crise du langage'

(‘Commitment or crisis of language’). However both of these essays, which build in references to a broad swathe of contemporary writers, and even the terms of interwar literary debate (particularly Jean Paulhan and the ‘terror’ of literature), can be considered to be clearing the way for the major study he dedicates to Robert Antelme’s *L’Espèce humaine*, ‘Robert Antelme or the Truth of Literature’.[34] As the title of this article suggests, there is no other work comparable for Perec to this account of survival in the Nazi concentration camps of Buchenwald and Gandersheim. Against claims that literature might be inadequate or irrelevant to the scale and nature of this persecution, he advances Antelme’s work as the re-foundation of the possibility of literature, premised on indefectible confidence in language, which will enable the transformation of the world from the alienated, obfuscating ‘chaos’ that prevails: ‘At this level, language and signs become decipherable once again. The world is no longer that chaos which words void of meaning despair of describing. It is a living, difficult reality that the power of words gradually [*peu à peu*] overcomes.’[35]

There are a number of echoes we can identify in this essay on Antelme with the extracts already quoted from *Species of Spaces*. The idea of despair in the mere accumulation of ‘brute’ matter and the insistence on the ‘return’ of meaning, which is what engenders a transformation of the world. But also more systematically the importance of the ‘peu à peu’, which points to a process of progressive revealing of pattern and significance, a building, that is, towards the sort of cusp I have just invoked. This analysis of gradual emergence constitutes the major insight Perec expresses in this essay. In contradistinction to many other testimonies and accounts, which he dispatches in passing, Antelme’s work does not ‘give’ the camp as a singular shocking fact or ‘a vision of the unbearable’ (‘une vision d’épouvante’), but rather ‘elaborates’ and ‘transforms’ his experience, allowing the ‘*evidence*’ of the camp to emerge, the ‘evidence of a total world’, which slowly imposes itself, not in the sense of ‘proof’, as if to answer scepticism or doubt, but rather as an obviousness or a suddenly salient realisation that *this* is what the camps were. The term ‘évidence’ is used recurrently, symptomatic of the difficulty Perec reveals here in tracing a line of demarcation between Antelme’s work and other forms of testimonial writing.[36] Perec’s emphasis is on ‘transformation’ as opposed to ‘accumulation’ or piling up. The latter he associates with literature that offers only a litany of horror. The mode of transformation is not, however, one of ‘explanation’. The terms he uses range rather from ‘désembrouiller’ or ‘to disentangle’ through to ‘unify’ and ‘rank’ and also ‘to betray reality’ (‘trahir’).[37] Antelme, he claims, builds a terrain for his own understanding and that of his readers through patient organisation.

Consciousness 'infiltrates' the anecdotes before giving way again to another element, each inseparable from the others in this 'total' account and yet 'scattered' ('éparpillé) from its conventional meaning by its place in this construction.

The multiplication of metaphors for this combination of 'integration' and 'dispersion' – a 'continual interplay', he writes – carry the effort of thinking about what it means to claim that Antelme's 'invention of a style' is of revolutionary bearing. And the emergence of a notion of betrayal – 'trahir la réalité' – suggests something of the 'wrench', which will also be his own, involved in abandoning the terrain of accumulation where 'false pity' ensures a legitimacy to the expression.[38] Fifteen or so years later, in 1978, in conversation with Frank Venaille just as he was about to embark on the Ellis Island project, Perec returned to this complex interplay between dislocation and consolidation in perhaps its tightest formulation. Discussing the process of composition of *W, or The Memory of Childhood*, he again insists on the transpersonal or collective nature of the reality and memory expressed in the work, evoking the metaphor of a 'cusp' again from which this composition-decomposition could topple towards generality, on the one hand, or singularity, on the other. And what ensures this momentary balance is precisely the progressive and meticulous approach towards the evidence that will emerge: 'Because the decomposition is so meticulous, something is revealed'.[39] The work of three decades of Perec scholars enables us now to know his extraordinary attention to the smallest articulations and connections through his texts, a process of patient calibration that he is himself able to point to more explicitly, though nonchalantly, in 1978 (drawing on 'the dictionary, the encyclopedia, the imagination, by the system of constraints'). In contrast, the analysis he offers of Antelme in 1962 still relies on largely metaphorical terms to describe the scattering and gathering. But what remains fundamental across the two 'ends' of his corpus is both the 'undoing' or dispersive drive expressed in the idea of 'de-composition' and that the horizon remains that of composing 'realist literature' in which the truth of literature *and* of the world suddenly emerges in 'sharp' intensity.[40]

Diaspora

The two preceding sections of this chapter have aimed to draw out a dynamic that is integral to Perec's work, which he claims in the 1962 Antelme essay can offer the means to 'dominate the world' in a refusal of the 'angst' of history and its 'modern cataclysms'.[41] Literature, as the re-finding of experience in language, is not 'merely' or flatly reconciliatory. Nor does it fix its anchor in the intimacy of the individual subject. It is interruptive, marked by sudden, inexplicable intensities or particular 'cusps' of conquest of meaning. Attentiveness to this dynamic, across the span from 1959–62 to the last texts, has the secondary effect of reconfiguring the chronology that is sketched in summary terms, for example, by Sturrock's footnote to the Antelme essay: 'This essay dates to a time when Perec was more political in his outlook than he subsequently became.'[42] That something happens in Perec's work in 1974–5 can be perceived, but its terms are not political/apolitical, as if there were a shift whereby the inclusive concept of the 'infra-ordinary' and its subsequent 'therapeutic' extension would replace the earlier critical edge. Rather, this moment is something closer to the 're-discovery' or 'retrouvaille' of a meaning that is *there* in all its evidence. The primary objective of this argument has been to figure this 'thereness' within the ever-present possibility, and even desirability, of dispersal as a form of 'crête', developing Perec's own attention to this 'figure' in an effort to displace the processes of accumulation or enumeration that have been so to the fore in much contemporary Perecquian experimentation.

As a figure for 'pattern' or composition across the surface of text and world it is intended first and foremost to illuminate the 'geography' that Perec announced in *Species of Spaces*. But what, if anything, does it offer to contemporary categories in human geography? By way of conclusion, I'll reconfigure dispersion as diaspora. This is merely following Perec again and his voice-over for the film *Récits d'Ellis Island* (1980), where we find a last framing of the figure of dispersion. Here it is not held out as a process to adopt or to 'set a higher value upon' ('privilégier la dispersion'), but rather as a truth of the world: 'What I, Georges Perec, have come to question here is wandering [*errance*], dispersion, diaspora.'[43] This statement opens onto his hesitant, perhaps even recalcitrant recognition that this island off the coast of New York is significant for his understanding of what it means to be Jewish:

> what for me can be found here
> is not in any respect landmarks, roots or traces,
> but the opposite: something unformed, barely something that can be said,
> something that I can name closure, or rupture,
> or cut,
> and which is for me very intimately and very obscurely
> linked to the fact of being Jewish.[44]

Nothing in the syntax of the final part of this sentence makes 'the fact of being Jewish' specifically Perec's claim. The passage as a whole functions in that state of syntactic suspension between the individual and the collective subject explored previously, continuing as it does by explicitly marking a distance between the personal pronoun and the verbal phrase 'être juif': 'ce que c'est / qu'être juif / ce que ça me fait que d'être juif' ('what it is / to be Jewish / what it is for me to be Jewish'). But what I would like to emphasise more in the closing phase of this particular discussion is the fact that 'being Jewish' is reached as a sort of provisional holding place, a cusp, that comes *within* dispersion, and does not precede it, as an identity would. It is not 'his' diaspora in any unshakeable way. Rather 'diaspora' is 'une évidence', he says, but an 'évidence mediocre', or what we might translate as 'a mediocre fact of life'. And it is perhaps useful to add that if the idea of 'une évidence', so insistently recurrent in the texts we have explored, is given in the dictionary as something that 'jumps towards the eyes' ('cela saute aux yeux'), mediocre signifies, of course, 'of the middle'. How diaspora emerges, thus, in Perec's work is as a fact of middling salience. This might be one point from which Perecquian geography can inform the complex layering that conditions expressions of cultural belonging in a world of shifting accumulations and dispersions.

There is no stable identity or place in Perec's work, as the end of *Species of Spaces* has already acknowledged. Instead, there is a pattern to be discerned, through the scattering and across the impediments of accumulation. This was what he found in Ellis Island, long before the heritage industry re-cemented the evidence of American ethnic diversity: an avenue from which he saw the possibility of being Argentinian, Australian, English or Swedish. And this strange cusp, figuring a certain evanescent trace across the globe, is the earthly writing or 'geo-graphy' of (his) reality.

Notes

1. Perec's principal discussion of realism in 'Pour une littérature réaliste' (1962) engages in particular with Georg Lukác's *Meaning of Contemporary Realism*, which had just been translated into French. See Robert Halpern's translation and introduction, 'For a Realist Literature', 28–39. Perhaps most useful in contemporary theorisation of realism for the reading of Perec here is Fredric Jameson's *The Antinomies of Realism*. Jameson's antinomies are other than our starting point here, but his differentiation between the 'scenic impulse' and storytelling (p. 11) establishes an analogous attention to what I am calling textual dynamics. Jameson also starts with Lukács.
2. Perec, *Species of Spaces,* 50–4.
3. Perec, *Species of Spaces*, 210.

4. Sheringham foregrounded the importance of 'Approaches to What?' in 2012 when he reviewed the genealogy of this attention to 'the everyday' in answer to Rabaté's questions in 'La vie quotidienne: Entretien avec Michael Sheringham'(*Europe*, 993–4 (2012), 52–61), also noting the signal influence it continues to have on contemporary production. Rabaté also underscores the 'seminal role' of Perec in contemporary literature as a form of 'patronage' in this interview, 59.
5. See, for example, Robin, *Le deuil de l'origine*.
6. Gefen, *Réparer le monde*, 194. My translation.
7. Gefen, *Réparer le monde*, 194.
8. Perec *Species of Spaces*, 79. Original emphasis. Gefen quotes Perec, *Espèces d'espaces*, 156, on p. 196 of *Réparer le monde*.
9. This therapeutic function extends evidently well beyond the literary sphere into cultural politics more generally in the post-1968 period. The emblematic example of this evolution in French urban politics is the Banlieues 89 project, launched in 1981 by *soixante-huitard* Roland Castro and transformed into an inter-ministerial mission in 1983. See the special issue of *Urbanisme*, 'De Banlieues 89 à Jean-Louis Borloo', n° 332, Sept–Oct 2003, for discussion of the modalities adopted to 'repair' the city and, for a broader account of this transformation of cultural politics, Cusset, *La décennie*.
10. Between 1959 and 1963 Perec and friends engaged in intermittent activity towards a review project particularly focused on questions of realism, which they entitled *Ligne Générale* in reference to Sergei Eisenstein's film of the same name. The group was constituted by numerous members of the French Communist Party though they tended to be dissidents from the Party line. The review never saw the light of day, and most of what remains of this project are the few texts written by Perec and published for the most part in *Partisans*. Here, we will refer particularly to 'Robert Antelme ou la vérité de la littérature', first published in *Partisans* in 1963, and re-printed in the collection entitled *L.G. Une aventure des années soixante*. John Sturrock's translation of the Antelme essay is contained in his 2008 collection, 253–66.
11. Perec, *Species of Spaces*, 59; *Espèces d'espaces*, 116.
12. Sturrock notes that the Poterne des Peupliers is 'a leafy place in the 13th arrondissement', which was no doubt true, but misses the level of the re-motivation of these names, ascribing referential meaning to the name as if it were an ideal place for making love, when the humour lies in the fact that 'poterne' refers to a hidden door in the wall of a fortified castle. The other allusions also work at this level of semantic displacement: 'dormir à Denfert': 'sleeping in Hell' and so on.
13. Sturrock corrects Perec's spelling of Harlem. The translation has been modified to correspond to Perec's anachronistic preference for Haarlem.
14. The delineation of arrondissements, and within them of *quartiers*, has been used as a tool of social control in a number of contexts, a prime example being the decision in 1860 to split the rebellious district of Belleville across four different administrative frontiers. Sturrock's translation of the opening of this section opts for a more varied register, losing the repetitive pattern in the original version. See p. 57 for the translation and p. 113 in the 2000 French edition.
15. Perec, *Species of Spaces*, 58.
16. Perec, *Species of Spaces*, 58; *Espèces d'espaces*, 115. Translation modified.
17. De Certeau, *The Practice of Everyday Life*.
18. De Certeau, *The Practice of Everyday Life*, 105.
19. Perec, *Species of Spaces*, 6.
20. Rabaté, '"Comme tout le monde, je suppose". L'individu collectif dans Espèces d'espaces', 44.
21. Pontalis, *L'amour des commencements*, 66–7: 'Et voici que [...] de cette recension sans fin qui n'eût dû rien laisser perdre, naissait en moi un sentiment poignant de l'absence. Les chambres de Pierre: plus je les voyais se remplir d'objets, plus elles me paraissaient vides; plus la topographie se faisait précise, plus s'étendait le désert ; plus la carte se peuplait de noms, plus elle était muette.'
22. Perec, *Species of Spaces*, 22.
23. Perec, *Species of Spaces*, 24. This passage echoes the reference to a plastic bowl and socks in Perec's earlier novel *Un homme qui dort* (1967), itself narrated in the second person singular. The latter novel is also an expansion on Proust's text, taking a micro-quotation from the beginning of *Combray* as its title.
24. In 1978, Perec made a parallel claim but in relation to *Je me souviens*. See Perec, *Species of Spaces*, 133.

25. Perec, *Species of Spaces*, 90.
26. Perec, *Species of Spaces*, 256.
27. Perec's work in this respect is a very prescient expression of the technocratic genealogies linking the concentrationary system of the Second World War to inter-war and post-war planning with its colonial and postcolonial 'hinterlands', such as have been explored by Rabinow in *French Modern*.
28. The English translation collapses this effect to some extent by placing 'Space' as a title at the top of the page rather that in the centre of an otherwise blank page.
29. Perec, *Species of Spaces*, 80.
30. Chambers, 'A Poetics of Quandary', 53–80.
31. Sturrock's translation has 'the coagulated sand of the desert' that has none of the graphic quality of 'crête'.
32. Lejeune, *La mémoire et l'oblique,* 87–91.
33. Mathews, *Le verger*, 26.
34. The reference to Antelme's text appears at the end of the first of these essays, offered as the conclusive example of how realism remains possible even in the face of the horror of the camps, while the second assert that *L'Espèce humaine* is 'the' answer to what Sartre and other contemporaries have failed to do, that is, to produce a literature that is fully in relation to the realities of the recent war and its aftermath. At this stage, Antelme's work was known to a small network of readers, having been published by a press created to this end by Duras and Antelme. Perec's essay 'Robert Antelme ou la vérité de la littérature' constitutes the first and for a long time the only serious engagement with this landmark work. These three related essays have been re-edited together in Georges Perec, *L.G: Une aventure des années soixante*. Antelme's text will also be decisive for Maurice Blanchot. Although he read it in 1950, his first mention of it only appears in 1962, in an article entitled 'L'Indestructible' in the *Nouvelle Revue Française*, then re-produced in 1969 in Blanchot, *L'entretien infini*.
35. Perec, *Species of Spaces*, 266.
36. Perec, *L.G.*, 94–6.
37. Perec, *Species of Spaces*, 265, 264 and 256; *L.G.*, 96, 94.
38. It is in the 1972 piece 'The Gnocchi of Autumn', subtitled in French 'answers to a few questions concerning myself', that Perec addresses the personal stakes of this 'betrayal' or 'unveiling' of (his) reality, work he suggests he has still to accomplish (*Species of Spaces*, 123).
39. Perec, *Species of Spaces*, 128; translation modified.
40. This is how the Antelme essays ends, while in the 1978 interview about 'The Work of Memory' he again claims the status of 'realist writer' (*Species of Spaces*, 132).
41. Perec, *Species of Spaces*, 265.
42. Perec, *Species of Spaces*, 253.
43. Perec, *Ellis Island*.
44. Perec, *Ellis Island*, 57–8. My translation.

Bibliography

Blanchot, Maurice. *L'entretien infini*. Paris: Gallimard, 2006.

Chambers, Ross. 'A Poetics of Quandary: Perec's *W ou le souvenir d'enfance* and the Figure of Assemblage', *French Forum* 31, no. 2 (2006), 53–80.

Cusset, François. *La décennie : le grand cauchemar des années 1980*. Paris: La Découverte, 2006.

De Certeau, Michel. *The Practice of Everyday Life*, translated by Steven Rendall. Berkeley: University of California Press, 1984.

De Certeau, Michel, Luce Giard and Pierre Mayol. *The Practice of Everyday Life, Volume 2: Living and Cooking*, translated by Timothy J. Tomasik. Rev. ed. Minneapolis: University of Minnesota Press, 1998.

Gefen, Alexandre. *Réparer le monde: La littérature française face au XXIe siècle*. Paris: Éditions Corti, 2017.

Halpern, Robert. 'For a Realist Literature', *Chicago Review*, 53:2/3 (2007), 28–39.

Heck, Maryline. 'L'"infra-ordinaire", une poétique du regard', *Europe: Revue littéraire mensuelle* 993/994 (2012), 62–70.

Hilsum, Mireille. *Comment devient-on écrivain? Sartre, Aragon, Perec et Modiano*. Paris: Éditions Kimé, 2012.

Jameson, Fredric. *The Antinomies of Realism*. London/New York: Verso, 2013.

Lejeune, Philippe. *La mémoire et l'oblique: Georges Perec autobiographe*. Paris: P.O.L., 1991.

Lucács, Georg. *The Meaning of Contemporary Realism*. London: Merlin Press, 1963.

Mathews, Harry. *Le verger*. Paris: P.O.L., 1989.

Perec, Georges. *Un homme qui dort*. Paris: 1967.

Perec, Georges. *W ou le souvenir d'enfance*. Paris: Denoël, 1975.

Perec, Georges. *Life: A User's Manual*, translated by David Bellos. London: Collins Harvill, 1987.

Perec, Georges. *W, or The Memory of Childhood*, translated by David Bellos. London: Collins Harvill, 1988.

Perec, Georges. *L.G.: Une aventure des années soixante*, edited by Cl. Burgelin. Paris: Éditions du Seuil, 1992.

Perec, Georges. *Ellis Island*. Paris: P.O.L., 1995.

Perec, Georges. *Species of Spaces and Other Pieces*, edited and translated by John Sturrock. London: Penguin Books, 2008.

Perec, Georges. *Espèces d'espaces*. Rev. ed. Paris: Éditions Galilée, 2010.

Pontalis, J.-B. *L'amour des commencements*. Paris: Gallimard, 2003.

Rabaté, Dominique. '"Comme tout le monde, je suppose": L'individu collectif dans *Espèces d'espaces*', *Europe: Revue littéraire mensuelle* 993/994 (2012), 43–51.

Rabaté, Dominique. 'La vie quotidienne: Entretien avec Michael Sheringham', *Europe: Revue littéraire mensuelle* 993/994 (2012), 52–61.

Rabinow, Paul. *French Modern: Norms and Forms of the Social Environment*. Chicago: University of Chicago Press, 1995.

Robin, Régine. *Le deuil de l'origine: Une langue en trop, la langue en moins*. Paris: Éditions Kimé, 2003.

Ruffel, Lionel. 'Un réalisme contemporain: Les narrations documentaires', *Littérature* 166 (2012), 13–25.

Ruffel, Lionel. *Brouhaha: Les mondes du contemporain*. Lagrasse: Éditions Verdier, 2016.

7

Islands, camps, zones: Towards a nissological reading of Perec

Amanda Crawley Jackson

The Perecquian corpus is shot through with innumerable allusions to islands and archipelagos, both real and imaginary. *W, or The Memory of Childhood* (1988 [1975; 2011 edition cited]) and *Ellis Island Revisited: Tales of Vagrancy and Hope* (1980 [1995]) the film Perec co-directed with Robert Bober, each use island settings to explore the entangled workings of power and memory. In *Le Voyage d'hiver* (*The Winter Journey*, 1993 [1979]), the first section of the fictional author Hugo Vernier's (missing) book unfolds on a mysterious island in the middle of a lake. *Life: A User's Manual* (1987 [1978; 1996 edition cited]) abounds with lists of the islands and atolls visited and imagined by the novel's protagonists, but also contains a plethora of intertextual references to island adventure stories, most notably Jules Verne's *L'Île mystérieuse* (*The Mysterious Island*, 1875). And yet, while scholars have, inevitably, considered the role and significance of the island setting in *W* and (to a lesser extent) *Ellis Island*, there has been surprisingly scant attention paid to the island as connective topos that runs throughout Perec's work. This chapter seeks to address that critical lacuna and, as such, proffers what I shall call a nissological (from the Greek *nisos* – 'island') reading of the Perecquian corpus. Bénabou and Reilly have pointed to 'the many different paths that Perec himself carefully established for his readers', with 'each of the indications [...] sufficiently discreet, numerous and ambiguous to afford each reader a large part of the responsibility in choosing which path to take'.[1] The 'Perecquian Path'[2] I propose to trace here thickens to encompass a series of cognates deriving from the French *île* ('island'): *îlot* ('islet', 'haven', 'block', 'blockhouse'), *îlot insalubre* ('slum', 'unhygienic precinct'[3]) and *îlotage* (literally 'islanding', but commonly used in both urban and military discourse to describe the sectorisation of a territory for the purposes of control and policing). Broadly speaking, the scope of this analysis will firstly enable us to reconsider utopian and disciplinary space in Perec's textual production, bringing to light their complex intersectionality. Specifically, it will allow us to think through a series of dichotomies, most notably utopia and dystopia, sanctuary and carcerality. Secondly, it opens up a space to have a renewed discussion of negation, ephemerality and what Paul Connerton has called 'repressive erasure' in Perec's work, particularly as these are played out in the urban memoryscape.[4] Thirdly, I will suggest that it is in the very ephemerality of the island form that Perec is able to locate an emancipatory writing practice.

Perec's interest in islands can be attributed in part to the books he devoured as a child (including, among others, Daniel Defoe's *Robinson Crusoe*, 1719; Jules Verne's *The Mysterious Island* [*L'Île mystérieuse*, 1874]; Jack London's *Jerry of the Islands: A True Dog Story*, 1917; and Charles Vildrac's *L'Île rose* [*The Pink Island*, 1924]), but also, in the context of his own trauma and displacement, to the resonance of the island as an idyllic, safe haven amid terrible storms. Bellos tells us that Perec's childhood bedroom at 18 rue de l'Assomption, where he lived with his paternal aunt, Esther Bienenfeld, and her family after the war, was 'kitted out as a ship's cabin. The bed was a bunk that when folded away turned into a little writing desk.'[5] The walls were adorned with nautical ropes, fishing nets, floats and a framed mariners' chart, which Perec would keep and refer to in both *Life: A User's Manual* and *Things: A Story of the Sixties*. In a short section of *Espèces d'espaces* (*Species of Spaces*) entitled 'The Bed', Perec writes: 'It was lying face-down on my bed that I read *Twenty Years After, The Mysterious Island* and *Jerry on the Island* [*sic*]. The bed became a trapper's cabin, or a lifeboat on the raging ocean, or a baobab tree threatened by fire, a tent erected in the desert, or a propitious crevice that my enemies passed within inches of, unavailingly.'[6] The bed is a haven, from the safety of which the child might begin to explore the world; it is 'the individual space *par excellence*, the elementary space of the body (the bed-monad), the one which even the man completely crippled by debts has the right to keep: the bailiffs don't have the power to seize *your* bed'.[7] For this orphan passed between family members, cast adrift in shifting diasporic sands, the bed is also 'the improbable place where I had my roots'; it is 'the space of dreams and of an Oedipal nostalgia', a provisional synecdoche for the rootedness of the 'paternal bed, massive, venerable, / Where all his kinsfolk were born and where they died'.[8]

Using an epigraph from Michel Leiris, '*Lit* = *île*' – 'bed = island'[9], Perec nests the bed (and the tent and lifeboat) in a broader configuration of insular spaces that mould themselves to the contours of the subject's body, protecting him from further trauma and harm amid the prevailing spirits of chaos and danger. They represent what Perec famously describes as 'space as reassurance'[10]: 'places that are stable, unmoving, intangible, untouched and almost untouchable, unchanging and deep-rooted: places that might be points of reference, of departure, of origin'.[11] In their ultimate impossibility, however, such spaces become the *utopia* (a word coined by Thomas More in 1516 that derives both from the Greek *ou-topos*, meaning 'no place' and its virtual homonym, *eu-topos*, designating a 'good place') that haunts the entirety of the Perecquian corpus. The insular '*village utopia*' described by Perec in *Species of Spaces*, in its bounded geography and quasi-cosmological self-completeness, is an exemplar of such a place. Written entirely in the conditional tense, the text describes a space in which place, community and family coincide, and in which you would know everyone and everyone would know you ('You'd have been at school with the postman'); in which each nook and cranny would be familiar to you ('you'd know the places where there are still crayfish') and the rhythms and history of the place would also be your own: 'You'd know each one of the trees in your orchard'; 'You'd know whether it was going to rain by looking at the shape of the clouds above the hill'; 'you'd go and fetch your wood from the communal woodlands'.[12]

We see the same striking use of the conditional and conditional perfect tense to express the fundamentally hypothetical nature of such a space – one that is anchored by deep roots, *a space where the self might have* (or *might have had*) *a space* – at other points in the Perecquian corpus:

> I would have liked to help my mother clear the dinner from the kitchen table. There would have been a blue, small-checked oilcloth on the table, and above it, a counterpoise lamp with a shade shaped almost like a plate, made of white porcelain or enamelled tin, and a pulley system with pear-shaped weights. Then I'd have fetched my satchel, got out my book and my writing pad and my wooden pencil-box. I'd have put them on the table and done my homework. That's what happened in the books I read at school.[13]

Levitas summarises Ernst Bloch's definition of utopia as 'the transcendence of alienation, the overcoming of antagonism between humanity and the world, [...] feeling at home in the world'.[14] In the extracts above, space is domesticated and arranged around the organising body of the child. Perec's utopia, like Bloch's, concerns the concordance and flourishing of the self in a world of which it is both origin and extension. These imagined memories in fact bear little resemblance to his actual (and largely delocalised) memories of being in the world as a child, as we see in this extract from *W*: 'I filled whole exercise books [with] human figures unrelated to the ground which was supposed to support them.'[15] Indeed, Perec continues, 'What marks this period especially is the absence of landmarks: these memories are scraps of life snatched from the void. No mooring. Nothing to anchor them or hold them down.'[16] In the imagined memory, the kitchen space and the child form a 'monad' of the kind described by Perec in *Species of Spaces*. There is something of the phenomenological view of spatiality here, in that the bed/island and the child (or, let's say, the village and the villager) are inseparable from each other and co-constitute each other's meaning. As Wylie puts it, according to this point of view, 'we are always embedded in the world, in a state of mutuality that cannot be disavowed. The very term *being-in-the-world* itself declares an indissoluble link, a mutual intrication of existence and location, such that one cannot legitimately conceive of these as separate entities. No being without world.'[17] In the notebook sketches, however, the unmoored figures point instead to 'the space of strangeness or estrangement … the land of those who have no land, who have lost their way'.[18]

Although Perec's work is shot through with the melancholy of loss (though more specifically, we should say a kind of grief for what *would* or *could* have been, and yet *never will be*), he is aware that this loss constitutes a perpetually vanishing horizon and, as such, puts the grieving subject at risk of falling into what would quite properly be called nostalgia – 'a longing for a home that no longer exists or has never existed.'[19] For Boym, '[n]ostalgia is a sentiment of loss and displacement, but it is also a romance with one's own fantasy.'[20] Perec is sceptical in much the same way of what he describes as the nostalgic aspiration to make good this loss by attempting to 'rediscover or fashion your roots, to carve the place that will be yours […] and build, plant, appropriate, millimetre by millimetre, your "home": to belong completely in your village'.[21] Such visions of an ideal belonging-in-place are structured by totalising (and ultimately dystopian) geometries of inclusion and exclusion, as Perec indicates elsewhere in *Species of Spaces*: 'All utopias are depressing because they leave no room for chance, for difference, for the "miscellaneous". Everything has been set in order and order reigns. Behind every utopia there is always some great taxonomic design: a place for each thing and each thing in its place.'[22] Nor, however, does he believe in what he calls the 'false' alternative to nostalgic recovery: 'to own only the clothes you stand up in, to keep nothing, to live in hotels and change them frequently, and change towns and change countries; [...] to feel at home nowhere, but at ease almost everywhere.'[23] Each of these propositions embodies its own risks, as will be seen in the works I now go on to analyse. I will suggest that it is only in the spatialised project of writing, rather than in space itself, that Perec will find a means of navigating a course between them.

The utopian project, as attractive as it may at first appear, presents Perec with a number of intractable problems. For Thomas More, writing in 1516, the island of Utopia was a space in which 'the rude and wild people' might be brought to 'that excellent perfection in all good fashions, humanity and civic gentleness'.[24] Of course, this benign vision is subtended by all the socio-spatial logic and violence of colonial modernity, something which Perec sardonically alludes to in *Life: A User's Manual* with his description of Bunny Macklin, a British missionary's wife living in the Solomon Islands in the 1950s: she 'looked after the village girls. She made them do gym practice on the beach, and every Saturday morning they could be seen dressed in pleated slips, embroidered hairbands, and coral bracelets, swaying in time to the tinny sound of a Handel oratorio.'[25] In *W,* Perec transposes this scene in the context of the concentration camps, drawing a straight line between colonial ideology and European fascism. The Athletes of the totalitarian island society of W are made to process through the great stadium to the sounds of Beethoven's *Ninth* (which, of course, was played at Hitler's birthday party and at the opening of the 1936 Olympic Games). They march 'in impeccable columns, their arms stretched outwards towards the official stalls where the great Dignitaries of W acknowledge them'.[26]

It is in *W,* that Perec most explicitly foregrounds islands as both 'material stage and spatial concept'.[27] *W,* comprises two alternating narrative strands, the first of which, written by Perec in 1970–4, is largely autobiographical. Shot through with gaps in knowledge and absent memories, it attempts to reconstruct Perec's early childhood, the time he spent in the Vercors during the Occupation, his mother's deportation to Auschwitz and his broader family history. The second strand concerns the fictitious island of W, based on a story written by Perec at the age of 12 or 13. Perec claimed he was reminded of writing this story during a visit to Venice in 1967, following six months of intensive (but fruitless) research into his family history.[28] This same 'Venetian anamnesis'[29] is reprised by the narrator of the 'W' story, Gaspard Winckler, whose fleeting encounter with a stranger 'in a cheap restaurant in the Giudecca',[30] an island in the Venice Lagoon whose name derives etymologically from the Latin *Judaica*, floods him with memories of his sojourn on W, where he encountered an insular society so terrible that its very existence would seem to many unbelievable. Venice, as Bellos reminds us, was 'the first state or city in Europe to confine its Jewish community to a little town within the town – *borghetto*, in Venetian dialect, now universally used in its contracted form, ghetto'.[31]

The two narratives are entangled in quite complex ways. In the story of 'W', the narrator – Gaspard Winckler – is told by a mysterious stranger, Otto Apfelstahl, that as a child he was given the name and identity of another young boy, a deaf-mute who disappeared when the vessel on which he was travelling with his mother was shipwrecked in the Tierra del Fuego archipelago. Despairing of her boy's condition, which the physicians had ascribed to 'some infantile trauma whose precise configuration remained obscure',[32] Caecilia Winckler, had decided to take her son on a journey around the globe, to see if he might be cured. They spent months at sea, convinced that 'there is, somewhere on the ocean, an isle or atoll, a rock or headland' where suddenly the miracle might happen.[33] Shipwrecked in the course of a violent storm, just off the Isla Santa Inés, which forms part of the Tierra del Fuego archipelago, all those on board die; yet when the vessel and corpses are recovered by the Chilean rescue team, it is discovered that Gaspard's body is missing. Apfelstahl wonders if the child was abandoned by his mother, the implication being, of course, that he may have been deposited for his own well-being on the ostensibly salutary island of W,[34] 'a land where Sport is king, a nation of Athletes where Sport and life unite in a single magnificent effort'.[35]

For Karl Popper, the political project of utopia is the result of a particular form of rationalism that posits 'an ideal state of society as the aim which all our political actions should serve'.[36] Thus, the ends always justify the means, and it will be the task of the engineers, or technicians, of utopia 'to construct means by which these ends can be realized'.[37] 'However benevolent its ends', utopian rationalism, argues Popper, 'does not bring happiness, but only the familiar misery of being condemned to live under a tyrannical government'.[38] The basic narrative arc in the story of W concerns the island society's descent from planned utopia into a Hobbesian dystopia. It was founded, Perec tells us, by a man named Wilson, who some speculate may have been 'a disenchanted Captain Nemo who dreamt of building an ideal city'.[39] Little else is known about the island's colonisers, though 'it is at least clear that they were white, Western, and moreover, exclusively Aryan: Dutchmen, Germans,

Scandinavians, scions of that proud class called WASPS in the United States'.[40] The island is organised and run in accordance with the principles enshrined in its Coubertinian motto: 'FORTIUS ALTIUS CITIUS' ('stronger, higher, faster'), which 'fashioned social relations and individual aspirations through and through'.[41] The island, which has at its centre a forbidding fortress, epitomises 'calculative rationality translated into space'.[42] Everyone who lives on the island is allocated a place within a deeply segregative grid, depending on their age, gender and performance. The techniques used by the regime to control and subjugate the bodies of the island's subjects multiply and proliferate, becoming progressively more detailed and refined as they regulate the very minutiae of corporeal existence. For example, the amount of food given to Athletes depends on their performance in trials and competitions, but this is subject to arbitrary review, in order to undermine complacency. The degree of spatial freedom accorded to them is differentially produced and depends precisely on their status within the community, although again this can be arbitrarily revoked and reviewed at any time. The brutality of this regime, grounded in the deliberate obfuscation yet rigorous implementation of rules, reduces the Athletes to 'skin and bone, ashen-faced, their backs permanently bent, their skulls bald and shiny, their eyes full of panic, and their sores suppurating'.[43] In all of this, of course, in the very space where bio-power and sovereign power intersect, 'There's no recourse, no mercy, no salvation to be had from anyone.'[44]

For Boyle, *W,* serves as an 'indictment of any administration where a systematic operation descends into inhumanity'.[45] While *W,* is frequently read as a metaphor of the Nazi camps (and certainly the text itself contains many passages in which allusions are clearly and specifically made), Perec notes that at the time of writing the book, US-backed military juntas were seizing power across Latin America: 'I have forgotten what reasons I had at the age of twelve for choosing Tierra del Fuego as the site of W. Pinochet's Fascists have provided my fantasy with a final echo: several of the islands in that area are today deportation camps.'[46] These included Dawson Island and Quiriquina Island, known as 'the Gymnasium'. As Mountz points out, 'islands and archipelagos recur in critical thought to spatialize understandings of power and politics beyond the spaces of islands'.[47] In fact, Perec points here to an enduring link between islands and exceptional operations of power. Insular geographies lend themselves to practices of quarantine and containment. The French had a long history of building *bagnes* ('penal colonies') on islands, some of which remained operational in the post-colonial era. Today, the form of the 'island prison' survives in what Derek Gregory astutely refers to as our 'colonial present', in the form of so-called offshore processing centres,[48] where sovereign states contain and screen involuntarily displaced peoples, effectively deploying what Hyndman and Mountz describe as a strategy of neo-*refoulement*, namely 'preventing asylum by restricting access to territories that, in principle, provide protection to refugees'.[49] It is in this sense that these insular sites, cut off, to use Arendt's words, 'from the world of the living', their inhabitants locked in a 'fundamental situation of rightlessness',[50] represent a specific, transhistorical form of power relations, one that is both arbitrary and absolute.

In *Ellis Island*, Perec effectively writes a prospective genealogy of contemporary migration management. Operational in the years 1892–1954, millions of migrants to the USA, 'the 'El Dorado of modern times',[51] passed through the Ellis Island migration inspection centre, which 'officialised, institutionalised, and to all intents and purposes, industrialised' migration control.[52] The centre was 'an American-style factory as quick and efficient as a Chicago pork butcher's. At one end of the assembly line, they would put an Irish man, a Ukrainian Jew or an Italian from Apulia, at the other end – after their eyes and pockets had been inspected, and they had been vaccinated and disinfected – there emerged an American.'[53] A threshold space, which regulated entry to the American utopia, 'It was not yet America, just an extension of the boat, a piece of rubble from Europe, where nothing was yet given, where those who had left had not yet arrived, where those who had left everything behind had not yet obtained anything.'[54] Only those who travelled in third class and steerage were triaged here, and they were subjected to a series of medical checks, the results of which were recorded on each individual's data sheet ('fiche signalétique'). When certain illnesses were identified, codes would be chalked upon the migrant's clothes, before they were sent for more rigorous and invasive tests: C for tuberculosis, TC for trachoma, K for hernia, L for a limp, X for 'mental infirmity' … .[55] Elizabeth Yew describes how medicine and (sometimes spurious) science were frequently used to justify the deportation of southern and eastern European migrants, who were considered racially different from northern Europeans and Americans. So-called 'immigrant diseases', like ringworm, syphilis and particularly trachoma (Bober's grandfather was refused entry to the US, based on a trachoma diagnosis), were, she adds, still associated with racially categorised living conditions, and 'viewed as symbols of the immigrants' low condition, greater susceptibility to disease, and congenital ignorance of hygiene'.[56]

The stigmatisation and management of migrants is a trans-historical phenomenon, materialised in the present according to the complex intersectionality of global, disciplinary space. When Perec and the film-maker

Robert Bober visit Ellis Island in 1979, Perec insists that, as a site of memory, the former American migration inspection centre belongs 'to all those whom intolerance and poverty have chased away, and continue to chase away, from the land where they grew up'.[57] He draws a connecting thread to the present, linking the historical migrants to the US and the Vietnamese boat people 'going from island to island in search of increasingly improbable places of refuge'.[58] Perhaps he is also thinking here of his mother, who fled the anti-Semitic violence of Poland for Paris, the 'city of light', where '[p]eople must have told her there would be no more massacres and no more ghettos, and money for everyone',[59] only to find herself detained within, and ultimately deported from, the Republic she believed would ultimately confer protective citizenship upon her.

As Mountz observes: 'One encounters islands everywhere. By this I refer not to the literal discovery that there are many islands in the world, but rather that the characteristics of islands as political spaces operate as a traveling metaphor, with broad applicability beyond the physical space of islands.'[60] In this final section of my chapter, I will look at the ways in which urban spaces are reconfigured through a process of 'islanding' (*îlotage*) and the impact this has on Perec's encounter with space. In French, *îlotage* designates a system of spatial gridding, used for the purposes of surveillance and policing. Adopted and systematised by the French military during the Algerian war of independence (when it was also referred to as *quadrillage*), it still plays a key role in contemporary counterinsurgency operations. However, the system of 'islanding' in the French urban fabric has a much longer history, stretching back to the early nineteenth century, when a series of laws were passed enabling the compulsory inspection, expropriation and demolition of areas deemed insalubrious. Lévy-Vroelant points out that, while these profoundly stigmatising spatial operations were ostensibly based on mortality rates and the incidence of cholera and TB, they in fact represented a complex intersection between contemporary hygienist discourse, moral judgements regarding class and promiscuity, race and capital interests.[61] In 1894, medical statistician Jacques Bertillon (the older brother of Alphonse Bertillon, who invented the mugshot and anthropometric profiling) designed a system of *casiers sanitaires* ('sanitary records') for each house within a designated insalubrious area. In 1904, the process of delimiting the areas themselves was codified, with the preliminary identification in Paris of 6 *îlots insalubres*, followed by another 11 in 1921. Of these, *îlots* 1, 7, 11 and 16 had large Jewish and migrant populations, and Backouche observes how the official designation of these 'sous-espaces' ('sub-spaces') made possible the discursive elaboration in the French press of 'Jewish ghettos'.[62] While each of the *îlots* was technically subject to a suite of exceptional planning laws designed to facilitate their demolition, the prohibitive costs associated with compulsory purchases had prevented substantial work from taking place. However, in 1941–2, and in *îlot* 16 in particular, the Prefect of the Seine exploited the round-ups and deportation of Parisian Jews in order to appropriate and redevelop their houses using existing French law.[63]

After the war, the question of insalubrity still dominated planning agendas, though medical discourse gave way largely to one of modernisation.[64] The 1957 *Plan d'urbanisme directeur* and the 1968 *Schéma directeur d'aménagement et d'urbanisme* framed and enabled the implementation of state policies of urban regeneration. It was from his vantage point in the capital's abandoned, 'forbidden territory' that Perec's contemporary, the poet Jacques Réda, ruminated on the birth of the neoliberal city, with all its attendant violence, iniquities and erasure.[65] Casting his eye over the skyscrapers and luxury apartment blocks that proliferated in Paris during Pompidou's presidency, he mourns the evacuation of industry, of the working classes and their homes. Whereas streets and buildings in the centre of Paris were typically restored under these new initiatives, those located in the *îlots insalubres* at the edges of the city were demolished and their occupants displaced. These newly vacant spaces, which initially fell into long periods of dereliction, were eventually given over to experiments with novel spatial and architectural typologies, including large-scale housing estates.[66]

For the first six years of his life, Perec lived with his mother in *îlot* 7, at 24 rue Vilin in the *quartier* of Belleville. From 1969–75, he revisited the street (which he had last seen in 1946, and then again in 1961 or 1962) on a yearly basis, as part of the uncompleted *Lieux* project, in an attempt to record a space on the cusp of disappearance.[67] The street is also mentioned in *W,*: 'Today [Perec is writing in 1974] Rue Vilin has been three-quarters demolished. More than half the houses have been razed, leaving waste ground, piling up with rubbish, with old cookers and wrecked cars; most of the houses still standing are boarded up.' In the notebook entries made for *Lieux*, we see the street gradually disappear, each of the houses giving way in turn to another demolition site. In 1974, Perec spots a notice stating the city authorities' intention to create a public open space on the cleared site.[68] This will be the Parc de Belleville, which finally opened to the public in 1982. All traces of the working-class and migrant communities that lived and worked there, of their homes, businesses, languages and memories, have disappeared beneath its fine lawns and luxuriant flora. As Paul Connerton so rightly comments, 'Repressive erasure need not always take malign forms [...]; it can be encrypted covertly and without apparent violence.'[69] Indeed, we are reminded here of the quiet work of the lexicographer, Cinoc, in *Life: A User's Manual*, whose job it was to eliminate obsolete words and meanings from the Larousse dictionary. When he retired, in 1965, after 53 years of service, 'he had wiped dozens of islands, hundreds of cities and rivers, and thousands of townships off the map', without anyone really paying any attention.[70]

Life: A User's Manual, like so many other texts in the Perecquian corpus, is 'strewn with archipelagos, islands, reefs and atolls, punctuated by the cries of seagulls and cormorants, shot through with shipwrecks, deficient lighthouse keepers and unheard mayday calls from ships in distress at sea'.[71] One of its central protagonists, Bartlebooth, spends nearly 20 years criss-crossing the oceans, stopping off at islands too innumerable to mention; a teenager daydreams in her Paris bedroom about the best islands on which to erect a radio signal tower;[72] while the actress Olivia Rorschach regularly visits such far-flung islands as New Caledonia in the course of her dozens of world tours.[73] The novel describes a single day (23 June 1975) in the life of a fictitious 100-year-old apartment block on rue Simon-Crubellier. It ends with the death of the artist, Valène, who leaves behind a blank canvas on which he had planned to paint a cross-section of the entire building, but also the (largely unremarked) departure of Cinoc, who, 'overcoming his fear of flying and of US immigration, which he thought still happened on Ellis Island, had finally responded to the invitations he had been getting for years from two distant cousins'.[74]

Embedded in the heart of the novel, there are several references to Verne's fictional Lincoln Island. We learn, for example, of a trunk in Bartlebooth's cellar, which 'contains, in modern form, all the contents Captain Nemo put together and had washed up on shore for the good-hearted colonizers of Lincoln Island, as these were listed in Gédéon Spilett's notebooks, along with illustrations of *L'Île mystérieuse*. All that was needed to survive on a desert island.'[75] On the wall of his apartment hangs 'a landscape entitled *The Mysterious Island*, signed L. N. Montalscot: it portrays a seashore the left-half of which presents a pleasant prospect with a beach and a forest behind, the other half, all rocky walls broken up into towers and only a single entrance in them, suggesting an invulnerable fortress'.[76] The intertextual reference to *W*, is, of course, unmistakeable. And then there is the decorated chest in Winckler's room, where Valène discovers 'miniature characters, the sea, the horizon, and the whole island, not yet named Lincoln, in the same way as the spacewrecked travellers, dismayed and challenged at the same time, had first seen it, when they had reached the highest peak'.[77] Like the convex 'witches' mirrors' that both adorn and reflect the entirety of Winckler's room, the decoration on the chest affords a tantalisingly omniscient bird's-eye view of the bounded totality of the island. Verne's mysterious island, the very emblem of the imperial, utopian fantasy of the whole, is thus nested in the very heart of the apartment block (*îlot*); the block itself is located in the Plaine Monceau district of Paris, which Haussmann wrested from a vast *terrain vague* with the ambition of creating 'not a new district', but 'an entire city'.[78] This entire city stands at the centre of a former empire. And yet, this concentric geography of imperial power now rather resembles one of the 'superseded maps' that Cinoc loves to find on the second-hand book stalls that run along the banks of the Seine.[79] All around the apartment block, which is stuffed to the gills with the dusty debris of empire, demolition and renovation work proceed apace. Valène contemplates the illusoriness of the building's apparent invulnerability, noting how 'the same fever which around eighteen fifty brought these buildings out of the ground from Batignolles to Clichy, from Ménilmontant to Butte-aux-Cailles, from Balard to Pré Saint-Gervais, will henceforth strive for their destruction'.[80] This 'galloping capitalization of space',[81] enabled by 'teamwork between government agencies and private ventures' promises 'a total restructuring' of the city.[82] The bourgeois apartment will be subdivided for profit and transformed into 'a charming pied-à-terre, two recept. + bedr., all mod. cons., open outlook, quiet'; streets such as rue Simon-Crubellier will become one of those 'uninhabitable spaces' described by Perec in *Species of Spaces*: privatised, securitised and overrun with 'cubes of glass, steel and concrete'.[83]

And what of the utopias promised by this new, neoliberal economy? Towards the end of *Life*, we learn of the Marvell Hostelleries group, whose plan it is to construct a series of 'entirely self-contained hotels, so that their guests would never have to set foot outside'.[84] The hotels will be built on islands, including two that will be artificially constructed. The beaches will be privatised and guests will be able to enjoy 'culture parks' and 'artificial clubs, villages, and holiday centres having no essential relationship with their physical and human environments'.[85] Heritage, which is difficult to relocate, will be conveniently represented in the form of 'quality replicas',[86] staffed by workers dressed in historical costumes. This archipelago of leisure will enable customers to experience the totality of the world's culture, without the need for making inconveniently long journeys from one end of the globe to another. In short, its unique selling point will be 'the pure and simple negation of space'.[87] If the camps were produced by the insular utopian logic of modernity, it seems Vegas and Dubai might represent the apogee of neoliberal spatial economics.

To conclude, I'd like to return briefly to the short piece on the bed in *Species of Spaces*. In French, 'lit' (bed) and 'île' (island) are reversed homonyms: /li/ – /il/. If, in the spirit of Perecquian playfulness, we operate another reversal, this time of Leiris' word order, what we hear is /il/ – /li/, which the Francophone ear would immediately hear and understand as 'il lit' ('he/she reads', 'is reading'). This inversion undoes the spatial fixity of the bed-monad, with all its attendant risks of nostalgia and emplacement, presenting instead a vision of space that is constructed processually, through the act of reading and in the creative imagination. Deleuze and Guattari's analysis of the refrain hummed by a frightened child in a dark bedroom seems apposite here: 'Lost, he takes shelter, or orients himself with his little song as best he can. The song is like a rough sketch of a calming and stabilizing, calm and stable, center in the heart of chaos.'[88] And yet, even as this domain, this *abode*, is mapped we are reminded that 'home does not pre-exist: it was necessary to draw a circle around that uncertain and fragile center, to organize a limited space'.[89] Perhaps it is in this kind of *islanding*, one which does not result in the vulnerable obsolescence of a finished spatial form, in an *image* of space, that Perec finds emancipation from the trauma of childhood dislocation. Perhaps the production of space and writing are indistinguishable from each other? After all, it is 'only by writing, by endlessly deferring that moment when I cease from writing', that Perec is able to suspend that moment of paralysing closure, when 'the image becomes visible, like a puzzle that has been inexorably completed'.[90]

Notes

1. Bénabou, 'From Jewishness', 21.
2. Bénabou, 'From Jewishness', 22.
3. Robb, *Parisians*, 391.
4. Connerton, *The Spirit of Mourning*.
5. Bellos, *Georges Perec*, 90.
6. Perec, *Species of Spaces*, 17.
7. Perec, *Species of Spaces*, 16.
8. Perec, *Species of Spaces*, 17.
9. Perec, *Species of Spaces*, 17.
10. Perec, *Species of Spaces*, 15.
11. Perec, *Species of Spaces*, 91.
12. Perec, *Species of Spaces*, 70.
13. Perec, *W*, 70. It seems that only with the finality of his father's grave does the conditional tense switch to the present: 'something like a secret serenity connected to this rooting in space, to this writing on the cross, to this death which had at last ceased to be abstract', 38.
14. Levitas, *The Concept of Utopia*, 111.

15. Perec, *W*, 68.
16. Perec, *W*, 68.
17. Wylie, 'A Landscape', 411–2.
18. Wylie, 'A Landscape', 415.
19. Boym, *The Future of Nostalgia*, xiii.
20. Boym, *The Future of Nostalgia*, xiii.
21. Perec, *Species of Spaces*, 71.
22. Perec, *Species of Spaces*, 191.
23. Perec, *Species of Spaces*, 71.
24. More, *Utopia*, 50.
25. Perec, *Life*, 347–8.
26. Perec, *W*, 26.
27. Mountz, 'Political Geography II', 641.
28. Bellos, *Georges Perec*, 371.
29. Bellos, *Georges Perec*, 371.
30. Perec, *W*, 3.
31. Bellos, *Georges Perec*, 371.
32. Perec, *W*, 23.
33. Perec, *W*, 24.
34. This story is mirrored in the autobiographical text, in which Perec tells us three times that in 1941, he was put on a train at the Gare de Lyon and sent by his mother to the Vercors region of France for his own safety. A natural fortress, thanks to its mountainous topography, the Vercors drew refugees and resistance fighters alike, becoming what Paul Dreyfus would describe, in 1959, as an 'island of salvation' ('îlot du salut') (see Aeschimann, 2004). Indeed, Bellos (*Georges Perec*, 63) suggests that Perec's description of the island of W in fact draws heavily upon the visual landscape of the Vercors.
35. Perec, *W*, 67.
36. Popper, 'Utopia and Violence', 6.
37. Popper, 'Utopia and Violence', 6.
38. Popper, 'Utopia and Violence', 7. Aimé Césaire (*Discourse on Colonialism*, 3) underscored the necessity of revealing to 'the very distinguished, very humanistic, very Christian bourgeois of the twentieth century that without his being aware of it, he has a Hitler inside him, that Hitler inhabits him, that Hitler is his demon, that if he rails against him, he is being inconsistent and that, at bottom, what he cannot forgive Hitler for is not crime in itself, the crime against man, it is not the humiliation of man as such, it is the crime against the white man, the humiliation of the white man, and the fact that he applied to Europe colonialist procedures which until then had been reserved exclusively for the Arabs of Algeria, the coolies of India, and the blacks of Africa'.
39. Perec, *W*, 66. The reference here is, of course, to the fictional Lincoln Island, the setting for Verne's *Mysterious Island*.
40. Perec, *W*, 66.
41. Perec, *W*, 67.
42. Giaccaria and Minca, 'Topographies/Topologies of the Camp', 5.
43. Perec, *W*, 161.
44. Perec, *W*, 140.
45. Boyle, *Consuming Autobiographies*, 92.
46. Perec, *W*, 164.
47. Mountz, 'Political Geography II', 637.
48. Boochani, '"The 'Offshore Processing Centre' I Live in Is an Island Prison"'. See also Gregory, *The Colonial Present*.
49. Hyndman and Mountz, 'Another Brick in the Wall?'.
50. Arendt, *The Origins of Totalitarianism*, 296.
51. Perec, *Récits*. My translation.
52. Perec, *Récits*, 15.
53. Perec, cited in Frances Jo Maddern, 'Spectres of Migration and the Ghosts of Ellis Island', 368.
54. Perec, *Récits*, 47.
55. Perec, *Récits*, 49.
56. Yew, 'Medical Inspection of Immigrants at Ellis Island', 494.
57. Perec, *Récits*, 63.
58. Perec, *Récits*, 63.

59. Perec, *W*, 31–2.
60. Mountz, 'Political Geography II', 638.
61. Lévy-Vroelant, 'Le diagnostic', 713.
62. Backouche, 'Rénover un quartier parisien sous Vichy', 115.
63. Backouche and Gensburger, 'Expulser les habitants de l'îlot 16 à Paris à partir de 1941', 167–95.
64. Lévy-Vroelant, 'Le diagnostic', 742.
65. Réda, *The Ruins of Paris,* 107.
66. Lévy-Vroelant, 'Le diagnostic', 740.
67. Perec began his ambitious *Lieux* project in 1969, the same year as he began to make notes on the novel that would become *Life: A User's Manual*. He abandoned *Lieux*, which he had originally planned to be a 12-year undertaking, in 1975, the year he published *W*,. 'La Rue Vilin' (the collated texts dealing with the street of the same name, taken from *Lieux*), which appears in *Species of Spaces*, was originally published in *L'Humanité* two years later, in 1977.
68. Perec, *Species*, 221.
69. Connerton, *The Spirit of Mourning,* 42.
70. Perec, *Life,* 288.
71. Rosenman, 'Georges Perec', 153. ('... est semée d'archipels, d'îles, de récifs, d'atolls, scandée de cris de mouettes et de cormorans, traversée de naufrages, de gardiens de phares défaillants et d'appels perdus de navires en détresse'.) Translation by author.
72. Perec, *Life*, 179.
73. Perec, *Life*, 395.
74. Perec, *Life*, 499.
75. Perec, *Life*, 345.
76. Perec, *Life*, 421.
77. Perec, *Life*, 26.
78. Olsen, *The City as a Work of Art*, 51.
79. Perec, *Life*, 289.
80. Perec, *Life*, 130.
81. Leak, 'Paris Created and Destroyed', 28.
82. Perec, *Life*, 129.
83. Perec, *Life*, 130.
84. Perec, *Life*, 424.
85. Perec, *Life*, 424.
86. Perec, *Life*, 428.
87. Perec, *Life*, 426.
88. Deleuze,and Guattari, *A Thousand Plateaus*, 311.
89. Deleuze and Guattari, *A Thousand Plateaus*, 311.
90. Perec, *Species of Spaces*, 143.

Bibliography

Aeschimann, Eric. 'Un havre de guerre', *Libération*, 18 May 2004. Accessed 29 May 2018. https://www.liberation.fr/grand-angle/2004/05/18/un-havre-de-guerre_479925.

Agamben, Giorgio. *Homo Sacer: Sovereign Power and Bare Life*, translated by Daniel Heller-Roazen. Stanford: Stanford University Press, 1998.

Arendt, Hannah. *The Origins of Totalitarianism*. New ed. New York: Harcourt Brace Jovanovich, 1973.

Backouche, Isabelle. 'Rénover un quartier parisien sous Vichy: "Un Paris expérimental plus qu'une rêverie sur Paris"', *Genèses* 73 (2008): 115–42.

Backouche, Isabelle and Sarah Gensburger. 'Expulser les habitants de l'îlot 16 à Paris à partir de 1941: Un effet d'"aubaine"?', *Le genre humain* 52 (2012): 167–95.

Baldacchino, Godfrey. 'Islands, Island Studies, Island Studies Journal', *Island Studies Journal* 1, no. 1 (2006): 3–18.

Bellos, David. *Georges Perec: A Life in Words*. London: Harvill, 1999.

Bénabou, Marcel. 'From Jewishness to the Aesthetics of Lack', translated by Brian J. Reilly, *Yale French Studies* 105 (2004): 20–35.

Bloch, Ernst. *The Principle of Hope, Volume 1*, translated by Neville Plaice, Stephen Plaice and Paul Knight. Cambridge, MA: MIT Press, 1996.

Boochani, Behrouz. 'The "Offshore Processing Centre" I Live in Is an Island Prison', *Financial Times*, 29 May 2018. Accessed 31 October 2018. https://www.ft.com/content/00620a94-5db2-11e8-ad91-e01af256df68.

Boyle, Claire. *Consuming Autobiographies: Reading and Writing the Self in Post-War France*. London: Legenda, 2007.

Boym, Svetlana. *The Future of Nostalgia*. New York: Basic Books, 2001.

Césaire, Aimé. *Discourse on Colonialism*, translated by Joan Pinkham. New York: Monthly Review Press, 1972.

Chevalier, Louis. *The Assassination of Paris*, translated by David P. Jordan. Chicago: University of Chicago Press, 1994.

Connerton, Paul. *The Spirit of Mourning: History, Memory and the Body*. Cambridge: Cambridge University Press, 2011.

Deleuze, Gilles and Félix Guattari. *A Thousand Plateaus: Capitalism and Schizophrenia*, translated by Brian Massumi. Minneapolis: University of Minnesota Press, 1987.

Emerson, Tom. 'From Lieux to Life ...', *AA Files* 45/46 (2001): 92–97.

Giaccaria, Paolo and Claudio Minca. 'Topographies/Topologies of the Camp: Auschwitz as a Spatial Threshold', *Political Geography* 30, no. 1 (2011): 3–12.

Gregory, Derek. *The Colonial Present: Afghanistan, Palestine, Iraq*. Malden, MA: Blackwell, 2004.

Huglo, Marie-Pascale. 'Mémoire de la disparition: *Récits d'Ellis Island*, l'album', *Protée* 32, no. 1 (2004): 7–14.

Hyndman, Jennifer and Alison Mountz. 'Another Brick in the Wall? Neo-*Refoulement* and the Externalization of Asylum by Australia and Europe', *Government and Opposition* 43, no. 2 (2008): 249–69.

Leak, Andrew. 'Paris Created and Destroyed', *AA Files* 45/46 (2001): 25–31.

Levitas, Ruth. *The Concept of Utopia*. Oxford: Peter Lang, 2010.

Lévy-Vroelagnt, Claire. 'Le diagnostic d'insalubrité et ses conséquences sur la ville: Paris 1894–1960', *Population* 54, no. 4/5 (1999): 707–43.

Maddern, Jo Frances. 'Spectres of Migration and the Ghosts of Ellis Island', *Cultural Geographies* 15, no. 3 (2008): 359–81.

More, Thomas. *Utopia*, edited by Susan Bruce. Oxford: Oxford University Press, 1999.

Mountz, Alison. 'Political Geography II: Islands and Archipelagos', *Progress in Human Geography* 39, no. 5 (2015): 636–46.

Olsen, Donald J. *The City as a Work of Art: London, Paris, Vienna*. New Haven: Yale University Press, 1988.

Paskins, Jacob. *Paris Under Construction: Building Sites and Urban Transformation in the 1960s*. New York: Routledge, 2016.

Perec, Georges. 'Georges Perec et Jules Verne', interview by Viviane Forrester, *Chemins*, Antenne 2, 22 March 1976. Video. Accessed 9 May 2019. http://www.ina.fr/video/I09365753.

Perec, Georges. *Things: A Story of the Sixties*, translated by David Bellos. London: Collins Harvill, 1990.

Perec, Georges. *Le Voyage d'hiver*. Paris: Seuil, 1993.

Perec, Georges. *Récits d'Ellis Island: Histoires d'errance et d'espoir*. Paris: P.O.L., 1995.

Perec, Georges. *Life: A User's Manual*, translated by David Bellos. London: Harvill, 1996.

Perec, Georges. *Species of Spaces and Other Pieces*, edited and translated by John Sturrock. London: Penguin Books, 1997.

Perec, Georges. *W, or The Memory of Childhood*, translated by David Bellos. London: Vintage Books, 2011.

Popper, Karl R. 'Utopia and Violence', *World Affairs* 149, no. 1 (1986): 3–9.

Réda, Jacques. *The Ruins of Paris*, translated by Mark Treharne. London: Reaktion Books, 1996.

Robb, Graham. *Parisians: An Adventure History of Paris*. London: Picador, 2010.

Rosenman, Anny Dayan. 'Georges Perec: Sauver le père'. In *L'oubli du père*, edited by Jacques André and Catherine Chabert, 147–72. Paris: Presses universitaires de France, 2004.

Wylie, John. 'A Landscape Cannot Be a Homeland', *Landscape Research* 41, no. 4 (2016): 408–16.

Yew, Elizabeth. 'Medical Inspection of Immigrants at Ellis Island, 1891–1924', *Bulletin of the New York Academy of Medicine* 56, no. 5 (1980): 488–510.

8

Textual, audio and physical space: Adapting Perec's radio plays for theatre

Christopher Hall

In an exploration of Georges Perec's geographies, it is important to consider the spaces of his texts and the spaces in which and through which they have been performed. This chapter examines the spatiality of two of Georges Perec's original radio plays: 'The Machine' (*Die Maschine*) and *The Raise* (*L'Augmentation*).[1] The layout and typesetting of these works on the page is an intrinsic component of their initial engagement and comprehension. The use of language in both creates meaning and narrative within their own separate conceptual landscapes and audio spatiality is key, particularly for 'The Machine'. The adaptation process through one conceptual and metaphorical space into the vocal area and further into the physical space of the theatre, as well as its attendant conceptual spaces, raises distinctly Perecquian opportunities and issues.

In this chapter, I discuss my own adaptation of these radio plays to the stage. 'The Machine' and *The Raise* were written for radio, for an audience to listen to in the private, informal, remote and individual environment of their own home. The first step of the adaptation process is the explicit understanding of the spatial, physical and conceptual relationships between the audience of radio listeners and how they are profoundly different from those of the theatrical audience. The process of transferring these two works from the aural to the theatrical presented to me and my collaborators a variety of opportunities and challenges as well as spaces for learning.

'The Machine'

One of the best, most concise summaries of 'The Machine' was written by J.J. White two years after the initial radio première and one year before the piece was published: '*Die Maschine* is a mixture of many levels of language, from the sublime to the ridiculous. From play to analysis, from destruction to political reformulation.'[2]

'The Machine' is written for four separate voices – Processors 1, 2 and 3 and System Control. Partially written originally in French by Perec, then further developed through collaboration with his German translator Eugen Helmlé, the original 1968 German version, when read on the page by a single person is difficult to comprehend (see Figure 8.1).

Speicher 1	*Speicher 2*	*Speicher 3*	*Kontrolle*
			Speicher in aufnahmebereitschaft
aufnahmebereit			
	aufnahmebereit		
		aufnahmebereit	
			TON Hier erato um ihre frage dirket durchzuprogrammieren, stecken sie bitte die perforierte karte in die lesespalte unde drucken sie die tasten a un d KLICKEN TON Titel des gedichts
wanderers nachtlied			
			entstehungsdatum
	6. september 1780		
			Autor des gedichts
		goethe johann wolfgang von, 17490-01832	
			originalspeache des gedicts
	deutsch		
			wortlaut des gedichts
	uber allen gipfeln ist ruh in allen wipfeln spurest du kaum einen hauch; die vogelen schweigen im walde. Warte nur, balde ruhest du auch.		

Figure 8.1 Georges Perec, *Die Maschine*, translated by Eugen Helmlé, 1968 (page 6). The opening section of the play shows the idiosyncratic page layout of the play. © Philip Reclam, Stuttgart

To accommodate this necessary but idiosyncratic layout, the original 1972 German print edition opts for a landscape rather than a portrait layout. A larger format journal, the *Review of Contemporary Fiction*, is able to accommodate this layout in portrait with Ulrich Schönherr's 2009 English translation, referred to as 'The Machine' (see Figure 8.2).

It was clear that the way to begin to solve the first part of the puzzle of adaptation – whether or not the piece was going to work for a theatre audience – was to hear it, as Oliver Bray notes:

> Therefore, the text needs to be spoken and requires multiple voices to reach a comprehensible form. Its realization depends on the three interrelated dimensions of performance: time-body-space.[3]

PROCESSOR 1	PROCESSOR 2	PROCESSOR 3	SYSTEM CONTROL
			processors ready to record
ready to record			
	ready to record		
		ready to record	
			SOUND this is Erato speaking. in order to program your question, insert the punch card into the reading slit and press buttons a and d. CLICK SOUND title of the poem
rambler's lullaby			
			date of origin
	september 6, 1780		
			author of the poem
		goethe, johann wolf-gang von, 1749–1832	
			original language of the poem
	german		

Figure 8.2 Georges Perec, 'The Machine', translated by Ulrich Schönherr, 2009 (page 36). The opening section of the English translation of 'The Machine' replicates the format of the German version. © Dalkey Archive Press

There are, however, irregularities in the page formatting of 'The Machine'. These irregularities presented challenges when maintaining the authenticity and integrity of the theatrical adaptation and raised issues about the consistency of the character traits of the separate Processors. An example is the difference between the Recapitulation section on page 54 of the published version, which is formatted differently to the original unpublished translation manuscript, creating a different interplay of language and voices. Early in 'The Machine', establishing Processor 2 as the mischievous component, we have the line 'Germany above everything in the world'.[4] Due to ambiguities in the formatting, this can be read either as Processor 2: 'Germany above everything' followed by Processor 3: 'in the world', or as Processor 2 having the whole line. In correspondence with Schönherr this ambiguity was resolved as the former of the two options. In rehearsal, the pacing and timing of the line and reaction from System Control made us feel that the latter of these options was correct for both the characterisation and to maintain the tempo and comedy of the wordplay.

These inconsistencies become important when considering the intervention of System Control during the section towards the end of 'The Machine' (page 82 in the English translation) defined by System Control as protocol number 4. This entails an explosion of quotes through free association, using poetry from a wide variety of world literature in an attempt to identify the essence of poetry. This intervention begins on page 86 as each of the characters, including System Control, read lines from a poem by Izumi Shibiku. We initially thought this was another formatting error. However, when considered from the perspective of System Control, this intervention is an acknowledgement of the increasing awareness that the Processors do not always strictly play by the rules laid down by the System Control. When considering the emotional arc of the play, this section begins to establish the ending of 'The Machine', acknowledging its own mortality.

This intervention or deviation from the Oulipian structure of 'The Machine' is an example of the implementation of the Oulipian clinamen: an error in the system. This conceit allows for deviation from the rigidly adhered to rules or structures. It further constructs the simultaneous, four-language passage that follows.

According to David Bellos, 'stereophonic sound keeps the language just sufficiently apart to permit overlaid translation between German, French, English and Japanese'.[5] Since it was initially written for broadcast radio, the original audience for 'The Machine' was remote and composed of individual listeners. This was markedly different from the immediate and communal experience of the theatrical performance. This difference is clearest when considering the ability of the stereophonic audio to split the four different languages between the two channels. Transcoding this effect and its implicit meaning into the theatrical space became an important component of the adaptation process of this section.

From the extant dual mono recording of the 1968 German broadcast it is not possible to tell whether or not this was achieved effectively. The recording does reveal that the simultaneous vocal stereo separation implied in the text of *Die Maschine* (see Figure 8.3) was not performed as such and is not spoken simultaneously but nearer to the way outlined in the 2009 English translation (see Figure 8.4). This presents a formatting inconsistency since the formatting of the original manuscript of Schönherr's translation is identical to that of *Die Maschine* (1972). In private correspondence, Schönherr made it clear to me that, despite the

SCHWEIGEN

Tsui ni yuku Michi to wa kanete	That is a road Which some day we all travel	Qu'il y ait un chemin Qu'un jour nous de- Vions tous prendre	Dass ed einen weg gibt Den wir eines tages all Nehmen
Kikishikada	I had heard before	Je le savais deja	Davon hatt' ich einst Gehort
Kino kyo to wa Omowazarishi	Yet I never expected To take it so soon myself	Mais je ne croyais Qu'il me faille le Prendre si tot moi- meme	Doch nie geglaubt Ihh selbst so bald zu Gehen
			Narahisa*

SCHWEIGEN

Figure 8.3 Georges Perec, *Die Maschine*, translated by Eugen Helmlé, 1968. This Narahisa (or Narahira) section of the German translation implies that all versions of the poem – all speaking parts – should be performed simultaneously. © Philip Reclam, Stuttgart

SILENCE
tsui ni yuku
dass es einen weg
qu'il y ait un chemin
that is a road
michi to wa kanete

Figure 8.4 Georges Perec, 'The Machine', translated by Ulrich Schönherr, 2009. The layout of the Narahisa (or Narahira) section of the English translation implies that the different version of the poem – the speaking parts – should be performed consecutively. © Dalkey Archive Press

formatting problems, he wished the published version of 'The Machine' to be viewed as the definitive English-language version. For the Crucible Theatre performance in 2012, developed through rehearsal, the performers spoke this section simultaneously.

The desire to adapt this intended and implied aural stereo experience efficiently to the physicality of the theatre presented us with another puzzle, establishing an informal and conversational approach required for certain components of the comedy to work. 'The Machine', for all of its Oulipian constraints and algorithmic scripting, is a comedy: variously silly, broad, absurd, satirical, obtuse and intellectual. For the staging, we found no opportunity to add physical comedy to the list, though performance and character became important parts of the theatrical audience experience. One of the mechanisms that non-physical comedy uses, for example stand-up, is the informal, conversational voice, amplified. This enables members of the audience to feel that they are part of the conversation and not witnesses to a routine.

We decided to use broadcast standard radio microphones, through a studio-standard PA system in order to replicate and approximate the one-to-one immediacy and individual experience of radio. The intention of stereo separation (more accurately a dual mono) effect could not be replicated by the four performers, but the personal connection with the voices of the performers could be achieved. The performers were able to speak lower and more from the larynx than the diaphragm, at less declamatory and more conversational volume.

The originally intended staging was simple, based on radio show recording session setups and, more obliquely, boyband performances – during rehearsals the distinct individual nuances and quirks of the personalities of the Processors became evident. There was the disruptive and mischievous nature of Processor 2; the intelligence and archness of Processor 1; and there was Processor 3 trying to keep up with the game playing and speed of the other two though never quite managing it. And finally System Control, the systematic leader and implementer of the rules, attempting to corral the occasionally wayward Processors, eventually throwing in the towel and joining in the fun.

The three different venues where 'The Machine' was performed in 2011 and 2012 were flexible studio-style spaces as opposed to traditional proscenium-arch theatres. This flexibility allowed for an intimate audience experience. The initial rehearsals in Sheffield's Bloc Space almost immediately inspired a change to the staging. Rather than a line of performers in front of an audience – the initial configuration – we arranged the four performers on the four corners of a square, among the audience (see Figure 8.5).

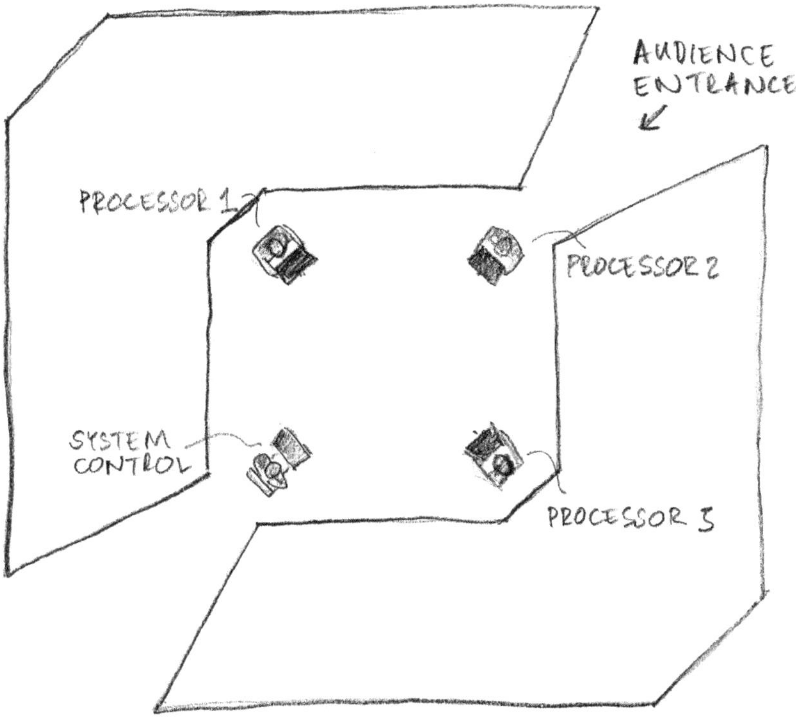

Figure 8.5 Sheffield Theatres, Crucible Studio Theatre layout, 2016. The diagram shows the four performers (System Control and Processors 1–3) and their positions at the four corners of the performance space. © Sheffield Theatres

Through a hybrid use of the studio space, we invited the audience to anticipate an event somewhere between combat or game play, music recital and theatre performance. The audience were placed partially within the action, where they would be aware of their proximity to certain performers and their distance from others. From this point of view, audience members had the opportunity to read the text/script/score, if they should wish to do so. The field of view was constrained such that each member of the audience could see the profile of one of their performers and the faces of the other three. Through these visual constraints, we sought to emulate or refract the constraints in the text.

This first performance was in the smallest space, seating an audience of 40 people. One audience member, in the front row, sat through the entire performance with their eyes shut. This was slightly disconcerting for the performers, but understandable if perhaps the audience member was seeking to experience the purity of the wordplay, attempting to negate the physicality of the performance and the communal experience of being in an audience. A second audience member told me that they felt like they were supporting the performer nearest to them. And, as one online commentator put it, 'The result was immersive, bringing the audience "into" the performance as avatar-like characters. Each of us was sat nearer one of the four performers in particular and felt like we were on their team.'[6] This comment underlines some of the fundamental differences between audience experiences of radio and theatre.[7]

Transposing the spoken and written text into a physical performance was an additional puzzle within the adaptation, forming an important part of the rehearsal and development process. Performers were lit only by their reading lamps. Performers could not move from the immediate vicinity of their music stands, on which their scripts were placed. Processors 1, 2 and 3 stood throughout. System Control remained seated throughout. It was necessary to make judgements on these matters because Perec did not provide instructions. On the contrary, he left it to others to decide how to stage 'The Machine'. Also, as I have explained, it is not possible to identify a single, definitive version of this play. The German version was initially broadcast in 1968; a written version, slightly different from the broadcast version was published in 1972.[8] The English translation was initially submitted to the publishers in 2006 only to be subtly changed by formatting errors when published in 2009. This variability and uncertainty gave us as theatre-makers an amount of licence to make decisions about how we wished to present the play, including its ending. 'The Machine' is challenging and disorientating for some audience members because it lacks conventional reference points such as narrative, plot, named characters or scene changes. Challenging plays are particularly challenging where they conclude, and any awkwardness that audiences experience may be intensified at this point.[9] With this in mind, we sought a logical conclusion to 'The Machine'. We gave the final sound to System Control: a prolonged breathing out, heightened of course by the use of radio microphones. This ending, inspired by Samuel Beckett's play *Breath*, is described by Beckett as an expiration (see Figure 8.6).

We began the play with a formalised ritual – the one-by-one turning on of the reading lamps and opening of the script – mirrored at the end by the one-by-one closing of the script and turning off of the lamps.

paz	paz	paz	paz
paz	paz	paz	paz
pzzz	pzzz	pshsh	pshsh
pshsh	shsh	shsh	shshshsh

Figure 8.6 The last word of Third Angel's production of 'The Machine' went to System Control, in the form of a prolonged breathing out or expiration. These final utterances are shown in this extract from the script (Perec, 'The Machine', 93). The final 'sh' could be interpreted as a reference to the sound of white noise or lack of radio frequency signal. © Dalkey Archive Press

The Raise

L'Augmentation, translated by David Bellos in an unpublished English version as *The Raise*,[10] was written for six separate voices. It also includes a news item with statistics about a measles outbreak. The structure of the play is derived from that of a fictional management decision flowchart (see Figure 8.7). Mapping the vicissitudes of an unnamed individual's attempts to secure a pay rise from their Head of Department, *The Raise* exhausts every decision, action, option, choice and consequence dictated by Perec's satirical management flowchart. Indecision, procrastination and the occasional circumperambulation around the nameless organisation's various departments repeatedly reign and continually impede the protagonist's progress towards their objective. The passing of time, during this drawn-out process, is reflected in changes to the Head of Department's job title: initially Section Head, he is later known as Supervisor, Team Leader, Task Force Convener, Head of Department and finally Lord and Master. Ultimately, having negotiated a series of obstacles and opportunities, the protagonist returns to the starting point. The play includes a great deal of repetition, with many returns to the initial position at the top of the flowchart or at a key position within the chart. The six main characters consequently have names reflecting the flowchart navigation and therefore the decision-making process. The first character to speak is known as '1. The Position', the second as '2. The Alternatives'. Each of the discrete sections – which cannot realistically be labelled scenes due to their brevity and similarity – start with the first two characters and continue in mainly numerical order. There is no apparent need for stereo signal separation, as *The Raise* lies more in the area of storytelling than the linguistic experimentation of 'The Machine'.

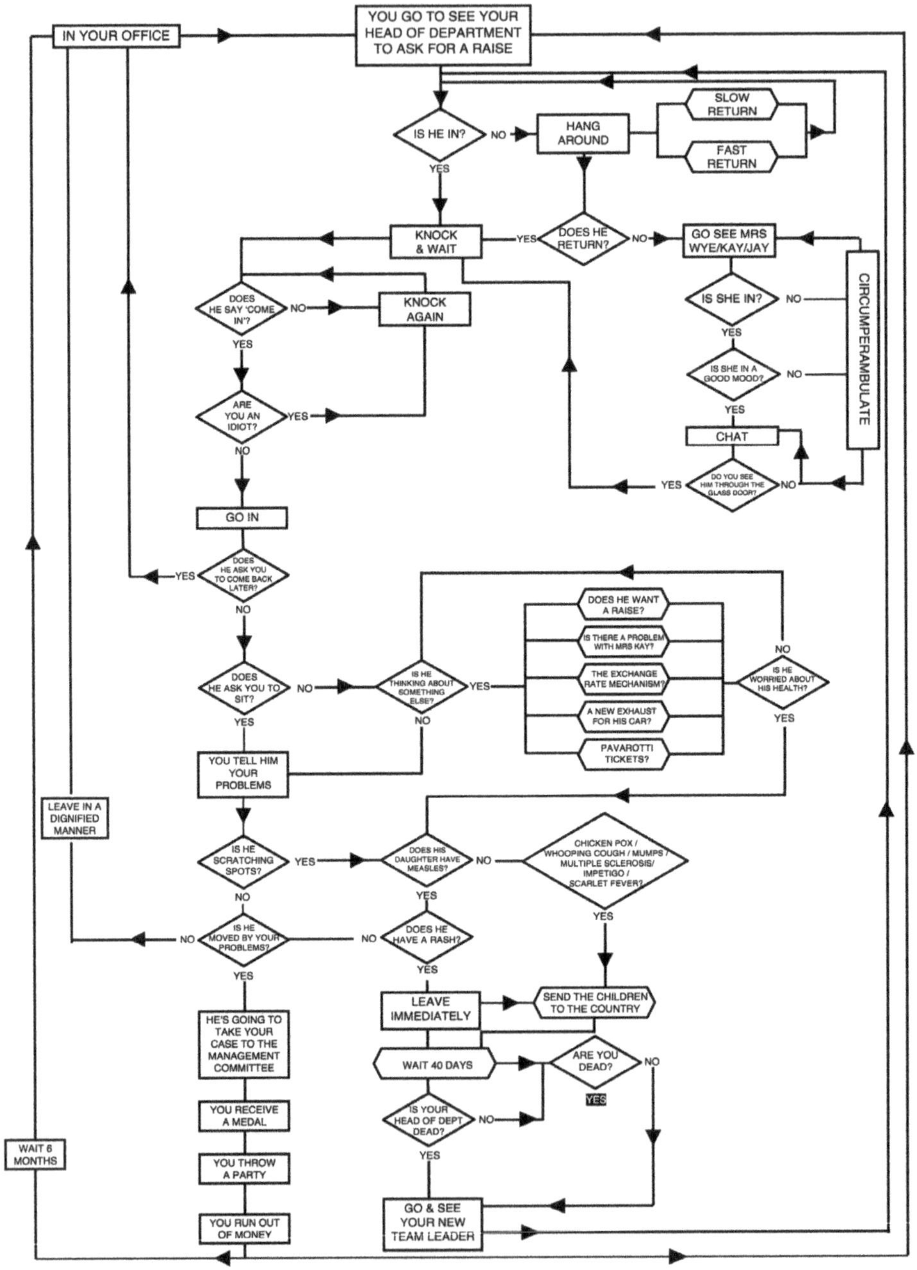

Figure 8.7 The structure of *The Raise* is derived from that of a fictional management decision flowchart. This image is taken from David Bellos's English translation of this text, originally published as *L'Augmentation*. Unpublished image. © David Bellos

The page layouts of the German *Die Gehaltsterhohung*, the French *L'Augmentation* and the unpublished English version, *The Raise*, provide no indication as to the manner in which the text should be spoken, not even a hint. The sole indicator, used by all three versions, is a five-pointed asterisk in the German version, a five-pointed star in the French, and a six-pointed asterisk in the English translation, between the different sections.

The prose adaptations, beginning with Perec's original 1968 version *L'art et la maniere d'aborder son chef de service pour lui demander une augmentation*, are a single unpunctuated monologue. From a theatrical perspective this would seem to hint at approaching *The Raise* as an almost Beckettian piece of rapid train of thought, as exemplified in *Not I*.[11] For a piece that can last somewhere between 40 and 60 minutes, following the pace and intensity of *Not I* would be more difficult for an audience to absorb and find entertaining. As well as being a denial of the humour inherent in the repetition and minor changes to the repetitions, this approach would have stifled any character development that the six separate performers could engender. The layout of the text of *The Raise* gave no hint as to how the piece could be adapted for theatre or indeed any indication of the general aural experience of the audience. There is no indication that the initial German broadcast of *The Raise* experimented with the stereo audio signal. The broadcast used expressionless voices, rhythmic regulations, almost intolerable repetitions.[12]

Adapting for a live theatrical physical performance, the audience seeing the performers and consequently making judgements about those performers, whether or not the vocal performance is expressionless, we set out to delineate the characters of the different functions and gain comedy of frustration from the repetitions.

The Raise is primarily a story told to the audience and the adaptation puzzle was how to get the audience to feel just the right amount of challenge, entertainment and comfort. With the 2016 production of *The Raise* at Leeds Beckett University Drama Studio, the audience needed to feel invested in the nameless protagonist 'you' – enough to be able to project their own feelings onto the character. Allowing the performers to inhabit the studio space logically, comfortably and in accordance with the text was, as with 'The Machine', a relatively straightforward process. The stage was set with chairs and tables, aping the form of one of the keystones of the bureaucratic process, so important in understanding *The Raise*: the committee meeting (see Figure 8.8).

Once the structure of the committee was established, the characters of the separate functions were allowed to develop and the enjoyment lay

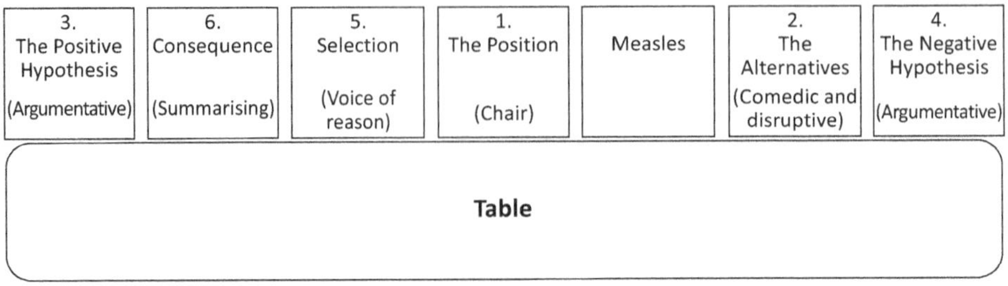

Figure 8.8 *The Raise* stage layout as performed at Leeds Beckett University in 2016. The layout was designed to be reminiscent of a committee meeting or a television panel show allowing the verbal interplay between the characters to have the arduous repetition of bureaucratic processes and gaining humour from the same repetition and the impact of different decisions. © The author

in the exhaustion of the myriad permutations. *The Raise* becomes a conversation/argument/meeting between the committee members in which the audience have little space to feel like participants, as they do in 'The Machine'. They are observers, passengers on the journey down the corridors of bureaucratic procedures and happenstance.

The seventh performer seated at the committee meeting plays the role of Measles: a role that has only two lines. We explored the idea of using video projection to deliver the statistics that Measles says. The comedy value of a performer remaining still and quiet throughout the piece, only to deliver two dryly comic lines, was too good to turn down. The sole physical constraint for the performers was that they should remain seated and defer to the chair, '1. The Position'. The major intervention into the studio space was that of acknowledging the algorithmic nature of the piece by projecting the flow chart on which *The Raise* is based, or including it in the programme notes (Figure 8.7).

If the audience members were listening to and engaging empathetically with the 'you' of the story, then the flow chart would allow them to recap, anticipate and work out the ending in advance of the protagonist. There would have been little in the way of surprise or delight gained from the circumperambulations of the protagonist's story.

The ending of *The Raise* is clear. The character known as '6. The Consequence', the performer who related most directly to the audience by summarising the sections, has the final line: 'Or by circumperambulating the diverse departments which together make up the whole or a part of that august Enterprise to which you have given, these many long years, the best part of your life …'.[13]

The English translation ends with a stage instruction, CURTAIN, both the German and French with the ellipsis.

Notes

1. I draw in this article upon audio recordings of the 1968 Saarländischer Rundfunk production of *Die Maschine* (1968), the Third Angel production of 'The Machine' (2012) and the Third Angel production of *The Raise* (2016).
2. White, 'Goethe in The Machine', 129.
3. Bray, 'Playing with Constraint', 44.
4. Perec, 'The Machine', 54.
5. Bellos, *Georges Perec*, 382.
6. Barker, 'Amusement Arcadia'.
7. Freshwater, *Theatre and Audience*, 7.
8. Bellos, *Georges Perec*, 381.
9. Freshwater, *Theatre and Audience*, 29.
10. *The Raise* is a translation of the *L'Augmentation. L'Augmentation* is itself an adaptation of an earlier piece by Perec, *L'Art et la manière d'aborder son chef de service pour lui demander une augmentation*, published in 1968. This prose piece was translated by Bellos as *The Art and Craft of Approaching Your Head of Department to Submit a Request for a Raise*, 2011. While *The Raise* is highly segmented and structured in its layout, *The Art and Craft …*, without punctuation or pause, uses a single narrative voice in one continuous sentence for over 100 pages and, as with *The Raise,* attempts to exhaust all of the options presented by navigating the fictitious management flowchart (Figure 8.7).
11. Beckett, *The Complete Dramatic Works*, 376.
12. Bellos, *Georges Perec,* 423.
13. Perec, *The Raise*, 31.
14. Other sources in the text include personal correspondence with Ulrich Schönherr and David Bellos.

Bibliography[14]

Barker, 'Amusement Arcadia', 2011. http://www.overlap.org.uk/790/amusement-arcadia-the-machine. Accessed 4 June 2019.

Beckett, Samuel. *The Complete Dramatic Works*. London: Faber and Faber, 1990.

Bellos, David. *Georges Perec: A Life in Words*. London: Harvill, 1995.

Bray, Oliver. 'Playing with Constraint: Performing the OuLiPo and the Clinamen-Performer', *Performance Research* 21, no. 4 (2016): 41–46.

Freshwater, Helen. *Theatre and Audience*. Basingstoke: Palgrave Macmillan, 2009.

Mathews, Harry and Alastair Brotchie, eds. *Oulipo Compendium*. London: Atlas Press, 1998.

Perec, Georges. *The Raise*, translated by David Bellos. Unpublished, undated.

Perec, Georges. *Die Maschine*, translated by Eugen Helmlé. Stuttgart: Reclam, 1972.

Perec, Georges. *Théâtre 1: La Poche Parmentier précédé de l'Augmentation*. Paris: Hachette, 1981.

Perec, Georges. *Die Gehaltserhöhung, Die Kartoffelkammer*. Frankfurt: Verlag der Autoren, 1990.

Perec, Georges. 'The Machine', translated by Ulrich Schönherr, *Review of Contemporary Fiction* 29, no. 1 (2009): 33–93.

Schwartz, Paul. *Georges Perec: Traces of His Passage*. Birmingham, AL: Summa Publications, 1988.

White, J.J. 'Goethe in The Machine: Georges Perec's Computer-Based Exercises with the Repertoire of "Über allen Gipfeln"', *Publications of the English Goethe Society* 41, no. 1 (1971): 103–30.

Part II
Perecquian geographies

9
Perecquian soundscapes

Alasdair Pettinger

Georges Perec was a 'man of letters' in more ways than one. Not only does the phrase conveniently capture the variety of literary genres in which he excelled; taken more literally it alludes to his fascination with lipograms, anagrams, heterograms, palindromes and crossword puzzles. But if this suggests that he had a particular affinity for 'things seen' – on the written page as well as the world around him – we should not allow it to obscure his interest in sounds and acoustic space.[1] This interest informs his practice across various media. I begin this chapter with a discussion of Perec's references to (mainly non-musical) sounds in his written texts, and his use of them in his work for radio, television and cinema. I then consider two examples of soundscapes explicitly influenced by him before going on to discuss the broader field of 'everyday' soundscapes, now being created in large numbers by amateur and professional phonographers, and consider to what extent they might be called 'Perecquian' too.

Perec's soundscapes

In the published and unpublished works that derived from his *Places* [*Lieux*] project, Perec dwells on what he sees rather than what he hears, and the other senses hardly figure at all. In the early 1970s, Georges Perec selected 12 places in Paris that were of personal significance to him and set himself the task of visiting each one twice a year for 12 years, once to write an on-the-spot description, and once to recall it from memory. This project applied a rigorous system that ensured that he visited them all in every month of the year.[2] One of his objectives was to test the limits of conventional empirical description – to document what is generally not noticed or noted. 'Force yourself', he writes, 'to write down what is of no interest, what is most obvious, most common, most colourless.'[3]

In the event, Perec never got close to completing his programme, and only a handful of descriptive texts were published.[4] The best known of them – printed separately as a booklet – was not actually composed in accordance with the rules of the project: *An Attempt at Exhausting a Place in Paris*, which itemises the comings and goings in place Saint-Sulpice over three days in October 1974.[5]

The photographer Pierre Getzler, who accompanied him on occasion, comments: 'No smells and, even more, no scents, no urine, no sounds, no shouts, he needs a taxi driver to tell him: "it was more noisy before the war", he's in a silent film, and it's in black and white (or just with some primary colours).'[6] To use a more contemporary image, we might compare him with someone monitoring a bank of mute CCTV screens.[7] Sounds are not completely absent from these writings. Here and there the silence is broken by church bells, police sirens, pinball machines, snatches of reported speech or music emerging from within a building:

> The Saint-Sulpice bell begins to ring (probably funeral chimes).
> A child slides a toy along the windowpane of the café (slight noise).
> A man stops for a moment to say hello to the big dog of the café.
> A baby in a baby carriage lets out a brief squawking.
> A meter man with a bad cough puts a parking ticket [...]
> Car horns.
> Ambulance goes by, siren blaring.
> I hear: 'it's a quarter after three.'
> Barking.[8]

But the *Places* project extends well beyond the written texts usually identified with it. In the preamble to one of his published descriptions, Perec wrote: 'The experiment stopped in 1975, and has been taken up and continued by other sorts of descriptions: poetic and photographic (*La Clôture*, about rue Vilin), cinematographic ('Les Lieux d'une fugue', about Franklin-Roosevelt), radiophonic (about Mabillon, in progress).'[9] And when describing his project in *Species of Spaces*, he refers to the interruption to it caused by the filming of *The Man Who Sleeps* – which nonetheless features most of the places he had planned to document, and may be considered within the orbit of the project too.[10]

The radio broadcast might seem to be the most promising source for a study of Perec's audio (rather than verbal) soundscapes. It is based on a six-hour recording made in a mobile studio parked at a busy junction with Perec itemising out loud the vehicles and pedestrians that pass by, trying to keep up with events in real time. Like a sports commentator, at times he must speak very fast indeed, at others he can enjoy pauses of several seconds, or permit himself a few words of elaboration. He then later compiled an inventory (totalling the numbers of cars and trucks of a certain colour or brand, for example) and edited the recording down to around two hours for broadcast on France Culture.[11]

But almost the only sound that can be heard is that of Perec's own voice, interrupted every few minutes by extracts from the inventory read in the studio by Claude Piéplu. The braking and accelerating of traffic, the idling engines, voices and footsteps of passers-by are only faintly audible, suggesting it is the practice of enumeration itself that is Perec's main concern here. One's attention is drawn almost exclusively to Perec's voice – the heroic level of concentration, to be sure, but also, and equally importantly (because not suppressed in the final, abridged, recording), the moments he lapses, betraying his fatigue with a sigh, or half-suppressing a giggle when his commentary stumbles.

The cinematographic descriptions offer richer sonic textures. *Scenes of a Flight* (*Les lieux d'une fugue*) (1976), made for television, is based on a semi-autobiographical piece written a decade earlier recalling the day the author ran away from home at the age of 11 and his wanderings in the vicinity of the Franklin-Roosevelt metro station.[12] The soundtrack is dominated by the overlain narration by Marcel Cuvalier (reading a barely edited version of the original text) and the recording of a pianist going over the same passages in Schumann's *Kreisleriana* that punctuate the film. Nevertheless, diegetic sounds (traffic, birdsong, train doors, typewriters, footsteps, the ticking of a watch, the shuffling of paper on a desk) are prominent at certain points, all the more so because they do not always match the images on screen or the words of the narrator but seem to belong to segments already – or not yet – seen. Sometimes, environmental sounds are unexpectedly withheld altogether, the activity on screen paired with an austere studio silence.

The opening of *The Man Who Sleeps* (1974), a film discussed in this volume by Julia Dobson, foregrounds a wide range of interior and exterior sounds – church bells, dripping tap, alarm clock, people at work in the street, *pommes frites* sizzling in a fryer – many of which feature prominently in the novella on which it is based, an edited version of which is spoken by a female narrator.[13] As in *Scenes of a Flight*, these sounds are often repeated, and do not always match the images and text, but in the film these motifs take on a musical as well as thematic significance. The diegetic sounds are gradually manipulated and absorbed into the more abstract electroacoustic score by Phillipe Drogoz and Eugénie Kuffler, the rhythmic drips, ticks and taps losing their distinctive timbres and eventually melding in a studio-created composition that incorporates separately-recorded vocal and instrumental motifs.

While this treatment of sound has some narrative justification – reinforcing both the sense of passing time and the way the unnamed protagonist ('you'), at first sharply defined in his room, slowly fades into the encroaching shadows of the metropolis – it also forces the audience to become listeners as much as viewers, to attend more closely than they would normally, to the presence and absence of sound. It should come as no surprise that the soundtrack has been broadcast independently on French radio.[14]

Perec was more than usually alert to the ways in which spaces and places nest inside each other. His extended essay *Species of Spaces* proceeds from the blank page before him to Alpha Centauri by way of (as the chapter titles have it) 'The Bed', 'The Bedroom', 'The Apartment', 'The Street' and so on. But he also reminds us that 'spaces have multiplied, been broken up and have diversified. There are spaces today of every kind and every size, for every use and every function. To live is to pass from one space to another, while doing your best not to bump yourself.'[15]

Of course, space is not just visible (to those who can see) but audible (to those who can hear). Sounds can enable us to map our surroundings, not only by means of sophisticated technologies such as sonar and radar, but also by the naked ear, especially for the blind or partially sighted.[16] But Perec's interest in sounds, no less than his interest in things seen, derives not from their ability to help him navigate three-dimensional space but rather for the personal and collective associations they elicit. As the two aspects of his *Places* project suggest, his phenomenological approach to space (transcribing sense-impressions as plainly as possible) is combined with a recognition of the emotional power of particular places; in Perec's case the familiar, safe, reassuring places he would inhabit and traverse every day. Even the apparently detached spoken and written enumerations seem to be suffused with a yearning to limit their unpredictability.

To understand this apparent paradox, it may be helpful to compare Perec's soundscapes with those recorded and theorised by the Canadian composer and acoustic ecologist R. Murray Schafer, who coined the term, on an analogy with the land- and seascapes apprehended by the eye. Schafer proposed a vocabulary that could be used to analyse soundscapes – 'keynotes', 'signals', 'soundmarks' – and proposed methods of notating and classifying non-musical sounds, and of understanding habits of listening and improving 'sonological competence'. But his overall approach is shaped by a nostalgia for natural and pre-industrial soundscapes whose disappearance he mourns.[17]

By contrast, Perec's preference is for contemporary sounds: his 'everyday' is very much in the here and now. To be more specific, the 'everyday' is the 'background noise' of 'what happens every day and recurs every day' – the 'infra-ordinary'– rather than 'the big event, the untoward, the extra-ordinary', such as, to use Perec's examples, train crashes and car accidents, 'tidal waves, volcanic eruptions, tower-blocks that collapse, forest fires, tunnels that cave in', all of which have sonic signatures that are almost completely absent from his soundscapes.[18]

Perec invites us to interrogate what we habitually do – as if asleep or anaesthetised – and if this questioning might take us in the direction of a certain sociological critique, it also awakens us to its positive value. For this infra-ordinary can only thrive under certain conditions. For those living in extreme circumstances, which give rise to fear, anxiety and hypervigilance, where the extraordinary *is* the everyday, the infra-ordinary becomes highly attenuated. Perec's quotidian is implicitly set against the very different everyday of the Second World War, to which it obliquely alludes. There is a poignancy to his almost obsessive fascination with the regular rhythms of traffic and pedestrians, the hourly peals of church bells, the timetabled circulation of buses and trains, signifying as they do a world free of the terrors of Nazi occupation and the unrelenting threat of imminent exposure, detention and transportation. In this respect, the 'background noise' Perec records and describes evokes something very precious and life-affirming.[19] While Schafer rails against the sonic vandalism of the internal combustion engine, displacing the richer soundscapes of an earlier age, Perec luxuriates in the itemisation and classification of motor vehicles, idling, braking, accelerating and changing gear, joyously celebrating the – precarious – normality of civilian routines.

Perecquian soundscapes

Perec's fascination with sound and the procedures he used to document his surroundings have influenced a new generation of field recordists and sound artists. Two examples may be indicative. One is explicitly inspired by Perec; the other, if not referencing Perec specifically, is probably unthinkable without his example.

Des Coulam, who describes himself as a 'professional listener', is the author of a blog, *Soundlandscapes*, which, over several years, has built up an impressive phonographic record of the French capital. In 2015, he marked its fifth anniversary with an homage to Perec's *An Attempt at Exhausting a Place in Paris* by posting a field recording he made outside the Café de la Mairie in place Saint-Sulpice, in a seat possibly once occupied by Perec himself.[20]

Acknowledging Perec as the main inspiration for his own 'detailed exploration and documentation of the contemporary sound tapestry of Paris', Coulam explained that Perec's 'quest for the infra-ordinary: the humdrum, the non-event, the everyday "what happens when nothing happens" could be replicated equally compellingly in sound'. As he sits he notices that the numbers of the buses have not changed since Perec meticulously recorded their movements 40 years before. Listening to it, we can also recognise many of the kinds of sounds Perec identified, if only sparsely. But there is one, almost continuous, sound that hasn't changed much since the 1970s and that is the sound of cups, saucers and glasses being washed, carried and delivered. And yet, while it dominates Coulam's homage, neither the sounds – nor even the activities that generate them – are acknowledged in Perec's descriptive text, beyond an occasional reference to the drinks he ordered.

While Coulam chooses to honour Perec with a fairly straightforward – apparently unedited – recording linked to him metonymically through place Saint-Sulpice, Mark Peter Wright's is a more indirect homage, which takes the form of a writing and recording project that echoes his love of constraints, particularly the rules he set himself for *Places*. *Tasked to Hear* takes the form of an illustrated booklet and downloadable soundfile documenting activities undertaken by Wright in 2013–4, which involved visiting the same location on the last Saturday of each month, noting the sounds he hears and some other particulars.[21]

To each visit are devoted two facing pages of the booklet. The right-hand page consists of two photographs (of the sky and a few inches of ground); the left-hand page offering a quasi-technical log that specifies the date and time, temperature, windspeed, some laconic 'physical' and 'psychological' observations (for example, 'pulsing in left eyebrow', 'thinking about other things'), and a short prose fragment that includes a different, repeated neologistic onomatopoeia for each visit. Thus, for 25 May 2013, we get: 'Tremulous liquid songs rising and falling above deep waves, emitting through and across, wailing, alarming, barking, close buzzing, *peet peet peet,* my throat croaking, heat rising in my left knee.'

As a soundscape, this has a more decidedly Oulipian flavour than Coulam's, nodding to the more playful, rather than ethnographic, aspects of Perec's work. The sensations it records are relatively decontextualised. While images of the café (then and now) are embedded in the blog post, here the place is not named, cannot be identified from the photographs, and only by looking up the given longitude and latitude can the listener-reader discover that the location he chose was the south side of the Tees estuary near Redcar in the north-east of England. The accompanying sound recording is not easily linked to any one of the logged events and seems to be a montage from several visits. But like the recording in Paris, there is something noticeable here that is, as it were, edited out of Perec's verbal soundscape: the sounds made by the listener himself, in this case, moving equipment on the grass, turning the pages of a notebook, or the rearrangement of his clothing as he shifts position. Indeed, listening to field recordings can often provide a salutary reminder of how easy it is to miss 'what is most obvious, most common', even for someone as attentive as Perec.

Soundscapes, constraints and the everyday

If these two examples are evidence of a continuing engagement with Perec, one might also consider ways in which his concerns have acquired a renewed salience in the creation of recorded soundscapes more generally. This is less a case of 'influence' than a sign of Perec's perspicacity, one which invites us to revisit his work and explore how it can illuminate these developments. Two (related) concerns seem to be of especial interest: the use of constraints, and the concept of the 'everyday'.

The constraints Perec sets himself in his *Places* project are partly designed to break the habit that usually draws our attention to the unusual rather than the ordinary. If there is a musical analogue for this, it would be the constraints of 12-tone or serialist composition without which the composer would easily slip into conventional melodies and harmonies.[22] But the constraints adopted for *Places* only relate to the broader choices of determining when the sites would be visited. What he does when he is there – what he attends to and how he chooses to write it down – is rather more informally guided by a series of illustrative imperatives: 'Describe your street. [...] Make an inventory of your pockets. […] Question your tea spoons.'[23] One of the pleasing aspects of his descriptions is the way he allows himself to interpolate comments on the physical and mental demands of the process: 'I want to clear my head […] I've lost all interest in them [buses] […] Weary eyes, weary words […] (fatigue).'[24]

The microphone relieves the sound recordist of comparable effort – and indeed can be left in place while the recordist goes off and does something else. It also, as we noted above, has the benefit of being able to capture sounds not noticed at the time. But still, difficult choices remain: when and where to record, what equipment to use, how to crop or otherwise manipulate the resulting sound file.

As affordable, digital, hand-held recording devices have become widely available, there has been an explosion of amateur phonography, if not quite as spectacular as that of amateur photography. Both might be said to have a special relationship to the 'everyday' – their affordability, ease of use and speed of dissemination mean that they are no longer restricted to special occasions. But the conventions of phonography are more fluid than those of photography – which for a long time now have been codified in mass-market magazines and advertising. For this reason, field recordings are open to a more diverse conception of the quotidian.

But this relative lack of conventions – concerning what to record – actually inhibits many practitioners who are spoilt for choice. Perhaps this is why many soundscapes which are posted online are often created within the set of self-imposed rules ('one-minute vacations', 'one sound each day') or as contributions to a collective project organised around a common theme or objective, most notably in the crowd-sourced 'sound maps' of towns, cities or countries.[25]

One such map is the British Library's UK Soundmap from 2010–11, which invited people to contribute short geo-tagged field recordings that together would form 'a permanent public record of everyday sounds'.[26] Over 2,000 recordings were uploaded by some 350 contributors. A browsing listener might begin by drinking coffee at Heathrow Terminal Three, then catch the sound of dogs in Suffolk and Arctic terns in Shetland, overhear bikers outside a café on the A4074 and someone opening a garage door on the Black Isle. They might go on to take a ghost train ride in Blackpool and a boat cruise in Cardiff Bay or wait for Prince Charles in Todmorden before baling hay in Gloucestershire.

The British Library tried to be as un-prescriptive as possible, but it is striking that the overwhelming majority of recordings were made in public spaces (transport hubs, cafes, shops, seaside resorts, etc.); very few in workplaces (those off limits to the public, that is) or the home (itself another workplace for many). The map's basic guidelines encouraged contributors to think of 'what your home, leisure and work environments sound like'. And yet, in practice, leisure trumped the other two – perhaps because the governing paradigm of 'the map' pre-disposes people to think primarily of public spaces (and notions of 'Britishness' probably played a part too).[27]

We might detect a similarity between these preferences and the sounds described or recorded by Perec, who chose, in the main, to describe and record the sounds of outdoor public spaces, echoing his fascination with the soothing and unthreatening aspects of everyday life. While this similarity does not in itself, perhaps, make these recordings 'Perecquian' – and we should be cautious of eliding the specific biographical and historical forces that shaped Perec's work – they offer a glimpse of where his concerns can lead us.

Two final examples of infra-ordinary soundscapes, more carefully crafted than the contributions to the UK Soundmap but informed by the same kind of preoccupations, hint at further possibilities. One develops the documentarist aspect of his work, the other is more aesthetic and playful, though they overlap.

The first is the work of Felicity Ford, who researched a PhD thesis on the 'domestic soundscape' and went on to devise and contribute to a wide range of projects – a sonic advent calendar, recordings of vending machines, and, more recently, *Knitsonik*, which explores the worlds of wool, textiles and knitting from the point of view of sound and vice versa – by means of installations, workshops, podcasts, and printed publications. One particularly Perecquian posting to the Knitsonik blog was not about wool at all. 'Adventures in Washing Up' is a collage of sound recordings of people doing the dishes and talking about the implements they use, the sequences they prefer and the objects they find especially hard to clean. The sounds of running taps, of brushing, of placing and stacking cutlery, cups and plates are prominent in the mix, and the whole piece is introduced by a specially composed tongue-in-cheek jazzy jingle.[28]

The second is a contribution to the *Disquiet Junto*, a project run by Marc Weidenbaum in San Francisco. Since January 2012, he has set a weekly challenge to which anyone is free to respond by posting a sound recording made in accordance with the constraints he specifies: 'Play your favourite musical instrument wearing gloves', 'Make a one-minute recording of a library', 'Combine four recordings of yourself walking', 'Make music from the ticking of a clock', and so on. One challenge, which

Weidenbaum dubbed 'Zola's Foley', invited participants to produce an 'artificial field recording' that sounds as if it was made in a large department store, but in reality is constructed from segments recorded elsewhere.[29] Mark Rushton's response was 'In Our Dream Department Store', which sampled extracts from a voice mail from a friend demonstrating a noise-cancelling microphone, recordings of a swimming pool, merry-go-round and political meeting, and various synth sounds. Rushton creates the illusion of a sound recordist wandering around a large store, approaching and then moving away from what might be an escalator, a lift, people in conversation, a security guard, a room in which music can be heard.[30]

Both these everyday soundscapes feature activities – housework, shopping – which might prompt reflections on their oppressive character. The title 'Adventures in Washing Up', together with the jingle, parodies the idealisation of feminine domesticity once common in television advertisements. And despite its attempted verisimilitude, 'In Our Dream Department Store' has an artificiality that can only underscore the alienation of the corporate retail experience, as its equally ironic title suggests. But what makes them Perecquian is the evident – and, to some extent, redemptive – pleasure they take in sonically enumerating familiar rituals so carefully that they begin to sound like something else. Music, perhaps?[31]

Notes

1. 'Things seen' is the declared subject of his radio broadcast, *Tentative de description de choses vues au carrefour Mabillon le 19 mai 1978*, discussed below. For more general studies of sound and spatiality see, for example, LaBelle, *Acoustic Territories*, and Gandy and Nilsen, *The Acoustic City*.
2. Perec, 'Places (Notes on a Work in Progress)' in *Species of Spaces*, 55–6. For useful background and analysis of the project see Lejeune, *Le mémoire et l'oblique*, 141–230; Bellos, *Georges Perec*, 417–21; Leak, 'Paris Created and Destroyed', 25–31; Schilling, *Mémoires du quotidien*, 129–76.
3. Perec, 'Practical Exercises', *Species of Spaces*, 50.
4. Perec, 'Scene in Italie', 'Glances at Gaîté', 'Comings and Goings in rue de l'Assomption', 'Stances on Mabillon', 'The Rue Vilin'.
5. Perec, *An Attempt*.
6. Depaule and Getzler, 'A City in Words and Numbers', 127.
7. Several shots of surveillance cameras appear in the film *The Man Who Sleeps* (1974); and surveillance is also a theme of the film he planned afterwards, *L'Oeil de l'autre*: see Virilio, 'A Walking Man',136; Bellos, *Georges Perec*, 558.
8. Perec, *An Attempt*, 14, 15, 15, 20, 20, 25, 30, 35, 46.
9. Perec, 'Scene in Italie', 34.
10. Perec, 'Places', *Species of Spaces*, 56.
11. *Tentative de description de choses vues au carrefour Mabillon le 19 mai 1978*, directed by René Farabet, broadcast by France Culture, 25 February 1979. See Bellos, *Georges Perec*, 640. The recording is included in Georges Perec, *Dialogue avec Bernard Noël; Poésie ininterrompue; Tentative de description de choses vues au carrefour Mabillon le 19 mai 1978* (Marseille: André

Dimanche, 1997), a set of four CDs and two booklets with useful supplementary documentation, including the text of the inventory, and an essay 'Carrefour Mabillon: "ce qui passe, passe"' by Bernard Magné.

12. *Les Lieux d'une fugue* (1976), directed by Georges Perec, broadcast on TF1, 6 July 1978; Georges Perec, 'The Scene of a Flight', *Species of Spaces*.
13. *The Man Who Sleeps* (film, 1974); Perec, *A Man Asleep*.
14. Bellos, *Georges Perec*, 739. Although beyond the scope of this chapter, Perec's interest in music was extensive, indicated by, for example, his collaborations with composers, his own compositional experiments, his reflections on jazz, and the systematic references to music in his novel, *Life: A User's Manual*. See Drogoz, 'Perec et la musique'; Bouchot, 'De la musique dans l'oeuvre de Georges Perec'; James, *Constraining Chance*, 115–21, 138; Perec, 'Je me souviens du jazz'; Perec, 'La Chose'; Perec, 'Souvenir d'un voyage à Thouars', 303–8.
15. Perec, *Species of Spaces*, 6.
16. Denny, *Blip, Ping, and Buzz*, 121–56; Hull, *Touching the Rock*, 99–100.
17. Schafer, *The Soundscape*.
18. Perec, 'Approaches to What?', 209–10.
19. For a discussion of the relationship between Perec's 'everyday' and the history and memory of the Holocaust, see Schilling, *Mémoires du quotidien*, 9–27.
20. Des Coulam, 'Georges Perec – Exhausting a Place'.
21. Wright, *Tasked to Hear*.
22. On Perec's references to, and uses of, serialist techniques, see Bouchot, 'De la musique dans l'oeuvre de Georges Perec', 108–20.
23. Perec, 'Approaches to What?', 210.
24. Perec, *Attempt*, 21, 29, 19, 24.
25. Quiet American, 'One Minute Vacation', http://quietamerican.org/vacation.html; Taylor Deupree, 'One Sound Each Day', no longer online, posts (but not audio clips) archived at https://web.archive.org/web/20100217131308/http://www.12k.com/onesoundeachday/. Among the more established crowd-sourced soundmaps are Radio Aporee, https://aporee.org/ and Soundcities, http://www.soundcities.com.
26. The call for submissions is no longer online but archived at https://web.archive.org/web/20100723084025/http://sounds.bl.uk:80/uksoundmap/takepart.html. The map itself may still be explored at https://sounds.bl.uk/Sound-Maps/UK-Soundmap.
27. For reflections on the UK Soundmap project, see Pettinger, 'Listening to Britain'; Rawes, 'Listening to Britain'.
28. Ford, 'Adventures in Washing Up'.
29. Weidenbaum, 'Disquiet Junto Project 0038: Zola's Foley'.
30. Rushton, 'In Our Dream Department Store'.
31. For further reflections on contemporary practices of listening and recording, see Carlyle and Lane, *On Listening*; Lane and Carlyle, *In the Field*; and Voegelin, *Listening to Noise and Silence*.

Filmography

Les lieux d'une fugue (France, 1978, Perec)
The Man Who Sleeps/Un homme qui dort (France, 1974, Queysanne)

Bibliography

Bellos, David. *Georges Perec: A Life in Words*. London: Harvill, 1999.

Bouchot, Vincent. 'De la musique dans l'œuvre de Georges Perec: Fréquentations, thèmes, structures'. In *Cahiers Georges Perec 4: Mélanges*, 97–120. Paris: Éditions du Limon, 1990.

British Library. 'UK Soundmap'. Accessed 8 May 2019. http://sounds.bl.uk/Sound-Maps/UK-Soundmap.

Carlyle, Angus and Cathy Lane, eds. *On Listening*. Axminister: Uniformbooks, 2013.
Coulam, Des. 'Georges Perec – Exhausting a Place', *Soundlandscapes*, 29 May 2015. Accessed 8 May 2019. https://soundlandscapes.wordpress.com/2015/05/29/georges-perec-exhausting-a-place/.
Denny, Mark. *Blip, Ping and Buzz: Making Sense of Radar and Sonar*. Baltimore, MD: Johns Hopkins University Press, 2007.
Depaule, Jean-Charles and Pierre Getzler. 'A City in Words and Numbers', translated by Clare Barrett, *AA Files* 45/46 (2001): 117–28.
Drogoz, Philippe. 'Perec et la musique'. In *Cahiers Georges Perec 1: Colloque de Cerisy (juillet 1984)*, 267–77. Paris: P.O.L., 1985.
Ford, Felicity. 'Adventures in Washing Up', *Knitsonik*, 17 February 2015. Accessed 8 May 2019. http://www.knitsonik.com/2015/02/17/adventures-in-washing-up/.
Gandy, Matthew and B.J. Nilsen, eds. *The Acoustic City*. Berlin: Jovis, 2014.
Hull, John M. *Touching the Rock: An Experience of Blindness*. London: Arrow, 1991.
James, Alison. *Constraining Chance: Georges Perec and the Oulipo*. Evanston, IL: Northwestern University Press, 2009.
LaBelle, Brandon. *Acoustic Territories: Sound Culture and Everyday Life*. New York: Continuum, 2011.
Lane, Cathy and Angus Carlyle. *In the Field: The Art of Field Recording*. Axminster: Uniformbooks, 2013.
Leak, Andrew. 'Paris Created and Destroyed', *AA Files* 45/46 (2001): 25–31.
Lejeune, Phillipe. *La mémoire et l'oblique: Georges Perec autobiographe*. Paris: P.O.L., 1991.
Perec, Georges. 'Je me souviens du jazz', interview with Philippe Carles and Francis Marmande, *Jazz Magazine* 272 (1979): 30–4.
Perec, Georges. 'Souvenir d'un voyage à Thouars'. In *Cahiers Georges Perec 1: Colloque de Cerisy (juillet 1984)*, 301–6. Paris: P.O.L., 1985.
Perec, Georges. 'La chose', *Le magazine littéraire* 316 (1993): 57–63.
Perec, Georges. 'Species of Spaces'. In *Species of Spaces and Other Pieces*, edited and translated by John Sturrock, 1–96. London: Penguin Books, 1997.
Perec, Georges. 'The Scene of a Flight'. In *Species of Spaces and Other Pieces*, edited and translated by John Sturrock, 103–12. London: Penguin Books, 1997.
Perec, Georges. 'Approaches to What?'. In *Species of Spaces and Other Pieces*, edited and translated by John Sturrock, 209–11. London: Penguin Books, 1997.
Perec, Georges. 'The Rue Vilin'. In *Species of Spaces and Other Pieces*, edited and translated by John Sturrock, 212–21. London: Penguin Books, 1997.
Perec, Georges. 'Scene in Italie', translated by Andrew Leak, *AA Files* 45/46 (2001): 32–41.
Perec, Georges. 'Glances at Gaîté', translated by Andrew Leak, *AA Files* 45/46 (2001): 42–53.
Perec, Georges. 'Comings and Goings in Rue de l'Assomption', translated by Andrew Leak, *AA Files* 45/46 (2001): 54–67.
Perec, Georges. 'Stances on Mabillon', translated by Andrew Leak, *AA Files* 45/46 (2001): 68–77.
Perec, Georges. *An Attempt at Exhausting a Place in Paris*, translated by Marc Lowenthal. Cambridge, MA: Wakefield Press, 2010.
Perec, Georges. *A Man Asleep*, translated by Andrew Leak. In *Things: A Story of the Sixties, with A Man Asleep*. London: Vintage Books, 2011: 127–221.
Pettinger, Alasdair. 'Listening to Britain', *Bulldozia*, 12 October 2010. Accessed 24 April 2018. http://www.bulldozia.com/adventures/index.php?id=603.
Rawes, Ian. 'Listening to Britain', *Sound and Vision*, 24 June 2011. Accessed 11 March 2018. http://blogs.bl.uk/sound-and-vision/2011/06/listening-to-britain.html.
Rushton, Mark. 'In Our Dream Department Store (Ask Me I Might Go)'. Accessed 8 May 2019. https://soundcloud.com/markrushtoncom/in-our-dream-department-store.
Schafer, R. Murray. *The Soundscape: Our Sonic Environment and the Tuning of the World*. Rochester, VT: Destiny Books, 1994.
Schilling, Derek. *Mémoires du quotidien: Les lieux de Perec*. Villeneuve d'Ascq: Presses universitaires du Septentrion, 2006.
Virilio, Paul. 'A Walking Man', translated by Clare Barrett, *AA Files* 45/46 (2001): 136–7.
Voegelin, Salomé. *Listening to Noise and Silence: Towards a Philosophy of Sound Art*. New York: Continuum, 2011.

Weidenbaum, Marc. 'The Disquiet Junto Project List (0001–0383 ...)', *Disquiet*, 27 January 2012. Accessed 8 May 2019. https://disquiet.com/2012/01/27/the-disquiet-junto/.
Weidenbaum, Marc. 'Disquiet Junto Project 0038: Zola's Foley', *Disquiet*, 20 September 2012. Accessed 8 May 2019. https://disquiet.com/2012/09/20/disquiet0038-asrealasitgets2/.
Wright, Mark Peter. *Tasked to Hear*. Corbel Stone Press, 2014.

10

Perecquian spaces for performance practice

Oliver Bray

Since 1960 Oulipo (Ouvroir de Littérature Potentielle or Workshop of Potential Literature) has used imposed structural constraints to generate writing. This chapter explores the influence of Oulipo and Perec on the spatial constraints of my own theatrical work *The Elision of Scaff*'.[1] This performance, a two-hander play performed three times at the same time, can be considered a site for the exploration of new terrain in contemporary performance-making.

Oulipians are lovers of highly structured and rational games, a quite different endeavour from the relative illogicality of the group's artistic parentage. Scott Esposito points out that 'over the years, the strength of the work produced by its members moved the group inexorably into the literary canon'.[2] Indeed, Perec has been hugely influential in this movement to literary recognition, authoring many of the Oulipo's most recognised works and, no doubt, contributing to the group becoming the longest-running literary movement in French history. Perec's adroit and pervasive work with constraints is highlighted by Daniel Levin Becker when he states that often an Oulipian will use a 'new' constraint and 'the would-be inventor doesn't realize that his or her invention has already been explored – usually by Perec'.[3]

The earlier years of the Oulipo were characterised by multiple investigations into short forms of literature. As more members, notably Perec in 1967, were co-opted into the group, emphasis shifted to include longer documentary and novelistic forms with a focus on exhaustivity. Perec's *An Attempt at Exhausting a Place in Paris* (1975 [2010]) is an example of such an Oulipian work focused on exhaustivity. The content of the book comprises Perec's documentation of ordinary things and happenings that he observed over three days sitting in cafés in place Saint-Sulpice in Paris. Although not a huge volume at first glance, the book's exhaustivity lends weightiness, in terms of words and pages. Another example of the longer form is the *Winter Journeys* (*Voyages d'hiver*) (2013) corpus, which started as a fictional short story, *Le Voyage d'hiver,* written by Georges Perec in 1979. The *Winter Journeys* collection comprises this story retold, extended and transformed by multiple Oulipian authors. Providing a fascinating insight into the writing voices of Perec and the other Oulipians, these short stories combine to create a serial novel that demonstrates the Oulipian and Perecquian penchant for both playfulness and rigour, serving as a kind of microcosm of their poetics. The group's shift towards the tendency of exhaustivity brought with it a more complete kind of literary work; indeed, the novelistic form occupies a greater literal space. Such works as the *Winter Journeys* corpus and Perec's masterpiece *Life: A User's Manual* (1978 [1996]) demonstrate how a constellation of constraints can be used in order to produce an 'Oulipo 'ard' volume that contains multiple constraining devices. Oulipo 'ard texts are labelled by Oulipians in contrast to their equally wryly nicknamed 'Oulipo light' works. Oulipo light texts are short examples of constrained texts often written for reading aloud. Oulipo 'ard refers to the longer, weightier and often novelistic tomes of Oulipian output.[4] The example of my own performance work, *The Elision of Scaff'*, approaches an equivalence to the more substantive, or 'ard, Oulipian work that considers the formal tendencies of the medium (literature/theatre) more overtly. Indeed, Perec's influence on the Oulipian sensibility towards the 'whole' text pushes the notion of space, both literal and conceptual, to prominence when considering how Perecquian constraints may be used to generate a theatre work. The inherent three-dimensionality of performance necessarily pushes the notion of composition to the forefront of a practice that exists beyond the two-dimensional space of literature. *The Elision of Scaff'* is a vehicle for the consideration of generative spatial constraint in a context of live theatre.

Constraints in performance

In *The Elision of Scaff'*, the structural oddities of the performance, that resulted from the various constraints I imposed, led the audience to consider the relationship between narrative and form. A great deal of Perecquian output explores the possibilities that applied constraint can have on the compositional properties of text on a page. However, the live space provides a complex synthesis of spatial concerns that result from the application of constraint on both narrative and form. In the case of performance practice generated under constraint, it is the particular blending of narrative and formal concerns that substantiate both. Spatial constraint leads to formal disruption that so swamps narrative that it changes and transforms it.

Though the results of some constraints were obvious in the performances of *The Elision of Scaff'*, such as *Simultaneous Play Triplication* for example (causing the play to be performed three times, with triplicate casts, at the same time), other constraints remained more subtly present, and in the moment of the performance would not be easily discernible or decipherable. The question of constraint visibility and revelation to the reader forms a major part of the discourse concerning Perec and the Oulipo, not just in the conversations following the publication of Oulipian texts, but in the more general philosophy of the covert/overt position of constraints that have impacted so prevailingly on the work generated. The late literary critic and translator John Sturrock notes:

> This is the classic dilemma of the practical joker: whether to play your joke and creep quietly away without revealing yourself, or to wait immodestly on the spot for the acclaim to start.[5]

Quoting Perec, Oulipian Daniel Levin Becker notes that 'the problem, when you see the constraint [...] is that you see nothing but the constraint'.[6] There is a dual concern here, raising consciousness of constraint for the writer in order to further control the variables is of course central to Perecquian philosophy, but the desire of the reader/audience to locate a constraint is another matter. This desire may overshadow and ultimately change the work itself, or at least take its interpretation in a direction undesired by the author. Unsurprisingly, Oulipo places most focus on the act of writing rather than the act of reading and the latter is perhaps a little overlooked by the group, if not their critics. In both performance and literature, the visibility of constraints is also dependent on the kind of constraints being used and the kind of work being produced. For example, a Snowball constraint[7] in a piece of poetry will certainly be more visible, to a casual observer at least, than taking a poem and submitting it to '*tireur à la ligne*'.[8] Significantly, Raymond Queneau, according to Warren Motte, felt that 'constraints must not overshadow the finished work, and pretext should never override text'.[9] This places a focus on constraint as a generative tool rather than an observational lens. Nevertheless, the impact on constraint visibility and revelation on readership is worth noting. The audience programme notes for *The Elision of*

Scaff' did not include a list of the constraints at play, deliberately muddying the waters of the hypothesis of intention. '[T]he reader's knowledge of a text's Oulipian status exacerbates the tendency to over interpret'.[10] This means that the mystification of revelation can lead to the creation of ghost-constraints that never existed in the first place, something which has occurred in Perecquian commentary.

Constraint as an observational lens means that an obvious or pronounced constraint has the potential to become the central thematic content of the work. In *The Elision of Scaff'*, the visually obvious constraint of *Simultaneous Play Triplication* may have been so overt in the performance as to render some of the other constraints invisible. This is in addition to potentially overshadowing the non-constraint-based content of the performance. Levin Becker observes that the observational lens of constraint may destroy the art object completely, describing how many readers opt out of reading *La Disparition* when they already know the lipogram by which it is constrained.[11] This posits a problem for those authors and architects of constraint who wish for recognition of their craft through revelation. Even though the work of a group that privileges potential, Oulipian poetics still demand application and practice, and results must at some stage be demonstrated. The *idea* of a novel in the lipogram of 'e' may be satisfying enough for the (non)reader, but it is not unreasonable to assume that Perec would have wanted people to actually read the book as well. This tension is echoed by individual Oulipians' desires either to publish their constraints, perhaps as evidence of artistry (or at least labour), or more confidently to make the reader aware of the complexity and cleverness contained within by letting them work out the constraints for themselves.

In any case, the application of constraint to a process leading to live performance amplifies the visibility of constraints considerably. The live moment of performance is a complicated, multi-dimensional and layered composition, involving bodies sounding and moving through uni-directional time in space. This, together with the nuances of observing (or reading) work within the conventions of theatrical observation, puts overt emphasis on form and space for the observer.

Audience engagement with constraints in *The Elision of Scaff'* may be considered in terms of Levin Becker's comforting assertion that awareness of the constraint, either by its observable mechanics or the possibility of its existence, is in the best cases:

> a question of making you, the reader, aware of your own effort and engagement, of putting you in control, of diminishing the distance between finding and making.[12]

This observation presents a rare occurrence of an Oulipian considering the position of the reader (audience) to generated material. As a maker of creative practice, I am only in control of the flow of information one way and my efforts at control are unescapably inexhaustive; my explanations of exactly how an audience may have read my work, or indeed the works of Perec, are of course inevitably speculative.

The Elision of Scaff'

The Elision of Scaff' was a theatre work comprising six performers (three couples) delivering a re-appropriation of an existing playtext titled *Enemies*, written by Neith Boyce and Hutchins Hapgood in 1921. The constraints used in the generation of the performance comprised existing Oulipian/Perecquian constraints appropriated to theatre, and others of my own design influenced by Oulipian poetics. What follows is an explanation of some of the constraints used during that project, which attempts to capture and reflect on how the application of spatial constraints can impact the generation of performance material.

Experimental poet Christian Bök refers to Oulipian structures and constraints as 'an array of rules for exploring an array of rules'.[13] The imposition of constraints on a theatrical process, specifically those concerned with time and space, led to the imposition of more constraints, such was the causal chain. Marcel Bénabou considers the results of the application of constraints:

> Linguistic constraints, for their part, granted their arbitrary exigencies, directly create a sort of 'great vacuum' into which are sucked and retained whole quantities of elements which, without this violent aspiration, would otherwise remain concealed.[14]

This metaphor of the vacuum is similar to my articulation of a constraint causal chain in a performance process, whereby one constraint decision leads to an unpredicted other. The multiple ingredients of theatrical composition – voice, body, space and time – make causal chains in this context extremely likely as constraint imposition can affect so many variables. While making this work, a constraint would quickly create a paradox, simultaneously demanding strict adherence while forcing me to select the appropriate generative tools to continue.

Threes in a vacuum

> If one can measure what one is talking about and express it in numbers, which constitute the sole reality, then one has some knowledge of one's subject.[15]

The number three has a pleasing locus in mathematics and art. Three is the first odd prime number, it features in the Fibonacci sequence and is the closest whole number to π. Three is the smallest plural odd number, it makes symmetry problematic and so presents compositional interests for me. My interest in the creative potential of *the number* links the mathematical fascinations of Perec and the Oulipo to Alfred Jarry's comment from *Dr Faustroll* (1898 [1996]) above, connecting to the Oulipo's traceable lineage from 'pataphysics. Jarry also conceived of the *Collège de 'Pataphysique* whose members included a number of the founders of the Oulipo. 'Pataphysics is notoriously difficult to define and Andrew Hugill notes that any attempt at definition should be approached with caution. However, a good attempt is the most famous of the 'Pataphysicians' own definitions, that 'pataphysics 'is the science of imaginary solutions'.[16]

As the fundamental spatial constraint in my process, it is appropriate to start with the previously mentioned *Simultaneous Play Triplication (SPT),* which dictated that the play would be performed three times at the same time. This involved using triplicate casts. This overt constraint was the most visible to the audience and disrupted their usual viewing experience. This constraint simultaneously involved all spoken text and actions of the play being performed three times. There was consequently the potential that, even though the narrative would be repeated and restated, the repetition would also make it difficult for an audience to comprehend the narrative in a usual way. *SPT* sucked into its vacuum additional number-three-based constraints. *SPT* created spatial problems that required resolution through the application of new constraints, in keeping with the Oulipo's most recognisable quotation: 'Oulipians: rats who must build the labyrinth from which they propose to escape.'[17]

Each constraint: a wall, a vacuum. The performance: the labyrinth, the map that determines escape. Each constraint imposed on the process led to further necessary impositions that again shaped the work created. The resulting performance work became evidence of spatial constraint, simultaneously existing as both map and destination – a pure inculcation of process in product – evidence of labour that encompasses both the labyrinth *and* the desire to escape it.

> Speculating about a constraint's potentiality involves discerning the extent to which it is apt to trigger variations and mutations; the extent to which it will naturally and productively participate families of constraints; and, finally, the extent to which it might evolve over the course of time.[18]

SPT was a constraint that triggered many more, it was the initial constraint that opened up the potential for myriad new possibilities.

An example of a constraint opened up by *SPT* is the *120° spatial wedging* constraint. This constraint dictates that each of the three versions of the play occupy a third of an in-the-round performance space. This constraint pins down a decision that might seem both obvious and/or unconventional, there are of course many ways that, scenographically, the space could have been configured to make sense of the *SPT* constraint. The naming of a constraint is firstly a testament to its open-ended, experimental, unpredictable nature, and secondly a demand that it be upheld. Bök points out that it simultaneously emancipates the artist from the infinite possibilities that could exist and the fact that only one can – and, if you don't take control, you will fall foul of convention.[19] A theatrical version of this philosophy can also be found in Anne Bogart's reflections on violent decisions, 'Art is violent. To be decisive is violent.'[20]

Space and time

The *180-year time span* constraint is also causally connected to *SPT*. Designed to explicitly create differences between the versions of the play, this constraint alters the year in which each version is set in graduations of 90 years. As a result, the first and last variants of the play are 180 years apart. The original play was written in 1921, approximately 93 years before the time I began working on the project. To keep the numbers clean, 93 years is rounded down to the nearest 10, ie 90. Adding 90 years to the original year places the middle play in the year 2011 (more or less a contemporary year) and the third play in 2101. The time graduations of 90 years and the total span of 180 years have clear, if coincidental, commonalities with the degree divisions of a circle although, in hindsight, deviations of 120 years may have been even more aesthetically gratifying by mirroring the thirds of the 360° of a circle.

180-year time span opened another vacuum to be populated by its unpredicted offspring. The conventional demands of theatre necessitate that the language and vocal qualities used by the actors in a play will, along with design decisions, scenography, costume, etc., indicate the period of the play. While there exists no rule to achieve this over three differing time periods at the same time, the notion that this is how time may be indicated led to the design of the *assumed period rewriting constraint.* This constraint meant that the first variation of the play, set in 1921, would remain true to the original text; the other variants would be re-written according to playwrights' assumptions of that period. The constraint was designed to mine the resource of the author's existing knowledge and know-how. This was not an automatic, surrealist inspiration exercise, rather a conscious acknowledgement of one's own subjective pre- or mis-conception, prejudice and general knowledge. *The assumed period rewriting* constraint was Perecquian in character, simultaneously limiting and liberating. Rather like *An Attempt at Exhausting a Place in Paris*, this kind of constraint makes the author/director operate according to their own limitations, tastes and tendencies. The structure is restrictive and clear, but the subjectivity and fallibility of the author/director is additionally important in terms of the content generated.

Writing the play to be set in 2011 involved the careful reading of the existing 1921 text and the modernising of it through re-writing in contemporary language. This included replacing cultural references where appropriate, through a kind of *isosyntaxism*.[21] The results of this relatively simple task of comprehension and translation were of course unique to me and based on my own expectations, tastes and rules of accessibility; no-one else would have made the exact translation that I made. In the writing of the 2101 version, the causal chain demanded an additional constraint. In this instance, I needed to address how I might predict the way in which the spoken text might sound in the future. I designed another constraint by devising a simple formula to alter the vowel sounds of words in order to generate a new accent. With an understanding that vowel sounds shift according to geographical barriers and the passing of time and that this, like any other kind of evolution, is due to the relative levels of success and sustainability of those sounds, it felt legitimate to use the following *accent modifier* (see Table 10.1) to alter the sounds of words.

Because the *accent modifier* was to have such a profound effect on how the text sounded, I decided to only alter the sounds of the words and not to alter the actual words as well (perhaps another kind of

Table 10.1 Accent modifier diagram. © Oliver Bray

2101 accent modifier

English RP	A	E	I	U
New Zealand English	E	I	U	A
NB - Each vowel sound moves to the left				

English RP	A	E	I	U
2101 English	U	A	E	I
NB - Each vowel sound moves to the right				

isosyntaxism), so no translation took place. The result was that the fundamental syntax of the 2011 and 2101 texts were the same. By positioning the 2011 version as a benchmark to aid the audience in listening to the 2101 version, an adherence was made to the theatrical convention that the audience should understand the sense of what they were hearing. This is a theatrical version of Esposito's assertion that Oulipian writing should 'withstand the strains of being made novelistic'.[22] *The Elision of Scaff'* was a constrained performance attempting to withstand the strains of being made theatrical. As discussed previously, theatre is a spatial medium. The manipulation of narrative time through the triplication of spoken material and the way that material sounds, meant that narrative time impacted on audience interpretations in performance time. The three spaces, notionally placed in three different time zones as well as three different parts of the performance space, produced a new space of understanding. The audience could not observe one-third of this work only, the collective reading of three simultaneous time zones side by side in one room (divided into three) produced a new triptychal narrative space that was unfixed in time and place. The spatial and textual constraints applied were realised as a kind of live map to their own complexity – the performers became cartographers of unpredictable new narratives and localities in the performance space.

Maths in space

This causal chain of development and permutation articulated previously is a result of the inculcation of the Perecquian inclination towards exhaustivity and the Oulipian forefathers' 'pataphysical desire to see out a hypothesis, however bizarre:

> Queneau and Arnaud [...] have traced the spirals of their own cognitive *gidouille*, deriving the reductio ad absurdum of an impossible hypothesis.[23]

However, not all constraints worked in such a directly causal way but were nonetheless inter-related and clearly influenced by Perec. For example, my theatrical tastes desired all six of the performers to occupy all of the different areas of the performance space that resulted from the *120 spatial wedging constraint*. Through studying George Perec's *Life: A User's Manual*, I became interested in Græco-Latin bi-squares.[24] Perec utilised these squares while designing the content of the chapters of his novel.[25] In my version below, which is not technically a true use of the Græco-Latin bi-square (see Table 10.2), I ensured that each performer occupied all possible spaces during the performance.

By placing section markers down the left axis of the square, I was able to map these pairings and space occupation in performance time. I was additionally attempting to achieve the satisfying aesthetic resolution of having the performers' locations end as they started. The bi-square takes the role of a set of instructions for the performance, a constraint map that

Table 10.2 Græco-Latin bi-square diagram. © Oliver Bray

	SPACE OCCUPIED AT START OF SECTION					
SECTION 1	PAST	PAST	PRESENT	PRESENT	FUTURE	FUTURE
SECTION 2	PAST	PAST	PRESENT	PRESENT	FUTURE	FUTURE
SECTION 3.1	PAST	PRESENT	PRESENT	FUTURE	FUTURE	PAST
SECTION 3.2	FUTURE	PRESENT	PAST	FUTURE	PRESENT	PAST
SECTION 4.1	FUTURE	FUTURE	PAST	PAST	PRESENT	PRESENT
SECTION 4.2	PRESENT	FUTURE	FUTURE	PAST	PAST	PRESENT
SECTION 5	PRESENT	PRESENT	FUTURE	FUTURE	PAST	PAST
SECTION 6	PAST	PRESENT	PRESENT	FUTURE	FUTURE	PAST
SECTION 7	PAST	PAST	PRESENT	PRESENT	FUTURE	FUTURE
	HANNAH	DAN	BETH	ADAM	SARAH	DAVE
SPACE OCCUPANCY (OUT OF 9)	5	3	2	2	2	4
	2	4	5	3	2	2
	2	2	2	4	5	3

can then be applied to existing material in order to transform it. In this way, the constraint of the bi-square became a spatial practice. Although primarily functional, the bi-square table, absent from the audience's reading of the performance, exists rather like a map or supplement to the performance, a trace or testimony to its existence. As a theatre-maker there is great pleasure in having visual material that sits alongside the ungraspable ephemerality that characterises live performance. In the context of a discipline that primarily exists in the live moment only, the bi-square sits pleasingly alongside the process of theatre-making – not as record or independent reflection, but as an integral example of process. This is perhaps reminiscent of a cartographer's map collection that reminds her not only of the place recorded, but of the process of considering and cataloguing.

Another example of a non-causally linked constraint includes *action according to body weight,* where each performer's body weight was used to determine the frequency that they got up from their chairs in the performance (see Table 10.3).

The *action according to body weight* constraint determined when each performer stood up from their chair in the performance. The constraint demonstrates an arbitrary attribute of the material of the performance (the performer's body), directly influencing the spatial composition of the theatrical work. This is the kind of constraint imposition that is simply not possible in a literary work. The author of literature may of course choose to impose the arbitrary maths of their own body to the composition of words on a page. However, the ability to manipulate the body that has provided that data directly *within* the performance text is unique to this kind of undertaking. The result is spatial constraint that has an embodied connection to the text. I am convinced that the relationship, of the spatial mathematical translation of physical attribute to performer action, gives the resulting performance moments a specific embodied legitimacy. This is a particular authenticity that is the result of the relationship between constraint, space and the body in performance.

The constraints of *The Elision of Scaff'* have at their core a relationship to my subjective, formal tendencies in theatre. It is the synergy between these tendencies and the imposed spatial constraints of the project that have led to the realisation of a holistic theatrical event. Perec's inclination towards the use of generative constraint to produce a substantive literary form paved the way for the consideration of imposing spatially oriented constraints on the generation of the event of theatre. The time and space made possible by the three-dimensionality of theatre allowed spatial constraints to affect both the form and content of a live viewing experience for an audience.

Table 10.3 Frequency of standing up formula. © Oliver Bray

Lines divided by time over weight.

or

$$\frac{\text{Total lines in the whole performance (L)}}{\left(\frac{\text{Total time of the performance in seconds (T)}}{\text{Performer body weight in pounds (W)}}\right)}$$

or

$$\frac{L}{\left(\frac{T}{W}\right)}$$

Resulting in the following frequency

NAME	TOTAL LINES	TOTAL SECONDS	BODY WEIGHT	Get up every...
HANNAH	396	1973	103	20.67308667
DAN	396	1973	140	28.0993411
BETH	396	1973	140	28.0993411
ADAM	396	1973	233	46.76533198
SARAH	396	1973	121	24.2858591
DAVE	396	1973	256	51.38165231
				...lines of your partnership text.

The causal nature inherent in the imposition of Perecquian spatial constraint on performance practice – the uncovering of further constraints through the discovering of their precursors – proposes a methodology for generation that effectively maps itself. Indeed, some of the diagrammatic and written reflective outcomes of my process do not only leave evidence and documentation of a constraint-driven process. Additionally, they exist as spatial traces, symptoms and (carto)graphic artefacts, that authenticate the ungraspable moment of performance.

> The intense difficulty posed by this sort of production … palls in comparison to the terror I would feel in writing ‘poetry’ freely.[26]

Spatial constraints have the ability, somewhat objectively and independently, to guide, record and reflect on a creative theatre-making process. Consequently, and provocatively, spatial constraints in performance exclude the possibilities for true, and perhaps deadly, artistic freedom.

Notes

1. Documentation of the performance can be viewed here: https://vimeo.com/241685687 (password : constraint).
2. Elkin and Esposito, *The End of Oulipo?*, 5.
3. Levin Becker, *Many Subtle Channels*, 33.
4. Levin Becker, *Many Subtle Channels*, 62–3.
5. Sturrock, *The Word from Paris*, 196.
6. Levin Becker, *Many Subtle Channels*, 80.
7. Snowball – a form in which each segment of a text is one letter longer than the segment preceding it. See Motte, *Oulipo*, 213.
8. *Tireur à la ligne* ('Puller on the line') – taking two sentences in a given text and interpolating a new sentence, then two new sentences in the interstices thus created, and so forth. See Motte, *Oulipo*, 213.
9. Levin Becker, *Many Subtle Channels*, 79.
10. James, *Constraining Chance*, 126.
11. Levin Becker, *Many Subtle Channels*, 84.
12. Levin Becker, *Many Subtle Channels*, 86.
13. Bök, 'Unacknowledged Legislation', 183.
14. Bénabou, cited in Motte, *Oulipo*, 43.
15. Jarry, *Exploits and Opinions of Dr Faustroll, Pataphysician*, 101–2.
16. Hugill, *'Pataphysics;* Shattuck, 'Subliminal Note'.
17. Queneau, cited in Motte, *Oulipo*, 22.
18. Levin Becker, *Many Subtle Channels*, 168.
19. Bök, 'Unacknowledged Legislation', 82.
20. Bogart, *A Director Prepares*, 45.
21. Isosyntaxism – or Homosemantic translation. 'A translation in which the vocabulary of the source text is changed while its sense is kept. At its simplest, it applies the procedure normally used to translate a text from one language to another to transforming a text within a single language.' See Mathews and Brotchie, *Oulipo Compendium*, 159.
22. Elkin and Esposito, *The End of Oulipo?*, 21.
23. Hugill, *'Pataphysics*, 68.
24. Græco-Latin bi-square – or orthogonal bi-square. 'Claude Berge ... defines it: "a Græco-Latin bi-square of order *n* is a figure with *n* x *n* squares filled with *n* different letters and *n* different numbers; each square contains one letter and one number; each letter appears only once in each line and each column, each number appears only once in each line and each column".' See Mathews and Brotchie, *Oulipo Compendium*, 154.
25. Bellos, 'Georges Perec's Puzzling Style', 63–78.
26. Perec, cited in Levin Becker, *Many Subtle Channels*, 182.

Bibliography

Bellos, David. 'Georges Perec's Puzzling Style', *Scripsi* 5, no. 1 (1988): 63–78.

Bogart, Anne. *A Director Prepares: Seven Essays on Art and Theatre*. London: Routledge, 2001.

Bök, Christian. *'Pataphysics: The Poetics of an Imaginary Science*. Evanston, IL: Northwestern University Press, 2002.

Bök, Christian. 'Unacknowledged Legislation'. In *Avant-Post: The Avant-Garde under "Post-" Conditions*, edited by Louis Armand, 178–93. Prague: Litteraria Pragensia, 2006.

Boyce, Neith and Hutchins Hapgood. 'Enemies'. In *The Provincetown Plays*, edited by George Cram Cook and Frank Shay. Cincinnati: Stewart Kidd Co., 1921.

Bray, Oliver. *The Elision of Scaff'*, directed by Oliver Bray. First performance April 2014.

Elkin, Lauren and Scott Esposito. *The End of Oulipo? An Attempt to Exhaust a Movement*. Winchester: Zero Books, 2013.

Hugill, Andrew. *'Pataphysics: A Useless Guide*. Cambridge, MA: MIT Press, 2012.

James, Alison. *Constraining Chance: Georges Perec and the Oulipo*. Evanston, IL: Northwestern University Press, 2009.

Jarry, Alfred. *Exploits and Opinions of Dr. Faustroll, Pataphysician*, translated by Simon Watson Taylor. Boston: Exact Change, 1996.

Levin Becker, Daniel. *Many Subtle Channels: In Praise of Potential Literature*. Cambridge, MA: Harvard University Press, 2012.

Mathews, Harry and Alastair Brotchie, eds. *Oulipo Compendium*. Rev. ed. London: Atlas Press, 2005.

Motte, Warren F., ed. *Oulipo: A Primer of Potential Literature*. Normal, IL: Dalkey Archive Press, 2007.

Perec, Georges. *Life: A User's Manual*, translated by David Bellos. London: Harvill, 1996.

Perec, Georges. *An Attempt at Exhausting a Place in Paris*, translated by Marc Lowenthal. Cambridge, MA: Wakefield Press, 2010.

Perec, Georges and the Oulipo. *Winter Journeys*. London: Atlas Press, 2013.

Shattuck, Roger. 'Subliminal Note'. In *Evergreen Review*, 13 (1960): 24–33.

Sturrock, John. *The Word from Paris: Essays on Modern French Thinkers and Writers*. London: Verso, 1998.

11

Embodiment and everyday space: Dancing with Georges Perec

Leslie Satin

Watching traditional Western concert dance, the spectator's gaze is typically directed towards the image or action the choreographer deems most important. Everything in the *mise en scène* participates in this 'guidance': the spatial positioning of still and moving performers, marking them as landscape or star; the movement lexicon, quality and design; the lights; the music – and viewers' familiarity with Renaissance-era conventions of stage space. When Merce Cunningham began choreographing in the mid-twentieth century, he resisted this over-determined relationship of stage and gaze. Instead he made dances characterised by open-field organisation of the performance space, which contained simultaneous non-matrixed movement episodes. In these, a still dancer was understood to take up as much space and significance, as a moving one and no area (say, centre), path (up-to-downstage diagonal) or facing (front) carried freighted meaning. One could look where one desired, with a broad, narrow or changing focus.

For some spectators, this remains uncomfortable: not having what Vasari called a 'magnet to the eye' feels disorienting rather than liberating.[1] Actually, though, this scenario parallels the experience of everyday life, especially in public places, where we endlessly make conscious and unconscious choices about what to look at, what to see and how to participate in social choreography.

Georges Perec wrote vividly about looking, seeing and space, most directly in *Species of Spaces* but regularly in much of his work. Perec is known primarily for his affiliation with Oulipo (Ouvroir de Littérature Potentielle or Workshop of Potential Literature), the interdisciplinary 'research team' founded in Paris in 1960 and devoted to conceiving and creating new, or 'potential', literature.[2] Much of that literature, and much of Perec's own work, was driven by literary 'constraints', Oulipo's term for a priori strategies narrowing a writer's options – e.g. omitting a language's most-used letter – and, thus, opening the imagination.

Perec was an avid contributor to, and exuberant practitioner of, Oulipo's compositional strategies. Buoyed by his pleasure in language, games and structures, he regularly addressed, across a wide range of literary genres, the critical importance of close observation, deep experiencing of space and, by extension, the physical phenomenon of being in the world. He paid particular attention to the space and spaces of daily life we so often overlook; he made clear that awareness-in-dailiness is a critical matter.

My explorations of Perec's perspectives on space, especially regarding everyday experience, fall into two broadly overlapping areas. One is this emphasis on paying attention to what easily goes unnoticed: this essay links Perec's spatial consciousness and experience with his articulation of his personal life and with the core role of embodiment.

The other, which emerges from my work as a dancer/dance scholar, is the correspondences of Perec's writing with dance, a pairing whose oddness resides in part in the abundance of language characterising Perec's work and the wordlessness – no longer assumed – long associated with dance. Here, I consider a Perecquian approach to spatial attention within the frame of an embodied practice. Dance, broadly conceived as bodies, space and time, is an ongoing, contingent process joining the spaces of the body – from cell to skeleton – to other spaces; to the sensations through which we perceive, experience and imagine these spaces; to the external environments – streets, studios, stages – in which we exist, with others, and in which we interact and endlessly remake ourselves and each other. I consider how dance practice functions as observation, reflection, generation and documentation, and how it interacts with and intervenes in spatial circumstance.

As far as I know, Perec's writing never addresses dance,[3] so the connections I make are laid over his words and ideas like a sheet of tracing paper, creating a posthumous interdisciplinary *pas de deux*.[4] I draw on work in human geography; affect, literary, autobiography and performance theory; phenomenology; the culture of the everyday and on contemporary arts practices, including my own embodied practice, integrating dance, writing, teaching and everyday life.

My practice is largely situated within Western concert/experimental dance and it is from this perspective that the essay emerges.[5] This dance continues, develops or actively diverges from the powerful lineage of mid-twentieth century compositional innovation, including Cunningham's choreography and early post-modernism. Perec was a young writer at the time – the early 1960s – that a particularly intrepid group of experimental dancers and choreographers in New York City (NYC), the Judson Dance Theater (JDT), led the charge to drastically revise what constituted dance. For two years (1962–4), the JDT investigated 'potential' dance: what choreography might be if it defied the aesthetic, performative, expressive, theatrical, physical and spatial conventions of classical modern dance, predominant since the 1930s.[6]

Had Perec seen or known about these pioneering dancers in NYC – or those in Europe investigating a somewhat different array of questions – he would, no doubt, have found kindred spirits challenging long-held definitions and boundaries of their form and creating dance-making strategies whose interventions into compositional practices were of an order with Oulipo's 'constraints', whose use of ordinary or vernacular rather than specialised movement and interest in non-theatrical performance venues reflected his own attraction to the everyday. And significantly, as I hope to show in this essay, he shared with them the centralness of space, time and the body.

The Perecquian perspective on space is inherent in multiple articulations of embodied experience: how we sense and how we represent our lives. In his 1973 'Approaches to What?', for example, Perec analyses and achingly protests the crush of media attention on the 'spectacular' and the salient, on everything but what matters: the everyday, the unnoticed. Seemingly overwhelmed, he asks, 'But where is our life? Where is our body? Where is our space?'.[7]

This line of thought continues in Perec's masterwork the following year, *Species of Spaces*. In this text, he stages the spaces of his life as a kind of archive; he organises them by size, from smallest to largest (the Page, Bedroom, Apartment Building, Neighbourhood, Town, Country, World, Space …) and represents each with a chapter, variously approaching its subject through multiple literary forms and modes of address, narratives, lists, tables, memories, meta-commentaries, facts, private images, stray observations. First, though, he offers two distinct spatial representations: 'Figure 1: Map of the Ocean (taken from Lewis Carroll's *Hunting of the Snark*)', an outlined empty square,[8] and facing it, then spilling onto the next page, a centred list, a visual chant of capitalised words, organised by the vertical line of SPACE, repeated over and over, accompanied by a modifier, the pairings pointing to space as quotidian (PARKING SPACE), historical (SPACE RACE), material, personal, evocative, absurd.[9]

Perec's spatial schema, however far it reaches as geographic fantasy, stays close to home – which I define here as Perec himself, his life, his body. Perec is drawn not to the 'void' but to 'what there is round about or inside it. [...] the space around us'. He is less concerned with imposed spatial configurations than with the spaces in and of which we 'live', 'dream', 'imagine'. Situating a person's life in spatial, corporeal terms – '[t]o live,' he writes, 'is to pass from one space to another, while doing your very best not to bump yourself' – he articulates his efforts to find his place in the world.[10] Through his extravagant merging of literary forms and styles, his multiple offerings of and dodges from personal detail, Perec continuously re-composes the vision and manual of his life.[11]

Perec's life was, in fact, framed by tragedy, ruptured from early childhood by loss and cut short by illness.[12] His biography provides a clear context for the profoundly personal, if often elusive, elements of Perec's work which underlie his playful, imaginative, insistent, lavish adventures in literary, linguistic and rhetorical strategy. A critical example is his 1969 *La Disparition* (The Disappearance), a lipogramatic novel composed (and translated into English, as *A Void*) without the letter 'e'.[13] As numerous scholars have noted, the 'disappearance' of the 'e' stood in both for Perec's own losses and for the enormous circumstance of loss – the 'disappearance' of Europe's Jews – in which they figured. No 'e' – in French pronounced '*eux*', or 'them' – meant no *mère* (mother), no *père* (father), no *je* (I), no *famille* (family); it meant, even, no *Perec*: an acknowledgement of his name and thus of himself, not being truly French, and a representation of his absence from his own autobiography.[14]

In a 1979 essay drawn from the Ellis Island film he made with Robert Bober,[15] Perec acknowledges the complications of his not-quite-French name[16] and more broadly characterises the project in complexly autobiographical and definitively spatial terms: Ellis Island is 'the very place of exile, that is, the place of the absence of place, the place of dispersal. [...] [It is] something without shape, at the limits of the sayable [...] which for me is very intimately and confusedly linked to the actual fact of being a Jew.'[17] David Bellos continues this image into the writing itself; Perec, he says, 'made gap or absence the constitutive device of all his writing. [...] [It] is explicitly built on nothing, on the absence that lies at the heart of language and which is the truest expression of the self.'[18] Not only *La Disparition* but his entire *oeuvre* of wildly clever, formally formidable, meta-narrative fiction and artfully incisive non-fiction is, too, Perec's 'underground' telling of the hole at the centre of his identity, his autobiography, his life.

This is a clue to the meaning-making possibilities of another text: the dancer's body. Such an undertext is germane to bodies, including dancing bodies, in ways both like and unlike the one described above. That is, how we 'read' bodies, including our own, reflects how we do and do not recognise or acknowledge the implication of discourse in embodiment.[19]

A dancer's practice comprises not only what she does with her body, or her cognitive understanding of bodies matrixed within webs of culture and representation, but the everyday experiences of her body in and as space. This is exquisitely complex: a dynamic merging of elements that are immediate, cumulative and known deeply by dancers while being largely inarticulable, or inexplicable or untranslatable, in language. The simultaneity of the dancer's cognitive/embodied experience, the non-Cartesian mind/body integration central to (understanding) the experience of space, takes place, as Perec wrote, at 'the limits of the sayable'.

Accordingly, over at least the last 20 years, dance scholarship as well as dance itself has changed. Auto-ethnographic, phenomenological, new materialistic and affect/performance-theory-derived perspectives identify dancers' experiences and locate them within the sphere of dancerly activity – itself connecting one's own moving to others with whom one shares space – and the larger spheres of sociopolitical circumstances. These perspectives, articulated throughout this text and emphasised in a series of inserts set in parentheses, also urge the dance writer/scholar/critic, like contemporary scholars of the everyday, not to fall back on assumed or generalised responses.

(In Rio de Janeiro, I led a workshop on dancing and talking. Since I spoke minimal Portuguese and the students had mixed levels of English fluency, a translator was hired. She never showed. I performed a little introductory dance; as I moved, I declared, in Portuguese, that I was Lula – then-president of Brazil – and asked the students, who knew that I was not Lula, what they could then find 'true' about my movement, my dance, my body.)

While not all the correspondences with dance are linked to Perecquian views of space *per se*, these spatial values are embedded within Perec's broader views. Consider the four approaches he attributed to his writing and their relationship to dance-making, outlined below.

In his 1978 'Notes on What I'm Looking For', Perec lays out the 'four modes of interrogation' characterising his writing: 'sociological: how to look at the everyday', 'autobiographical', 'ludic' and 'fictive'.[20] These 'fields' are largely parallel to certain primary compositional practices of historical post-modern dance and suggest ways to understand relationships of dance-making and dance-viewing, then and now, to their dance-historical and cultural circumstances. That they are admittedly 'arbitrary' and overlapping[21] as choreographic and literary options points to the personal and cultural intersectionality informing the processes of creating art and participating in its meaning-making. While 'intersectionality' is generally used in a sociological context to join the invisible interweaving social forces through which agency and identity are formed, I use it here to join those forces to the mix of individual artistic practice and personal history inherent in these processes.

Perec links his 'sociological/everyday' category to works such as his early novel *Things* (1965), which tells a couple's story through description of their objects; to *Species of Spaces*, through its extensive nuanced portrayals of multiple spaces; and to those works directly recognising the everyday. The corresponding use of everyday and un-stylised movement material in early post-modern dance included extremes of repetition; movement generated by tasks; disrupting hierarchical views of the dancing body; casual and 'backstage' behaviour onstage; non-heroic or specialised self-presentation; resistance to conventions of energy and dynamics and to the performer's seduction of the spectator.[22]

The contemporary incorporation of non-technical movement investigates new physical options and responds to updated definitions and limits of dance and performance. Some experimentation emphasises spatial elements: in addition to site dance, which foregrounds its venue and other dances in non-theatrical spaces, dances call attention to the typically hidden parts of a space or radically undo familiar spatial organisation. Some dances are less about movement, or more about resisting movement, or have a focus on time (through, say, extremes of duration, or speed) which produces altered experiences of space and the meaning-making of bodies in space.[23] Everydayness figures, too, in dances that interrogate long-held beliefs about gender, race, ethnicity, power and other social frameworks of identity, through deconstruction of movement itself and the material components which contextualise it and through inclusion of performers whose physicality extends beyond stereotypical 'perfect' bodies to variously abled as well as less obviously trained dancers.

'Autobiographical' works most directly invoke Perec's actual life (however altered), like *W, or The Memory of Childhood* (1975), or *La Boutique Obscure: 124 Dreams* (1973); beyond specifically labelled texts, though, what is significant is those many works containing 'traces of the autobiographical'[24] – and, to me, those *evoking* Perec's presence-in-process through works of 'implicit' rather than 'explicit' autobiography. Perec's genre-bending adaptation of autobiography, which fictionalises or elides personal history, resists chronological and narrative conventions and experiments with the teller's voice and position is germane, too, to post-modern dance (and other art-forms).[25] Sometimes incorporating (or substituting) language, sometimes not, choreographers stage narrative and narrative-resistant mergings of autobiographical fiction and non-fiction, flaunting or flouting the invitation to the spectator to identify with or appropriate the central 'character', creating a momentary self-in-performance or leaving the viewer to wonder what 'really' happened, or to whom.

The 'ludic' category includes those works most fully exemplifying Perec's devotion to Oulipian games and other compositional devices – the 'palindromes, [...] pangrams, anagrams, isograms, acrostics, crosswords',[26] the literary acrobatics pushing the linguistic/semantic ideals while retaining the tactility and accessibility of his writing. This approach was important across mid-twentieth-century experimental art-making, including John Cage's music, Cunningham's choreography, Fluxus's multi-arts actions and objects. Judson dancers used choreographic scores, or blueprints and games, some featured in the dance itself rather than hidden 'off-stage'. Putting the modes of composition up front and centre, as it were, rather than producing an illusion of pre-set wholeness at once disrupted the formality of performance, the relationship of performer and viewer and the ideals of artistic process. Since then, choreographers have generated, organised and deployed material by first composing scores, which – like Oulipo's devices – limit the artist's choices and encourage access to unfamiliar choices. These exemplify, too, Viktor Shklovsky's ideas of 'defamiliarization' – art's project of making perception conscious, making known phenomena new – and 'recover[ing] the sensation of life' – through a range of evident strategies, or what he called 'baring the devices'.[27] Cage spoke about work made using chance operations and indeterminacy as resisting the likelihood of falling into one's habits, as well as what he often called one's 'likes and dislikes'.[28] West-coast artists Anna Halprin (choreographer) and Lawrence Halprin (landscape architect) devised the RSVP Cycles, a system for articulating the creative process, positioned as inherently ludic and socially/politically progressive.[29]

Perec applies his 'fictive' category, a mode inherently overlapped with others, to stories – texts read for sheer pleasure. He allocates this to *Life: A User's Manual* (1978), a wildly complex 'story' whose literary *modus operandi* is a game in which the reader – directed not to a particular experience but to experience/perception-producing acts of involvement (translational, structural) with the text and its internal conundrums – is situated. This active, interruptive experience probably diverges from some readers' notions of enjoying 'the sort of books that are devoured lying face down on your bed'.[30]

Full-on story dances had little play in early post-modernism, but work including elements of narrative while changing the terms of its creation and reception, such as the dramatic and theatrical choreography of Pina Bausch, appeared in the 1970s in Europe. And choreographers have continually explored ways to offer, suggest and/or resist the 'closure' of traditional narrative (and autobiography) through a range of spatial, chronological, structural, dramatic, textual and generally 'paranarrative' strategies.[31]

Choreography is only one element of dance characterised by relationships to Perec's spatial values. The rest of this essay largely addresses space as experience for the dancer, who is called on to be acutely aware of every physical detail, however subtle or extravagant and every quality of movement, however nuanced or dramatic. At the same time, she is expected to let go of that vigilant watchfulness, to transcend that ongoing analysis of herself as a subject of information and awareness in order to actually *dance*: to be absorbed in the movement, the performance, the space and time of the experience rather than to be its observer.

This is for some dancers an ideal. Others, whose practice is based in somatic techniques (e.g., Alexander, Klein, Feldenkrais), image- or anatomy-directed improvisation (e.g., Contact Improvisation, Gaga, Authentic Movement), performative walking, or (other) phenomenological approaches to movement, may focus on maintaining their sense of interiority while staying aware of external elements.

That said, dancers often complete a preparatory ritual before class or rehearsal, instead of or in addition to the 'body scan' with which a teacher or choreographer might begin the day's work. Many components are common to people in a specific class or company, e.g. stretching particular body parts, maybe using specific equipment (*barre*, weights). I consider here those moments of 'stillness' in which the dancer completes a 'catalogue' of her body, a rundown of all its parts as they align with each other and connect to the space around/above/below them. Performed over and over, this is a continuing opportunity to renew and revise one's embodied experience, a process joining past and present, building on layers of memory – itself embedded in systems of spatial awareness such as proprioception and visualisation – in locating the nuances of this moment's affects and sensations.

This acknowledgement/sensation of the body as parts and whole is one route through which I connect dance, at the most intimate body level, to Perec. The catalogue at once echoes the lists and other archival expressions of material characterising Perec's writings, especially those recounting his observations of spaces and evokes the personal, cultural and phenomenological complexities within them. And like his writings, it at once takes place in the present, encompasses the past (the archive/body's 'sensational' histories) and again restages the terms of embodied experience.

The dancer's catalogue, however many parts it contains, typically assumes either the person's sense of a body's wholeness or the desire to experience that wholeness. But Perec's catalogues – especially those directly referring to his or a character's body – often present something fragmented, or fractured: a body-in-parts, a *corps morcelé*. In the 1967 novel *A Man Asleep*, for example, the predominant image is a body, perhaps but not definitively that of the profoundly depressed narrator, its anatomical segments repeatedly, minutely and analytically described as though from an outside vantage point – like that of a disembodied trauma victim observing his or her torture.[32] That sense of observing, of properly and complexly characterising the narrator's view as it is created by the juxtaposition of a thumb or foot or knee with the other 'things' in its sphere, is tied to his drastically reduced sense of himself: 'nothing more than an eye'. He can see his body but 'will never again be able to get back to it', this body that insists on staying, however distorted or detached from the most basic sensation of physical integrity.[33]

My own daily catalogue emerges from years of gradually developing an understanding of my anatomical structure within the terms of my own dancing. That is, my anatomical map is derived from 'objective' and applied knowledge of my body's systems – i.e., skeletal, muscular, visceral – and from the dance systems, or techniques, that have become embedded in my experience of my body. Marcel Mauss describes, in 'Techniques of the Body', 'the ways in which, from society to society, men [*sic*] know how to use their bodies', in action and repose, posture and gesture.[34] This socially/culturally-derived 'training' exists invisibly in everyday life; more blatantly, variously visibly and in ways minutely attentive to each technique's attributes, this technical training is central to dance study.

My spatial orientation is typically vertical: I stand, my feet in parallel position under my hip sockets, my eyes closed, and sense my head floating on top of my neck. I move, in my mind's eye, through my torso, finding its volume, feeling the openness of my chest; locating the length of my spine, letting my tailbone drop, feeling the shoulders-over-hips-over-knees-over-toes stack up. I feel the weight of my hanging arms; I sense the two long lines of my legs, the weight going down through my feet into the floor. I pay attention to my breathing, often just noticing. My energy simultaneously goes up and down. Nothing is static; I move in tiny increments or make larger adjustments to find balance, recognise gravity, get to what feels spatially organised that moment. Contact Improvisation founder Steve Paxton calls this the Small Dance, or the Stand, identifying it as meditation and improvisation – as *dance,* rather than preparation.[35]

The spatial terms of this catalogue are multiply contingent as well as 'objective'. For instance, I experience myself in here-and-now materiality. Imagining my head stretching up and my weight dropping into my feet, I think of 'ceiling' and 'floor'. 'Place is palpable', writes dancer/environmentalist Andrea Olsen, whose own spatial context is more expansive, assuming 'a sensuous relationship of body and earth';[36] deconstructing 'Bipedal Alignment', she identifies it as one of the primary Underlying Patterns through which we interact with space – with the *earth*.[37] I embrace Olsen's perspective. Still, my corporeal self-imaging/experience predominantly reflects my immediate spatial circumstances – and my aesthetics, training, personality. The metaphorical dimension more often arises later, in writing.

The catalogue I have described is, essentially, how I begin to prepare before the start of technique class (usually Cunningham), which directly continues, through its central concepts of anatomical geography and the movement lexicon based on that model, the body design of my catalogue's 'script'. My 'hybrid' version reflects, too, additional spatial practices and studies: Klein, other somatic techniques; Trisha Brown-based movement; West African dances; and I consciously adjust when I am alone or in classes whose techniques assume a different spatial/anatomical model. Daily, I lie supine, breathing into my body's weight, accepting the welcome of gravity, the opening of my joints, directing my breath towards whatever stiffness I notice.

(One teacher of somatic-inflected movement intones as we lie on the floor, 'Do absolutely nothing'. This is impossible, of course, but I gratefully take the opportunity to 'just be' on the floor. I borrow her words when I teach and watch my students melt; I have seen tears.)

The space in which a dancer sets/re-sets her body orientation figures into the anatomical model. Class itself is social; what happens there happens among others, who serve concurrently as colleagues, competitors and witnesses – in compliance (consciously or not) with an array of mutually agreed-on values, beliefs and behaviours about bodies and space.

Among these: class happens in a specific place, in which students individually and collectively enact spatial narratives merging territory, habit and convention. Dancers often have a favourite spot in class, a doubly significant locale in the *actual* room and the *virtual* one. In the actual room, the dancer adapts to accommodate other dancers and their moving bodies, acknowledging that studio's and technique's accepted views of necessary space surrounding each person. She accommodates, too, the image of her partner/self in the virtual room: the mirror, site of a charged and often vexed relationship to one's body, communicator of (flawed) technical/spatial information (about, say, placement), physical 'shortcomings' (technical and personal: weight, age, beauty) and by extension, the overlapping crossover of personal and cultural identity (race, gender, ethnicity, able-bodied-ness).

And, as Claudia Brazzale argues, a technique's (here, Cunningham's) literal/philosophical spatial implications extend to spheres of identity, economics and politics. Even our casual descriptions of movement/spatial quality – 'eating space', 'cutting through space' – are imbued with metaphorical significance. No dancer conflates – mid-air – her *grand jeté* with colonialism, but the deep pleasures of dancing and watching dancing are often at odds with fully encountering choreography.[38]

(A still-young man who danced, beautifully, with Cunningham tells me that as both mover and viewer, he finds dance without the technical virtuosity of what he used to do boring. I love to dance-till-I-drop in class, but I have always loved making and watching dances defined by slowness, quiet, interiority.)

Perec's relationship to dance is signalled throughout his writing in his continual references to the body, to his body, to the embodied baseline of his experiences of space and time – central, of course, to dance – as well as to the personal history that colours and contextualises the writing of his life. In particular, writing after writing characterises Perec's embodied experience of space: observing it, creating it, directing it, controlling it, being in it and understanding his life and actions, in spatial terms. For instance, in his 1976 [2008] 'Reading: A Socio-physiological Outline', he applies Mauss's ideas on technologies of the body to the physicality of reading.[39] Always, he urges readers and himself, to be present, awake to unfamiliar encounters and responses.

Perhaps Perec's best-known entreaty to readers to look closely at what is around them is the *Species of Spaces* chapter 'The Street'. 'The Street' coaxes us not only to look at the place's components, large and small – its buses, pavements, fashions, dogs – but to look without choosing, without assuming familiar hierarchies of significance. He urges the frustrated viewer who is struck by nothing to 'set about it more slowly, almost stupidly'.[40]

'Stupid' is an unflattering epithet, but Perec was guiding readers towards a condition of openness, not pre-determined by expectation or desire. The word he famously used, in 'Approaches to What?', to describe or acknowledge elements of everyday life is 'endotic', as distinguished from 'exotic'.[41] His brief essay packs a punch, addressing systems of public communication whose reportage, consumed with 'the big event, the un-toward, the extraordinary', hides the underpinnings of these spectacular circumstances. 'What is scandalous', he writes, 'isn't the pit explosion, it's working in coalmines.'[42] Forty-six years later, the Internet and other systems of mediated information have only made this loss of connection to what is happening in and around us even more extreme and perhaps made Perec's efforts at suturing our experiences and knowledge more necessary. He asks, 'What's really going on, what we're experiencing, the rest, all the rest, where is it? How should we take account of, question, describe, what happens every day and recurs every day: the banal, the quotidian, the obvious, the common, the ordinary, the infra-ordinary, the background noise, the habitual?'[43]

These words recast Perec's everyday 'mode of interrogation' as not only observation but resistance: defying the systemic robbery of 'what's really going on' through insistence on the value of the everyday. Taken together, 'The Street' and 'Approaches' present Perec as feeling for clues, seeking through the visible and the felt, the spatial – what is in him and around him, what is elusive: 'where is it?' – for what matters. The dancer, too, inhabits and constructs a world of meaning through the mix of exploration, observation, generation, reflection and attention to one's own experience and to what (and whom) we encounter in the space around us.

A dancer's visual sense of space is critical, of course – but not all of a dancer's experience of space is accessed through vision; one crucial element of dancing is the *feel* of it, the sensing of other people's proximity, of breathing together: the proprioceptive elements of experiencing ourselves in and as space. 'Proprioception is, literally, how we "sense ourselves"', writes performer/scholar Louise Steinman. It has three primary prompts: *kinesthesia* 'is the feeling of movement derived from all skeletal and muscular structures' and 'the feeling of pain, our orientation in space, the passage of time, and rhythm. *Visceral* feedback consists of the miscellaneous impressions from our internal organs. *Labyrinthine* or *vestibular* feedback [is] the feeling of our position in space.'[44]

Sensitivity to these bodily messages plays a critical role in the experience of dancing, ranging from the moments of relief and release on the floor, eyes closed, air on the face, hair, feet, to the rhythmic rush of leaping across the studio in a pack. A similar sensitivity participates in the spectatorial experience, adding to the visual field inviting the viewer into the scenario the kinesthetic charge that reproduces in *her* body the sensation of the suspended leaps, the languorous falls, the tense stillness – and the performance space filling and emptying, or a dancer alone in the dimness and then another suddenly lit.

It also exemplifies dancer/phenomenologist Susan Kozel's descriptions of the reciprocity of embodiment inherent in moving with others. Linking the elements of embodiment, inter-subjectivity and inter-corporeality, she says, 'We're embodied through other bodies.'[45] That is, we know and understand our own embodied experiences through our interaction with other people, other bodies. Elsewhere, Kozel expands the parameters of her attention to both the performance of everyday life and the experience of 'choreographing the flow of data' via social media, thus expanding the concepts of kinesthesia, improvisation and phenomenology to address the internality supported by these devices: changing the questions a dancer might ask herself or another dancer from 'what are you doing?' to 'what are you sensing/feeling?'[46]

This increased awareness of our bodies, especially its small shifts of affect, is integral to the experience of dancers in and out of the studio, in our daily lives. Some dancers (more in the UK than the US, where I live) have reconceived their everyday walking-in-public as dance. Fiona Bannon, for instance, joins walking as practice-led research to reflection and documentation, individual choreographic practice to social choreography, 'the material practice of [...] slow art' to improvisation and generally 'engag[es] with space, pace and rhythm'.[47] Many others, dancers and non-dancers, direct Perecquian concern for noticing the unnoticed to public spaces, investigating the pedestrian patterns, the cars and advertisements and coffee-cups in urban streets and 'non-places', their own psychogeographic experiences.

(A student performs almost-invisible 'secret dances' on subway platforms. Her movements are quite small, uninflected, not unlike the fidgety gestures of other commuters waiting for the train. She looks around, finds a place

that feels right, not too crowded, not too tense. Paying close attention to her actions and sensations, consciously affecting the space in which she moves, she is quietly complicating the terms of her embodied encounter with this place that is typically ignored or tolerated, these people whose faces and bodies we merely glance at, if that. She walks to a new spot if she thinks anyone notices what she is doing.)

Notes

1. Steinberg, *Other Criteria*, 7.
2. Bellos, *Georges Perec*, 349.
3. Interestingly, however, several of Perec's works have been adapted for the theatre, notably *Je me souviens* (a famous production starring Sami Frey). Perec also wrote several *Hörspiele* which were translated to the stage (e.g. *Die Maschine*), as well as the two plays that have been performed quite often: *L'Augmentation* and *La Poche Parmentier*. See Hall in this volume.
4. In other essays, I address different elements of the Perec/dance relationship. See Satin, 'Georges Perec and On Kawara' and 'Dancing in Place'.
5. This essay reflects my personal experience, largely in the Western concert lineage and exploratory/somatic techniques. While I believe that many of the essay's ideas are representative of other dance forms, I make no over-arching claims.
6. The detailed history of the JDT best known in the US is Banes's *Democracy's Body*. See also Burt's *Judson Dance Theater*. Burt's view of choreographic experimentation, which includes European contributions, differs from Banes's more American-centric perspective.
7. Perec, 'Approaches to What?', 210.
8. Perec, *Species of Spaces*, 2.
9. Perec, *Species of Spaces*, 3–4.
10. Perec, *Species of Spaces*, 5–6.
11. The reference is to *Life: A User's Manual*, Perec's massive, remarkable novel merging stories, puzzles, images and games focused on a single moment in a fictional Paris apartment building.
12. Perec's life has been sensitively recounted in Bellos's comprehensive biography, *Georges Perec: A Life in Words*.
13. Perec, *A Void*.
14. Marcel Bénabou, David Bellos, Warren Motte, Benjamin Ivry and Dan Stone are among the many Perec scholars who have addressed not only this specific literary act, but the broader area of Perec's relationship to his Jewishness.
15. Perec, 'Ellis Island'. This essay is derived from the script, which was read as a voice-over in the film and published in book form: Perec, *Ellis Island*.
16. Perec, *Ellis Island*, 136.
17. Perec, *Ellis Island*, 136.
18. Bellos, 'The Old and the New', 18.
19. See Foster's *Reading Dancing* for a discussion of understanding dance through literary tropes, semiotics and critical theory.
20. Perec, 'Notes on What I'm Looking For', 141–3.
21. Perec, 'Notes on What I'm Looking For', 142.
22. See choreographer/writer Rainer's articulation of these principles, tying them to her ground-breaking dance, *Trio A*, in her 'A Quasi Survey of Some "Minimalist" Tendencies'.
23. See Lepecki's *Exhausting Dance*.
24. Perec, 'Notes on What I'm Looking For', 142.
25. These examples depart from what Lejeune called the 'autobiographical pact', assuring the sameness of the tale's teller and text. Conventional autobiography, he wrote, was 'a retrospective prose narrative written by a real person concerning his own existence, where the focus is his individual life'. Lejeune, *On Autobiography*, 4.
26. Perec, 'Notes on What I'm Looking For', 142.

27. Shklovsky, 'Art as Technique', 12–13.
28. When asked, 'In using chance operations, did you ever feel that something didn't work as well as you wanted?', Cage responded, 'No … I thought the thing that needs changing is me … If it was something I didn't like … I could change toward the liking rather than getting rid of it'. See Cage, 'Interview of John Cage: Laurie Anderson'. http://www.jimdavies.org/laurie-anderson/work/interviews/cage.html.
29. Halprin, *The RSVP Cycles*, 1969.
30. Perec, 'Notes on What I'm Looking For', 142.
31. In the eponymous 1982 NYC festival, choreographers experimented with up-ending conventions of narrative in dance.
32. Perec, *A Man Asleep*.
33. Perec, *A Man Asleep*, 193.
34. Mauss, 'Techniques of the Body', 78.
35. Paxton, 'Why Standing?', 37–40.
36. Olsen, *Body and Earth*, 202.
37. Olsen, *Body and Earth*, 17–22.
38. Brazzale, '(Un)covering Ground', 107–18.
39. Perec, 'Reading'.
40. Perec, *Species of Spaces*, 50.
41. Perec, 'Approaches to What?', 210.
42. Perec, 'Approaches to What?', 209.
43. Perec, 'Approaches to What?', 209–10.
44. Steinman, *The Knowing Body*, 11.
45. Kozel, 'Susan Kozel: Across Bodies and Systems, New York'.
46. Kozel, 'The MEDEA Talks'.
47. Bannon, 'Articulations', 97–109.

Bibliography

Banes, Sally. *Democracy's Body: Judson Dance Theater, 1962–1964*. Durham, NC: Duke University Press, 1993.

Bannon, Fiona. 'Articulations: Walking as Daily Dance Practice', *Choreographic Practices* 1, no. 1 (2010): 97–109.

Bellos, David. *Georges Perec: A Life in Words*. London: Harvill, 1999.

Bellos, David. 'The Old and the New: An Introduction to Georges Perec', *Review of Contemporary Fiction* 29, no. 1 (2009): 11–20.

Brazzale, Claudia. '(Un)covering Ground: Dance, Space and Mobility', *Theatre, Dance and Performance Training* 5, no. 2 (2014): 107–18.

Burt, Ramsay. *Judson Dance Theater: Performative Traces*. London: Routledge, 2006.

Coe, Robert. 'Taking Chances: Laurie Anderson and John Cage', *Tricycle* (Summer 1992). Accessed 9 May 2019. https://tricycle.org/magazine/taking-chances/.

Foster, Susan Leigh. *Reading Dancing: Bodies and Subjects in Contemporary American Dance*. Berkeley: University of California Press, 1986.

Halprin, Lawrence. *The RSVP Cycles: Creative Processes in the Human Environment*. New York: George Braziller, 1969.

Kozel, Susan. 'Susan Kozel: Across Bodies and Systems, New York', YouTube, 19 August 2009. Video. Accessed 18 February 2018. http://www.youtube.com/watch?v=y8FsjeDUcnQ.

Kozel, Susan. 'The MEDEA Talks: Susan Kozel'. Video. 2012. (no longer available).

Lejeune, Philippe. *On Autobiography*, edited by Paul John Eakin and translated by Katherine Leary. Minneapolis: University of Minnesota Press, 1989.

Lepecki, André. *Exhausting Dance: Performance and the Politics of Movement*. New York: Routledge, 2006.

Mauss, Marcel. 'Techniques of the Body (1935)'. In *Techniques, Technology and Civilisation*, edited by Nathan Schlanger, 77–96. New York: Durkheim Press, 2006.

Olsen, Andrea. *Body and Earth: An Experiential Guide*. Hanover, NH: University Press of New England, 2002.

Paxton, Steve. 'Why Standing? Steve Paxton Talks about How the Stand Relates to Stage Fright and Entrainment in Contact Improvisation', edited by Karen Nelson, *Contact Quarterly Journal* (Winter/Spring 2015): 37–40.

Perec, Georges. *Life: A User's Manual*, translated by David Bellos. Boston: David R. Godine, 1987.

Perec, Georges. *W, or The Memory of Childhood*, translated by David Bellos. Boston: David R. Godine, 1988.

Perec, Georges. *A Void*, translated by Gilbert Adair. London: Harvill, 1995.

Perec, Georges. *Species of Spaces and Other Pieces*, edited and translated by John Sturrock. London: Penguin Books, 2008.

Perec, Georges. 'Species of Spaces'. In *Species of Spaces and Other Pieces*, edited and translated by John Sturrock, 1–96. London: Penguin Books, 2008.

Perec, Georges. 'The Street'. In *Species of Spaces and Other Pieces*, edited and translated by John Sturrock, 46–56. London: Penguin Books, 2008.

Perec, Georges. 'Ellis Island: Description of a Project'. In *Species of Spaces and Other Pieces*, edited and translated by John Sturrock, 134–38. London: Penguin Books, 2008.

Perec, Georges. 'Notes on What I'm Looking For'. In *Species of Spaces and Other Pieces*, edited and translated by John Sturrock, 141–43. London: Penguin Books, 2008.

Perec, Georges. 'Reading: A Socio-Physiological Outline'. In *Species of Spaces and Other Pieces*, edited and translated by John Sturrock, 174–85. London: Penguin Books, 2008.

Perec, Georges. 'Approaches to What?'. In *Species of Spaces and Other Pieces*, edited and translated by John Sturrock, 209–11. London: Penguin Books, 2008.

Perec, Georges. *A Man Asleep*, translated by Andrew Leak. Boston: David R. Godine, 2010.

Perec, Georges. *Things: A Story of the Sixties*, translated by David Bellos. Boston: David R. Godine, 2010.

Perec, Georges. *La Boutique Obscure: 124 Dreams*, translated by Daniel Levin Becker. New York: Melville House, 2012.

Perec, Georges with Robert Bober. *Ellis Island*, translated by Harry Mathews and Jessica Blatt. New York: New Press, 1995.

Rainer, Yvonne. 'A Quasi Survey of Some "Minimalist" Tendencies in the Quantitatively Minimal Dance Activity Midst the Plethora, or an Analysis of *Trio A*'. In *Work 1961–73*, 63–9. Halifax: Press of the Nova Scotia College of Art and Design, 1974.

Satin, Leslie. 'Dancing in Place: Exhaustion, Embodiment, and Perec', *Dance Research Journal* 47, no. 3 (2015): 85–104.

Satin, Leslie. 'Georges Perec and On Kawara: Endotic Extravagance in Literature, Art, and Dance', *Literary Geographies* 3, no. 1 (2017): 50–68.

Shklovsky, Victor. 'Art as Technique'. In *Russian Formalist Criticism: Four Essays*, translated by Lee T. Lemon and Marion J. Reis, 3–24. Lincoln: University of Nebraska Press, 1965.

Steinberg, Leo. *Other Criteria: Confrontations with Twentieth-Century Art*. New York: Oxford University Press, 1972.

Steinman, Louise. *The Knowing Body: The Artist as Storyteller in Contemporary Performance*. Berkeley: North Atlantic Books, 1995.

12
Seeing more flatly: *The Regional Book*

David Matless

Hoveton Great Broad

An isolated broad and nature trail in the Bure valley, between Wroxham and Horning

Aromatic, a broad and carr reserve gained only by water, a small Bure north bank quay. Tree and fen bar land access. Tie up and take the boardwalk, a sleeper path of half a mile, looping from entrance to exit, single file. Visits elective, no stray humans. Public authority trails nature, national reserve maintained. The warden has a hut.

Signs warn not to stray, muddy danger lurking. Experience sensibly channelled. Hides give on the broad, free of navigation, birds undisturbed. Mud accumulates shallows. Chained binoculars see terns, platform nesting. Coot graze. Kingfisher darts.

Petrol engines made this grow. Hay lost horse demand, and cutting ended. Signs mark succession, and intervention, deflecting for sedge. Numbered posts match guiding text, for moss and fern, peat solid and thin, turf ponds and the greater broad. Bird life passes by, or perches. Branches frame a sunlit tawny.

Boat noise fades into wood, traffic forgotten. River water nose drops, carr scent rising. The fruits of damp, sweet gale of fen. Currant, wild. Reserve confinements, aromatic.

This descriptive account of Hoveton Great Broad is taken from *The Regional Book*, published in 2015.[1] The book was written after many years of interest in and experience of the region concerned, the Norfolk Broads in eastern England, and the form of writing deployed to recount the region was in part prompted by the work of Georges Perec. The description of Hoveton, part of a national nature reserve accessible only by a boardwalk trail from a river mooring, is characteristic in attending to modes of encounter, sensory engagement, recommended and channelled movement, specialist language, manifest traces of the past, and presences animal, vegetable and mineral. This essay reflects on the writing of *The Regional Book*, and the way in which Perec, among others, shaped its forms of geographical description. The first part reflects on histories and conventions of geographical description, the second discusses description and field observation. Further extracts from *The Regional Book* conclude the essay. Perec's injunction in *Species of Spaces* to 'Force yourself to see more flatly' acts as a motto for the book, in part punning on the very flat landscape of the Norfolk Broads, with which *The Regional Book* is concerned, but also suggesting a virtue in cutting across styles of seeing claiming conventional hierarchical authority.[2] The injunction to 'see more flatly' serves as a motto for constant notice, respectful looking, the spotting of unlikely material significance in things that are 'most obvious, most common, most colourless'.[3] The cover of the book (see Figure 12.1) shows the grazing marsh landscape near Wickhampton, with cattle, bush and redundant drainage mill.

Geographical description

In geographic outline, Broadland (see Figure 12.2) is a region defined by waterways, with six rivers flowing, some into one another, and all waters ending in the North Sea at Great Yarmouth.

To make up the 'Southern Rivers', the Chet joins the Yare just upstream of Reedham, and the Yare and Waveney meet at Breydon Water. For the 'Northern Rivers', the Ant joins the Bure west of Horning, the Thurne and Bure meet north of Acle, and the Bure continues, joining the Yare below Breydon. Only the Yare keeps its name to the sea at Yarmouth. The broads are shallow lakes distinctive to the region, filled-up medieval peat diggings whose artificial industrial origin was figured out with some surprise 60 years ago.[4] Some broads sit to one side of the rivers, linked by dug channels, some occupy the river as if it had simply 'broadened' in its flow. The map shown here, by which the accounts given in this chapter may be located, is from Anna Bowman Dodd's 1896 travel book *On the Broads*. Its reproduction there 'By Permission of The Great Eastern Railway' indicates the role of railways in opening up the region

Figure 12.1 Front cover of *The Regional Book*, by David Matless, photograph of the Halvergate marshes, taken by the author, 28 May 2011. © The author

for tourism in the late nineteenth century, thereby expanding the audience for regional literature.[5]

The Regional Book describes the Norfolk Broads, gathering descriptions of 44 sites around the region. After a short introductory essay, the pieces are ordered alphabetically, with a list of recommended reading and a gazetteer with map at the end. Six of the accounts were aired at a conference, 'Living Landscapes', on landscape and performance, at Aberystwyth in 2009, and subsequently published within a paper in *Performance Research*.[6] A subsequent book, *In the Nature of Landscape:*

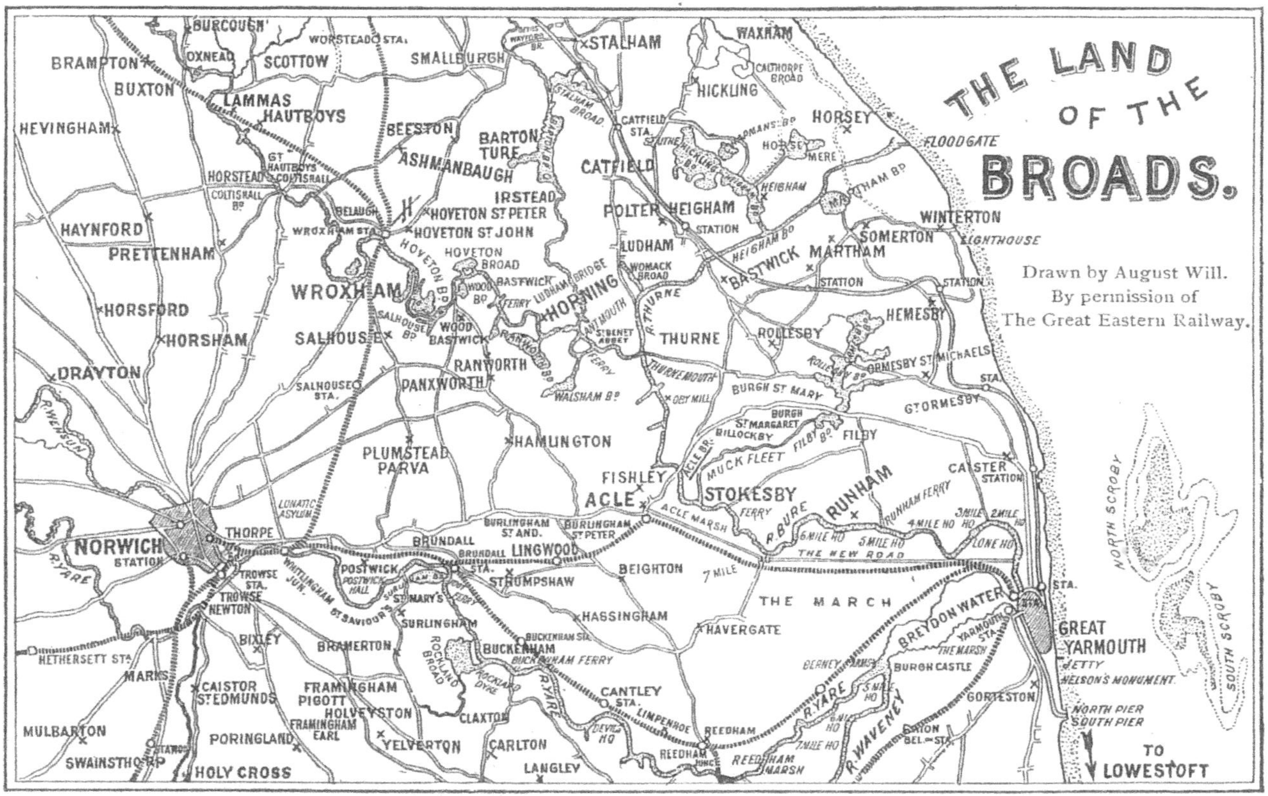

Figure 12.2 'Map of the Broads', from *On the Broads* by Anna Bowman Dodd (1896). This map, originally produced for the Great Eastern Railway, was used as a location guide in a regional travelogue by American travel writer Anna Bowman Dodd. It is reproduced here as a location guide for this essay.

Cultural Geography on the Norfolk Broads, extended their coverage.[7] That book is structured around key themes in regional geography and history – origins, conduct, animal landscapes, plant landscapes, regional icons, and the ends of landscape – with six descriptions given at the end of the opening chapter, and six more at the end of the book. The opportunity to develop such works of description for publication in a different format, at the invitation of Colin Sackett at Uniformbooks, was welcome.[8] Sackett's own work has been marked by an inventive, attentive reworking of twentieth-century British geographical sources, such as works by Geoffrey Hutchings, Dudley Stamp and Alfred Steers.[9] Uniformbooks also includes in its publication list neglected works of modernist landscape writing, including Ronald Johnson's 1967 *The Book of the Green Man*.[10]

The Regional Book is titled in part as a plain description of its content, but also as a nod to earlier regional topographies, notably 'The Regional Books' issued by publisher Robert Hale during the 1950s, including RH Mottram's *The Broads*.[11] These guides could be unusually reflexive concerning regional definition; thus Mottram included a chapter entitled 'The Broads become Self-Conscious'. Hale also issued a 'County Books' series, but the Regional Books stretched more conventional and administrative units of geographical coverage, titles including *The Channel Shore, The Southern Marches, Sedgemoor and Avalon*, and *Holiday Lancashire. The Regional Book*, and *In the Nature of Landscape*, are, like those earlier Hale volumes, studies of regional cultural landscape. This term may be familiar as a theme, if not always as an exact phrase, from earlier modes of geographical enquiry, and from a wider extra-scholarly topographical literature, and may be revisited following the re-theorisation, across a range of disciplines, of each of its constituent parts: region, culture, landscape. What happens if region, culture and landscape, in their various ways rethought, meet again, and what kinds of geographical account might follow?

As an exercise in geographical description, *The Regional Book* also taps a geographical genealogy, the disciplinary terms of which deserve review in part for the way in which narrative possibilities are identified and literary models evoked. Perecquian elements even turn up in unlikely spots. Thus in P.W. Bryan's 1933 *Man's Adaptation of Nature: Studies of the Cultural Landscape*, a discussion of 'Almost Uninhabited or Very Thinly Peopled Areas' is illustrated by four square maps of 'house patterns', three from Surrey-Berkshire, Norfolk and Pembroke, with sparse dot patterns, and the fourth showing '9 Square Miles of Country Without a Building' (see Figure 12.3).[12]

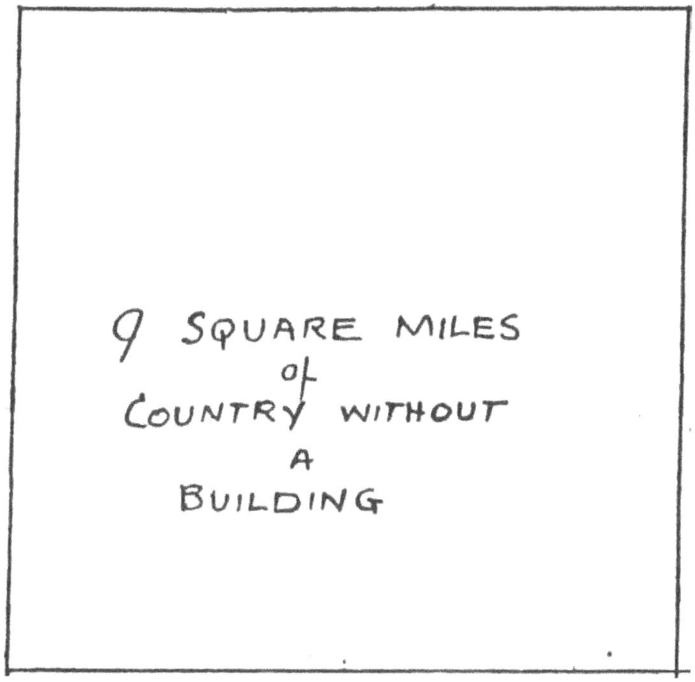

Figure 12.3 '9 Square Miles of Country Without a Building', from *Man's Adaptation of Nature: Studies of the Cultural Landscape* by P.W. Bryan (1933). Geographer Bryan illustrated his discussion of 'Thinly Peopled Areas' with four maps of 'House Patterns' in different parts of Britain. Alongside maps of Norfolk, Surrey and Pembrokeshire, this map shows inhabitation thin to the point of vanishing.

Perec's *Species of Spaces* famously begins by presenting a perfectly blank 'Map of the Ocean', derived from Lewis Carroll's 'The Hunting of the Snark', an empty square discussed elsewhere in this volume by Andrew Leak, and comparison of these mappings of blankness may be instructive. Bryan's map indicates blankness against a country background with the caption, written within the map, clarifying the unobvious. Perec's Carroll map, shown as Figure 1 in *Species of Spaces*, is referenced in the opening sentence of Perec's foreword: 'The subject of this book is not the void exactly, but rather what there is round about or inside it (cf Fig. 1).'[13] Perec's blank square may in one reading appear to indicate the void, but his 'cf' might also allude to figuration, the inside and round about. Here may simply be, after Bryan, '9 Square Miles of Ocean Without a Boat'. The ocean is, of course, hardly unmapped space, its frequent charting a response to its material variation, nautical charts aiding navigation, showing deeps and shallows, lanes and roads, hazards and buoys. As David Bellos notes, *Species of Spaces* was first published 'in covers with a wrap-around illustration of a mariner's chart', a detail from a sixteenth-century map of the coast of Guinea, oriented to set east at the top of the page.[14] The reader of the blank map held cartographic covers dense with maritime detail. As ever with Perec, jokes open space.

Two 'classic' papers are commonly cited in discussions of description in the discipline of geography, 'The principles of geographical description' (1915) by eminent US physical geographer William Morris Davis, and 'The problem of geographical description' (1962) by British historical geographer Clifford Darby. Davis set out exhaustive principles, with 'regional description' identified as the synthetic goal of geography, requiring 'extended mental equipment' and 'serious preparation', including 'training in analytical and systematic geography through all its many branches': 'pure regional geography is the final object of a geographer's efforts'.[15] Towards the end of his lengthy essay, Davis departed from his physiographic specialism to suggest what urban geographical description might entail:

> It may however be suggested that 'What does it look like?' is as good a question with which to begin the geographical study of cities as of landscapes, and that in answering such a question not only the manner in which the city lies on the land, not only the nature and advantages of its situation, should be presented, but also the general appearance of the city itself, day and night, summer and winter. Trains of passengers and of freight arriving and departing, processions of men and women on their way to work in the morning and returning home in the evening, streams of children going to and from school in forenoon and afternoon, and many other similar features, should all be included, for these are all visible responses to the fundamental influences of light and darkness, and of warmth and cold, on the rotating, revolving earth. How many additional matters should be treated in the description of a city I shall not attempt to say.[16]

Davis asserted a disciplinary boundary between a geography concerned with the present, and a geology or history concerned with the past; Darby, while acknowledging Davis's essay, argued for 'a historical ingredient in geographical description'.[17] If, however, Davis set out regional description as the summit of geography, description emerges from Darby's essay as a disciplinary problem. Indeed, whatever geography's etymological claim to 'earth writing', 'descriptive' has often been a pejorative term, denoting lack of analysis, a bland surface accounting, something less to strive for than to move beyond in a search for scientific credibility. Darby commented: 'We look in vain for – to use an old-fashioned word – a "likeness" of, say chalk downlands or clay vales or mountain uplands. What we do sometimes encounter is a kind of verbal cartography, as unattractive as it is unrevealing.'[18] Darby reflected: 'It is a humiliating experience for the geographer to try to describe even a small tract of country in such a way as to convey to the reader a true likeness of the reality. Such description falls so easily into inventory form in which one unrelated fact succeeds another monotonously.'[19]

In 1978, humanistic geographer Yi-Fu Tuan, a key figure in promoting place and 'topophilia' as core geographical themes, echoed Darby in an essay on 'Literature and geography', invoking Balzac, Eliot, Tolstoy and Forster as literary models for the geographer, against other modes of writing:

> It is ironic to note that some of the shoddier specimens of geographical description bear a superficial resemblance to French novels of the 'New Wave'. In geography texts, we have all encountered the dry itemization of streets, shopping centres, and other land use patterns as though they somehow add up to a living portrait of the city. At the other extreme, the interest in viewpoints and perspectives may be carried so far that it dissolves the external world and makes it impossible to depict a unit larger than the fragmented worlds of the committed individual actors.
>
> The model for the regional geographer of humanistic learning is neither Beckett nor Robbe-Grillet but the Victorian novelist who strives to achieve a synthesis of the subjective and the objective.[20]

Perec is also likely to have figured as a non-model for Tuan. An outlook more open to modernism might, however, find Darby's lamented 'verbal cartography', or Tuan's 'dry itemization', more intriguing than dull. Description carries other cultural possibility. As Svetlana Alpers suggested in her 1983 study of seventeenth-century Dutch painting, a complex 'art of describing' may challenge distinctions between description and narrative action: 'northern images do not disguise meaning or hide it beneath the surface but rather show that meaning by its very nature is lodged in what the eye can take in – however deceptive that might be'.[21]

Description thus gives an account of landscape in the sense of both itemisation and action proceeding, carrying a dual performative sense of, on the one hand, distanced representation – the observer set back, however closely, from a scene – and on the other inscriptive enactment – the instrument engraving, describing, a line.

Field words

In *Species of Spaces*, outlining 'practical exercises' for describing a Paris street, Perec proposed exhaustive itemisation to take description beyond expected or conventional forms of notice, stating: 'Force yourself to see more flatly.'[22] Perec's accounts themselves move between matters of fact, digression, memory and reverie, and show inventories to be neither plain nor simple. As Richard Phillips notes, writing here becomes 'a form of fieldwork practice in itself, not simply a way of reporting fieldwork findings'.[23] *Species of Spaces* also attends to the past and its presence, and mulls over the language of geography, with its clichés and nuances of scale; Perec working over words such as neighbourhood, town, country, and countries. The physical landscape is also noted, as Perec offers geologically precise counterpoint to general Situationist slogans evoking the beach beneath the paving, concluding his 'practical exercises': 'Underneath, just underneath, resuscitate the Eocene: the limestone, the marl and the soft chalk, the gypsum, the lacustrian Saint-Ouen limestone, the Beauchamp sands, the rough limestone, the Soissons sands and lignites, the plastic clay, the hard chalk.'[24]

All this, and the flatness of Broadland topography, made Perec's phrase an apt epigram for *The Regional Book*, which variously attends to pleasure craft, geological formation, road signs, freshwater biology, shops, etc. *Species of Spaces, An Attempt at Exhausting a Place in Paris*, and Perec's attention to the 'infra-ordinary' and the 'endotic', shaped a particular regard for geographical presence.[25] The infra-ordinary becomes variously rhythmic, dynamic, light, weighty, inert, with presence also shadowed by absence. For Perec, loss shapes a project to notice and mark things, however trivial or slight, while they still remain, before they pass. Perec carries a propensity, in approaching such material, to enfold the banal and lyrical, inventory and imagination, the seeming certainties of factual record and the doubts and glitches which such records prompt. Words may convey all this, and are placed in print. At the end of the section on 'The World' in *Species of Spaces*, Perec evokes 'the familiar rediscovered, a fraternal space', beyond sights of conventional grandeur and fame:

> And with these, the sense of the world's concreteness, irreducible, immediate, tangible, of something clear and closer to us: of the world, no longer as a journey having constantly to be remade, not as a race without end, a challenge having constantly to be met, not as the one pretext for a despairing acquisitiveness, nor as the illusion of a conquest, but as the rediscovery of a meaning, the perceiving that the earth is a form of writing, a *geography* of which we had forgotten that we ourselves are the authors.[26]

At the end of *The Regional Book*, there is a list of 'Recommended Reading': works in alphabetic author order, with no separation of works by genre, all in their way pertinent to the book's making; Broadland authors, landscape writers, and novelists. Perec's contemporary, Italo Calvino, is included, with the observational fables of *Mr Palomar*.[27] The *Journals* of poet R.F. Langley are there, opening up the possibilities of landscape description.[28] Wherever (geographically, intellectually) the reader comes from to the book, the list moves across sources familiar or otherwise. Perec is thus sandwiched between Pevsner and Patterson: the authoritative architectural historical inventory of Nikolaus Pevsner's Norfolk regional guide, and Yarmouth autodidact naturalist Arthur Patterson's 1905 *Nature in Eastern Norfolk*, with its lists of birds, fishes, mammals, crustacea and mollusca met around the port town.[29] Might a reader thereby move from Patterson to Perec, or Perec to Patterson, reflecting on the naturalistic eye? Patterson's *Nature in Eastern Norfolk* conveys species becoming apparent in various spaces; 'C' indicates common, 'R' rare, 'RR' rather rare:

> Chiffchaff (*Phylloscopus rufus*). – C.
>
> Used to be abundant in the Market Gardens in the month of March. Its cheery, vivacious song is, to my mind, one of the delights of early spring.[30]
>
> Pennant's Swimming Crab (*Portumnus variegatus*). – R.
>
> I have met with very few specimens of this Crab; have taken it from a Cod's maw, and on one or two occasions found examples at the tidemark.[31]
>
> Green Woodpecker (*Gecinus viridis*). – RR.
>
> Dead examples of this beautiful and harmless bird are occasionally brought to market.[32]

Greater Pipefish (*Syngnathus acus*). – C. 'Snake-fish.'

Numbers are taken in the shrimpers' nets. Shrimpers often dry and varnish these fish, placing them on their 'overmantels'.[33]

Juxtaposition with Patterson may cast Perec as a naturalist of urban space.

While *In the Nature of Landscape* was concerned with the multiple voices which have spoken of and for Broadland, including figures such as Patterson, the accounts in *The Regional Book* are mono-vocal, deliberately singular, responding in part to an assumed request to describe a landscape without reflex resort to the commentary of others. Past accounts can be read, the contrasting answers to questions acknowledged, but what follows if, after all, the plain request is for a description? This assumed request may have been prompted in part by participating in artist Simon Pope's 2007 W.G. Sebald-inspired project *The Memorial Walks*, where various commentators scrutinised paintings in Lincoln and Norwich museums, before being driven into the nearby countryside, walked over fields, and asked to describe the painting they had viewed. The Norwich walks included Broadland sites, but I participated in Lincoln, describing *Landscape with Tree* by Nicholas Van Schoor while standing in a field, somewhere near the village of Scothern.[34] The experience of description out of situ, the insistence that a detailed account of the painting, saying what you had seen and nothing more, was all that was required, may have shaped the mode of descriptive attention in *The Regional Book*.

The 44 pieces in *The Regional Book* range across the Broads' varied constitution: nature reserves, towns, riversides, marshes, seasides, waterways broad and narrow, broads landlocked and connected. Alphabetically ordered varieties practise a cross-regional democracy, with locations and objects treated in non-hierarchical fashion (though with attention to the ways in which hierarchies operate). Flat sight descriptions cut across, while also recognising, and occasionally inhabiting, forms of attention, and styles of seeing, claiming conventional authority, notably those touristic and conservationist outlooks which have shaped the narration and management of the region. To conclude this essay, seven entries from *The Regional Book* follow, considering in turn: the north shore of the estuarine Breydon Water, inland from the port and resort town of Great Yarmouth; Cockshoot Broad on the south side of the Bure valley, a nature reserve owned by the Norfolk Wildlife Trust where the broad's waters have been isolated from the main river for ecological restoration; Coltishall, a village with riverside pub and the current head of navigation on the Bure; Patterson Close, a cul-de-sac in Great Yarmouth named after Arthur Patterson; Horning, a village on the north bank of the Bure just upstream from Cockshoot, with river and banks developed for commercial, residential and leisure use; Muck Fleet, a now un-navigable stream connecting the Bure to the 'Trinity Broads' of Filby, Rollesby and Ormesby; and St Benet's Abbey, a ruined medieval abbey gatehouse by the Bure with a windmill stump built in. In setting and topic the selection indicates regional variety. If Broadland is a flat landscape, with few rises, it remains possible to see more flatly.

Breydon Water: North Shore

The north side of the estuary inland from Great Yarmouth

Yare's broadening, an estuary contained. Blue and brown commingle, flats intertidal, waders tapping. Naturalists and wildfowlers co-sponsor signage. Posts channel navigation, warning stakes submerged, dodging mud grounding.

Dyke and river conjoined or aloof by pump and sluice. One capped tower stands for older drainage. Houseboat remains stave shore mud.

Trains follow Breydon west to a divide, the Reedham branch twice more touching shore. Livestock level cross. Rolling stock moves small and flatly under sky.

Yarmouth contains, outflow deflected by two miles of towned spit. Sea blades turn as if landed. Nelson and chimneys, church and rollercoaster, line sky; and sky loops back to water colour.

Cockshoot Broad

In the Bure valley between Horning and Ranworth, a broad isolated from the main river

No boat to Horning Ferry inn, across the Bure from the marsh road end. Tantalising lights of an evening. Talk crosses water on still days. The southern bank makes other sound; angling shufflings, leaves and calls. Moored craft clunk piling on passing wash.

A five minute path finds another mooring, at Cockshoot Dike. A boardwalk bridges and tracks, to Cockshoot Broad, a hide giving on water for lilies and birds. Loops take in carr.

Notice the water. The footbridge crosses a blockage, river water cloudy, dyke and broad clear. Biomanipulative, mechanical; algae chomped, mud pumped. Boats barred. Plant life viewed in confinements. On flows the river's obscurity.

Coltishall

A large village at the head of navigation on the Bure

Going up the Bure as far as can be gone. Pass properties of substance, view the Rising Sun in the west. Navigation's social head. A staithe stretches out to wait. Common grass invites rest and play. Sitters water-gaze to an unbuilt bank. Things gather to a picture by a B-road.

Upstream, backwaters bend right forked to a navigational end. Twenty years ago, lingering disuse made an old painting from these parts, all tree banks, leans-to and wood wrinkles. Now newer gates lock neat closure.

Great Yarmouth: Patterson Close

A cul-de-sac in Great Yarmouth

The sign marks the common haunt of residents. The footbridge from Vauxhall and a main road crossing finds it, the river and Breydon not far. Patterson Close, for Arthur, autodidact naturalist, observer of things common and strange.

White capitals on green, with white trim, seven bolts between letters and trim top and bottom. Signs fixed each side of two grey two foot metal posts. Paint peeled to rust at bases. Looking from the yellow-lined gutter, a lean left of five degrees. Variation in levels of sign and post top suggests barging, human or vehicle, rather than sinking. Verge grass worn around the left post, pavement feet straying. On the left post, below the sign, a sticker for dog clean-up. A lamppost three feet from the right post, perpendicular: choice of facilities. Canine visits likely. Spiders web between metal; two signs make a sheltered trap. Passerines land at a pinch.

Horning

A village on the Bure

Upstream from the Ferry Inn to the west end, northern banks are well appointed. Property as substantial as can be, hard by water, looking across to trees, south bank carr. Public space intrudes awhile at a sharp bend, the Swan Inn and staithe, small grass and moorings.

Parked up, a paddle boat. Cruises leave for Ranworth, spring through fall, incongruous platform for spying wet woodland. Light refreshment and waterborne licence, Mississippi-on-Bure. Jazz swings, a sailor tacks away. Loons display in bobbing wash, blithe to ragtime. A local habitation, use multiple, indifference virtuous.

Muck Fleet

The formerly navigable waterway connecting the Bure and Filby Broad

Off the A1064 along the 'New Road', not on the 1910 map but there by 1932, running straight to Stokesby with one bend, over Bure marshes grazed and cropped. You might miss the Muck Fleet. White painted metal railings mark a bridge, the road barely rising over something once sailed.

One hundred years an ex-navigation; to think boats came this way, making for the Trinity Broads, now out of circulation. Above the bridge, a sluice backs a pool, weed green. Below the bridge, plant life overgrows. Railing signs state Canoeing Prohibited; somebody must have tried, injunctions warning the intrepid. A minor road crosses a dyke, road navigating over river.

St Benet's Abbey

The remains of a medieval abbey on the Bure, between the mouths of the Ant and Thurne

Leave tarmac at Shangri La and bump across the marsh. Or moor up on the Bure, by hints of bank flint. On a low rise, abbey remains.

Low banks mark major structures, Benedictine livings to tower over the flat, commanding Ant, Bure and Thurne, demanding fish and turf, carving future broads. Surrounding small heights could not but see. The newer church stamps a cross on the rise, 20 wooden feet of claim. PEACE de-ruins atmosphere. A bishop is still an abbot.

One gatehouse arch, brick mill stump conjoined. Old painter-haunted. Tufty grass on masonry jags. Lion and warrior weathered, France and England worn. Names etch the gate, hearts of old love scratched.

Over a stile, under Gothic span, to the stump door. Enter to a brick-circled sky. Eyes bright for cloud observance: scud, glide, procession. Sharper and duller from shifts beyond; whites to greys, shiny blues, rare bright blacks. Stiff-necked reverence of weather. Exit in transfigured light.

Notes

1. Matless, *The Regional Book*, 28.
2. Perec, *Species of Spaces*, 51.
3. Perec, *Species of Spaces*, 50.

4. Matless, 'Original Theories', 354–78; Matless, *In the Nature of Landscape*, chapter 2.
5. Dodd, *On the Broads*. On Dodd, and the 'discovery' of the region for tourism, see Matless, *In the Nature of Landscape*; Clarke, *The Broads in Print*.
6. Matless, 'Describing Landscape', 72–82.
7. Matless, *In the Nature of Landscape*.
8. Matless, 'Writing Regional Cultural Landscape', 9–25.
9. Sackett, *Englshpublshing*; Sackett, *The True Line*.
10. Johnson, *The Book of the Green Man*.
11. Mottram, *The Broads*.
12. Bryan, *Man's Adaptation of Nature*, 141.
13. Perec, *Species of Spaces*, 5. The 'Bellman's Speech' in Carroll's poem presents a map representing the sea as a 'perfect and absolute blank'.
14. Bellos, *Georges Perec*, 532.
15. Davis, 'The Principles', 61–105; quotations from pages 64, 92, 93 and 62 respectively.
16. Davis, 'The Principles', 98.
17. Darby, 'The Problem', 1–14; quotation from page 12.
18. Darby, 'The Problem', 1.
19. Darby, 'The Problem', 2.
20. Tuan, 'Literature and geography', 194–206; quotation page 204–5.
21. Alpers, *The Art of Describing*, xxiv.
22. Perec, *Species of Spaces*, 51.
23. Phillips, 'Georges Perec's Experimental Fieldwork', 171–91; quotation from page 185.
24. Perec, *Species of Spaces*, 54.
25. Perec, *An Attempt*. Extracts from *L'Infra-ordinaire*, a collection first published in 1989, of pieces issued between 1973 and 1981, are included in Perec, *Species of Spaces*, 203–45.
26. Perec, *Species of Spaces*, 79.
27. Calvino, *Mr Palomar*.
28. Langley, *Journals*.
29. Pevsner and Wilson, *Norfolk I*. Patterson, *Nature*.
30. Patterson, *Nature*, 117.
31. Patterson, *Nature*, 328.
32. Patterson, *Nature*, 152.
33. Patterson, *Nature*, 304.
34. Pope, *The Memorial Walks*. At the time of writing the field recording retains an online presence behind painting number four at: http://www.waterlog.fvu.co.uk/simonpope/ (accessed 5 February 2018).

Bibliography

Alpers, Svetlana. *The Art of Describing: Dutch Art in the Seventeenth Century*. London: John Murray, 1983.

Bellos, David. *Georges Perec: A Life in Words*. London: Harvill, 1995.

Bryan, P.W. *Man's Adaptation of Nature*. London: University of London Press, 1933.

Calvino, Italo. *Mr Palomar*, translated by William Weaver. London: Secker and Warburg, 1985.

Clarke, David. *The Broads in Print: The Days of Discovery: Early 1800s to 1920*. Norwich: Joy and David Clarke, 2010.

Darby, H.C. 'The Problem of Geographical Description', *Transactions and Papers (Institute of British Geographers)* 30 (1962): 1–14.

Davis, W.M. 'The Principles of Geographical Description', *Annals of the Association of American Geographers* 5 (1915): 61–105.

Dodd, Anna Bowman. *On the Broads*. London: Macmillan, 1896.

Johnson, Ronald. *The Book of the Green Man*. Axminster: Uniformbooks, 2015.

Langley, R.F. *Journals*. Exeter: Shearsman Books, 2006.

Matless, David. 'Original Theories: Science and the Currency of the Local', *Cultural Geographies* 10, no. 3 (2003): 354–78.

Matless, David. 'Describing Landscape: Regional Sites', *Performance Research* 15, no. 4 (2010): 72–82.
Matless, David. *In the Nature of Landscape: Cultural Geography on the Norfolk Broads*. Chichester: Wiley-Blackwell, 2014.
Matless, David. *The Regional Book*. Axminster: Uniformbooks, 2015.
Matless, David. 'Writing Regional Cultural Landscape: Cultural Geography on the Norfolk Broads'. In *Reanimating Regions: Culture, Politics, and Performance*, edited by James Riding and Martin Jones, 9–25. London: Routledge, 2017.
Mottram, R.H. *The Broads*. London: Robert Hale, 1952.
Patterson, Arthur H. *Nature in Eastern Norfolk*. London: Methuen, 1905.
Perec, Georges. *Species of Spaces and Other Pieces*, edited and translated by John Sturrock. London: Penguin Books, 1997.
Perec, Georges. *An Attempt at Exhausting a Place in Paris*, translated by Marc Lowenthal. Cambridge, MA: Wakefield Press, 2010.
Pevsner, Nikolaus and Bill Wilson. *The Buildings of England: Norfolk I: Norwich and North-East*. New Haven: Yale University Press, 2002.
Phillips, Richard. 'Georges Perec's Experimental Fieldwork: Perecquian Fieldwork', *Social and Cultural Geography* 19, no. 2 (2018): 171–91.
Pope, Simon. *The Memorial Walks*. London: Film and Video Umbrella, 2008.
Sackett, Colin. *Englshpublshing: Writing and Readings, 1991–2002*. Exeter: Spacex, 2004.
Sackett, Colin, ed. *The True Line: The Landscape Diagrams of Geoffrey Hutchings*. Axminster: Colin Sackett, 2006.
Tuan, Yi-Fu. 'Literature and Geography: Implications for Geographical Research'. In *Humanistic Geography: Prospects and Problems*, edited by David Ley and Marwyn S. Samuels, 194–206. London: Croom Helm, 1978.

13 Endotic Englishness: Meades, Perec and the everyday curiosities of place

Daryl Martin

By reading Georges Perec alongside another post-war writer with whom he has affinities – Jonathan Meades – this chapter brings 'everyday curiosities' into focus. These curiosities, which both Perec and Meades exemplify and inspire, revolve around memory, materiality and place – interconnected themes that are illustrated and unpacked in the course of this chapter. Meades is a writer whose work since the 1980s has encompassed novels, short stories, food writing and architectural criticism for literary journals and British broadsheet newspapers. Since the 1990s, he has been best known for his sequence of BBC film essays, primarily on architecture. These films avoid the clichés of much mainstream arts broadcasting and instead offer visually inventive commentaries on built environments and their cultural histories. The originality of his approach across media, and the variety of forms in which he contributes creative and robust critiques of architecture and its orthodoxies, indicate the ease with which Meades crosses intellectual traditions. The scope and span of Meades's interests, I will argue in this chapter, share the inter-disciplinary reach of Perec's work,[1] and similarly illustrate the value of adopting a curiosity-driven approach to our everyday materialities and landscapes,[2] in order to re-animate our understanding of them.

Meades and Perec make for an odd couple, at first sight. Their writings cover different geographies and have different affects – their work is temperamentally dissimilar, with nothing in Perec's *oeuvre* matching the abrasiveness of Meades's early novels and stories.[3] And yet, Meades's ongoing interests in dissecting conventional understandings of Englishness in its many varieties, and topography more generally, makes for an intriguing point of comparison with some of Perec's literary and documentary strategies. By suggesting a connection between the two writers, I do not wish to claim a sustained influence on Meades by Perec; although Meades has read Perec, there are no substantive grounds for making such a strong claim.[4] In interviews, Meades has professed the influence of figures associated with the 'nouveau roman', especially Alain Robbe-Grillet,[5] and writers such as Michel Tournier,[6] rather than pointing to Perec or other members of the Oulipo group. There may well be writers who have inspired both Meades and Perec, but this chapter does not embark on a genealogy of their common literary reference points. Rather, I want to place their works into dialogue with each other in order to show how both writers use similar techniques for rendering a sense of place, and describing the materialities that accumulate to compose a sense of historical time. Their works argue that moments of cultural memory should be sought within the fragments of everyday material cultures, rather than the extraordinary events that bolster glossed-over narratives of particular places. At root, Meades and Perec act as advocates for retaining a 'space for curiosity' in how we describe, imagine and interpret our social worlds.[7]

I begin by drawing on examples within both writers' work that show the inter-relatedness of individual memories and cultural histories, and reflect on the unreliability of authorship in autobiographical writing. Then, I move on to compare how their work treats the role of everyday materialities, or the stuff of material culture,[8] in the shaping of our understandings of place. Finally, I suggest an affinity between both writers in their delight in banal landscapes: for both Meades and Perec, ostensibly boring places are valuable in helping us to look at our social worlds more precisely, with greater curiosity and understanding. Throughout the chapter, I will draw from Meades's recent memoir *An Encyclopaedia of Myself* and his landscape photography collection *Pidgin Snaps*. I will read these alongside Perec's varied writings on space, memory and the anthropology of everyday materialities, in order to locate resonances between these apparently unrelated writers.

Memory

An Encyclopaedia of Myself is a memoir of post-war life in Wiltshire which is limited to the first two decades of Meades's life. In offering a deeply textured sense of place inscribed through the micro-memories and embodied perspectives of a child, Meades avoids any tendency to neatly subsume the detail of events and spaces within an over-arching narrative trajectory. In her review of the book, Bee Wilson suggests that Meades's memoir is 'not so much an autobiography as a series of detailed inventories of English provincial life in the 1950s' and that, despite its title, 'this is not an encyclopedia of Meades himself so much as of a particular people and its strange and complicated value system'.[9] Meades's eye for the particularities and vanities of provincial England at the time is sharp; we get eight chapters in his memoir devoted to the 'non-family army majors of his locale' that tell us little of Meades's upbringing but rather more about their own humdrum routines. The effect of such excessive description of individuals marginal to the experience of Meades as a child is not to further any narrative line. The overall effect of such dense character detail is to disrupt narrative development and, instead, conjure up a mood rather than conform to biographical conventions. The evocation of an atmosphere rather than a narrative line in Meades's memoir is also achieved through an encyclopedic structure, with the chapters arranged in alphabetical order, abandoning the typical trajectories of biographical genres.

The fallibility and inconstancy of memory is a theme shared between Meades – who writes that his 'earliest memory is loitering in False Memory Lane',[10] within a chapter devoted to multiple first memories – and Perec, who acknowledged that his autobiographical book on cultural memory, *I remember*, was 'stuffed with mistakes'.[11] In its subtle epigraph – 'Nothing wilfully invented. Memory invents unbidden'[12] – Meades recalls the sincere unreliability of the author and subverts the misery memoir tradition through his borrowing, then disavowal, of its major tropes. The unreliable author, constrained by the contingencies of subjective recall, is also a feature found in Perec's *W, or The Memory of Childhood*, a book which frustrates typical expectations of childhood memoirs.[13] In the preface to the Vintage edition of this book, Perec identifies the centrality of remembrance, and its failures, to literary practice itself, locating his autobiography as resting on 'the *points of suspension* on which the broken threads of childhood and the web of writing are caught'.[14] The falsity of memory in these works is also indicative of a common ludic sensibility and writing strategies that frustrate formulaic genre norms. Like his television essays, which subvert expectations of how documentary films should be structured, Meades's memoir shares with Perec a systematically playful approach. The chapter titles are red herrings, spurs to a discombobulated rendering of the past: so, the opening chapter 'Abuser, Sexual' indicates only that the younger Meades was *not* subject to abuse (and there then follows a list of various paedophile stereotypes who did *not* subject him to abuse). We have lists by Meades not only of names from his youth, but also of names that he did *not* encounter in his youth:

> Why were people called Salmon, Pike, Gudgeon, Whiting, Chubb, Grayling, Roach, Haddock, Spratt, Bass? But not Tench, Minnow, Eel, Lamprey, Perch, Carp, Huss, Plaice [...]
>
> Why were people called Hill, Vale, Field, Wood, Ford, Rivers (always plural), Bridge, Brook, Park, Street? But not Road, Track, Path, Stream, Ditch, Garden, Copse, Canal.[15]

For Meades the younger (and the older writer), these are the idiosyncrasies of English culture that pique his curiosity; this curiosity forms the basis for his account of his youth, rather than a need to present a neat narrative of his family history. The literary playfulness continues further: Meades inserts a faux indexing system of organisation, which mirrors Perec's use of indexes as 'anti-indexes' in a book such as *I Remember*, in order to 'make plain not the neat orderliness, but the unending messiness of life itself'.[16] As David Bellos notes, the purpose in Perec's somewhat estranged and erratic presentation of the past in *I Remember* was 'not to give a documentary history of the popular culture of his teenage years, but to give an honest and authentic map of his *memory* of those years'[17] – errors, fiction and all. Such purpose is similarly present in *An Encyclopaedia of Myself*: in the chapter 'No food, future food', Meades presents a roll-call of forgotten food combinations and flavours which echoes Perec's 'repeat-formula' in *I Remember*,[18] with the recurring phrase 'I would miss' followed by further detail of his mother's, father's and friends' cooking. Such passages corroborate Wilson's description of the book as 'an attempt to pin down what can be recollected of an obsolete way of life before it disappears entirely'.[19] As I will show in the next section, more often than not, Meades's evocation of this time and place is most powerfully mediated through references to popular culture, its everyday expressions and materialities.

Materialities

Meades's memoir is an account in which we learn about many personal events in the first two decades of his life, with experiences of school, unjust accusations of shop-lifting and early sexual adventures recounted – maggots and all.[20] We are party to intimate information about family members, including extra-marital affairs. Nevertheless, although we receive such detail, far more is understood about Meades's family through the description of the types of foods they cooked, how they dressed, and so on. We understand Meades's father more fully through the detail of his attitudes to cheeses and curries[21] than we do through information about his career as a biscuit salesman. Similarly, our knowledge of his mother is only slimly constituted through details of her teaching work, and far more through the litany of the types of meals, indigenous to English life, made by her throughout the 1950s, until changing fashions introduced new packaged foods.[22] To evidence this changing food culture, and to much the same effect as Perec's descriptive strategies in his early novel *Things*,[23] Meades provides painstaking lists of these new branded goods, as in the 'Period product inventory' of his nearest shop, which begins with:

> Weston's Wagon Wheels; Nestle's segmental chocolate bars with green mint filling and green wrappers; Fry's segmental chocolate bars with white mint filling and navy wrappers; Fry's Turkish Delight; Crosse and Blackwell Russian Salad; Trex; Robinson's Lemon Barley Water; Kia-Ora (which meant good health – it was everyone's single word of Maori); Walls' disgusting pork sausages; Millers' even more disgusting pork pies […] bottled sauces – A.1., HP, OK, Daddies, Heinz Salad Cream and ketchup […] Rowntree's Fruit Gums (which caused mouth ulcers) and Fruit Pastilles (which didn't) […][24]

And so the list goes on, spread over two pages. Such thorough detail situates the child and his curiosities in tension with his elders. So, if we get to know of his father through his opinions on particular cheeses, then relatedly we gain a keener sense of generational change through Meades's own sheepish admission of a fondness for processed cheese and how he 'succumbed, shamefully, to Primula, Dairylea triangles, citric Philadelphia, Huntley and Palmers cheese footballs' as a boy.[25] In many ways, Meades's book is an essay in what David Matless has termed the 'historical complexity of relationships between Englishness and the modern'.[26] This underlying strain runs throughout the book, whether in the frequent discussions of cars at that time, changing fashions in clothing and music, or the wonderfully observed discussion of the Mistral typeface, a French font smuggled into provincial newsagents because of its use in the Playfair cricketing magazine.[27]

The effects of Meades's frequent lists that are meticulous in their description of food, clothing and the materialities of other consumer goods are similar to the uniform enumeration of French popular culture in Perec's

I Remember. In his comments on Perec's book, Howard Becker notes the representational potency of unembellished lists that lack any explication of their content.[28] Perec's flat descriptions of salvaged cultural references all add up to a 'benevolent project'[29] that itemises the France of his youth at a time when it was opening to imported goods and trends, among more indigenous names and brands. For Michael Sheringham, *I Remember* is central to unravelling the problematic of the everyday, where the 'memories which truly render the "tissu du quotidien" ... cannot be purely personal (what happened to me) or factual (what happened to be the case)'.[30] Rather, the function of memory in tracing the everyday is less tied to questions of accuracy and more to the communication of common experience. Perec himself described the book as like a trampoline: to fiction, to something akin to nostalgia and 'to a kind of sympathy'.[31] This intriguing suggestion of sympathetic writing, tied to the sensation of nostalgia and the fictive documenting of the past, is found again in another interview, where Perec explains the book is 'in sympathy with its readers', because it 'starts out from a common memory'.[32] This is, Becker suggests, how an ethnographically rich portrait of a culture comes to be in Perec, through the clarity and verisimilitude of a list of ordinary things recognisable to the reader as the background of everyday habits, encounters and experiences.[33] What we glimpse in Perec and, I argue, in Meades too is an elicitation of a complete culture through the cumulative effect of the everyday and its materialities.

Through their concentrated considerations of the materialities of culture in, respectively, post-war France and 1950s England, we see in Perec and Meades a distilled and somewhat elliptical continuation of Francis Ponge's detailed focus on things as 'mute objects of expression'.[34] Through doing so, they train our curiosity for our surroundings in their materialities and mundanities. Although it would be a mistake to think of these writers as uninterested in larger historical figures and events – mentions of political figures recur throughout *I Remember*, and *An Encyclopaedia of Myself* is punctuated by furious asides about Tony Blair – there is an unmistakable kinship in both writers with quotidian geographies. It is to their shared impulses in recording banal landscapes that I turn in the next section.

Curiosities

Meades's reputation rests most recently on his television essays for the BBC, which primarily are films on architecture or, more correctly, on questions of place. As Owen Hatherley observes, Meades's work is engaged in a defamiliarisation of those spaces which we feel we know so well that we no longer see them. 'Architecture', Hatherley writes, 'isn't quite mundane enough to be made strange' and so, instead, the focus of Meades's vision is on 'Place, somewhere architecture happens'.[35] Meades himself admits to an 'obsessive preoccupation with places' and, in particular, 'British places, with their ingredients, with how and why they were made, with their power over us, with their capacity to illumine the societies that inhabit them and, above all, with the ideas that they foment'.[36] His analysis is especially astute when focused on English places and spatial cultures. Throughout *An Encyclopaedia of Myself*, Uncle Hank's and Uncle Wangle's equation of Englishness with bucolic ideals and rural landscapes is a point of contention for their nephew. Against their valorisation of the limestone cottages of the Cotswolds – an aesthetic that is hardly typical of England more generally – Meades prefers scrappier, scrubbier places that are less homogenous, less gentrified and less culturally consecrated. The Vale of Evesham is highlighted as a more effervescent landscape than the Cotswolds because it is 'an *unofficial* landscape', an under-appreciated 'accretion of intimate details, dense with incident'.[37] It is a more eccentric landscape than that of the Cotswolds, with more visible markers of industrial history in its fields and towns. This landscape is, thus, a neat illustration of Matless's arguments about the 'conjunction of Englishness and modernism' that undermines picturesque narratives of rural England.[38] In line with this, Meades argues instead for the re-evaluation of neglected places; it is telling that in his memoir he very briskly passes over the most extraordinary architectural work in Salisbury, its Cathedral, in order to devote much more space to modest and ordinary buildings of the city.

Meades's inclination towards the everyday buildings of his youth prompts comparison with Perec's own preference for the interstitial spaces of Paris over its monumental architecture, and for the insignificant over the significant.[39] This is famously stated in Perec's *An Attempt at Exhausting a Place in Paris*, his field-notes recorded in place Saint-Sulpice over three days in October 1974. In his short introduction to the book, Perec declares that he will elide the already inventoried buildings of the street in favour of 'that which is generally not taken note of, that which is not noticed, that which has no importance'.[40] The resulting slim volume of notes has been justly admired as one of his most original contributions to documenting the infra-ordinary aspects of our social worlds, an endotic approach to ethnographic investigation and the over-arching problematic of the everyday in contemporary culture.[41] Much has been written in response to Perec's attempt in this study to record meticulously the idiosyncracies of this particular place during these three days. For example, Paul Virilio likened Perec's attempt to record everything to the working of CCTV[42] and, indeed, Adair goes so far as to wonder if 'Perec, then, [is] a camera?'[43] Leak suggests we understand Perec's forensic textual descriptions of various places in their particularities as 'snapshots',[44] urging us to see them anew, and to read their infra-ordinary aspects more precisely.

Perec suggested that our reading habits resemble those of 'a pigeon pecking at the ground in search of breadcrumbs'.[45] It thus seems appropriate to turn to Meades's recent collection of landscape photography, *Pidgin Snaps*, in order to offer examples of his own attempts to document the interstitial spaces of town, city and country – in England but also elsewhere. When describing his photography, Meades equates the concentration needed to take images to that used in writing; for him, photography 'makes the (potential) photographer look more intently. You don't passively survey: you gape, you stare. And you reinvent the world, you shape it.'[46] He goes further, to argue that photographs are 'a way of making the seemingly banal fascinating and calling into question the very idea of banality. Perhaps banality doesn't exist.'[47] Meades's suggestion of photography's potential to question the idea of banality itself aligns perfectly with Perec's imperatives in his 'Approaches to What?' essay, wherein he challenges us to see differently and to 'question the habitual', its spaces and its places.[48] The unobtrusive image-making in *Pidgin Snaps* offers one example of how to answer Perec's challenge of how best to notice and represent common things and our encounters with them.

So, this image of Westminster underground station (see Figure 13.1) in London, can prompt a closer inspection of a social space frozen in time, and make us see more creatively and critically. Following Becker's advice,[49] we can use photographs to cultivate a closer practice of repeated observation, looking actively for longer periods each time we look at the image. Attending to an initial enumeration of people, colours, light, spatial depth, the geometry of architectural elements and their materialities allows us to transpose our attention to a more creative, affective and empathic register in later viewings of the picture. When we itemise what we can see in this snapshot of the underground station, the embodied movements of those moving in the space and how these are shaped by the physical features of the station, then this act of attention gives us licence to ask different types of question, related to the emotional and imaginative aspects of inhabiting spaces such as these. It stimulates our curiosity about the human experiences of this place, and the non-human networks that it enables. It allows us to move beyond interrogating how

Figure 13.1 Westminster underground station, London. An example of a space which enables the everyday movement of thousands of people, and is designed to be taken in habitually, at speed. By slowing down our visual attention and looking with more curiosity, it is possible to highlight the extraordinary social complexity of this place. Image originally published as postcard 1 in 'Pidgin Snaps'. © Jonathan Meades

this space seems to be used at this moment and to more openly question why, for whom and for what reasons it might be used in these ways. It may even prompt us to reflect on the particular version of English high-tech architectural modernism that lurks beneath the heritage stage-set spaces of Westminster above ground. Looking carefully and repeatedly at photographs results in a greater retention of the image in one's memory and, indeed, a more precise observation of what the eye might otherwise overlook.[50]

Becker's exercise in seeing puts us in mind of the fluctuating attention described in Perec's accounts of observation and imaginative recall in his texts on the infra-ordinary, whether the popular cultural recount of *I Remember* or the scrutiny of place Saint-Sulpice in the cold autumn. Behind both projects is Perec's aspiration to create work which is attuned to the materialities of social worlds and spatial cultures, and which is in sympathy with its audiences. The translator of the place Saint-Sulpice study, Marc Lowenthal, notes that Perec's attempts to 'communicate everything, to describe everything'[51] speak to an underlying generosity in his work. This tendency to communicate comprehensively is also present in Meades's work; although generosity is not a word typically associated with his writing, it should be. Again, Owen Hatherley's commentary is astute, characterising Meades's work as 'so generous, so rich and so obviously contentious' in its instinct to 'praise things, especially things that are habitually ignored'.[52] Meades focuses our attention on the overlooked, as can be seen in the image below (see Figure 13.2), which I read as his own attempt to concentrate our gaze on the everyday experiences of many Parisians and, in doing so, to question our knowledges of the habitual, the ordinary and the infra-ordinary life of the city today. Richard Phillips has argued that we best further Perec's fieldwork not through imitating his working methods exactly, but rather by exploring infra-ordinary places and apparently boring landscapes with new observational approaches.[53] Without suggesting a direct influence, I contend that Meades's snapshots share an affinity with Perec's portraits of place, given their essayistic mode, as they wander lightly between disparate sites, and with their attention on the unremarkable materialities of the everyday. Fleeting as it is, Meades's image of Paris below is entirely in keeping with Perec's curiosity about the city's ordinary places, and yet it also moves us on, beyond the familiar city, by throwing into relief the new spatial forms and cultures that we routinely overlook.

Figure 13.2 Parisian road network, to the south of the city. The infra-ordinary sites of urban experience today, often overlooked, may be found less in the culturally over-determined centres of cities, and more on their outskirts. Image originally published as postcard 44 in 'Pidgin Snaps'. © Jonathan Meades

Conclusion: emplacing curiosity

In this chapter, I have brought together two seemingly unrelated writers, Jonathan Meades and Georges Perec, in order to highlight their affinities and to consider their combined importance for contemporary notions of landscape, biography, materialities and their inter-relations. Their works can help us to animate present-day understandings of the connections between biographies and buildings, people and place, everyday encounters and what Perec termed the endotic method of anthropological observation. Their works offer forensic analyses of the geographically near – or, to follow the meaning of Perec's words, anthropologies of the inner ear – and move us within and beneath the surface of the everyday. I have outlined some shared analytical strategies that characterise their work, including their ludic approaches and writing tactics that disrupt genre conventions. The themes of memory and autobiography have been particularly important in teasing out the fecundity of their representations of places at particular cultural moments, and how these are brokered by mundane materialities and the stuff of everyday life. Separately and together, Meades and Perec perfectly illustrate Robert Walser's dictum that 'We don't need to see anything out of the ordinary. We already see so much.'[54]

Perhaps the best lesson we can take from the example of both writers relates to their ceaseless curiosity about their everyday environments and social worlds. Sheringham describes Perec's memory experiments in *I Remember* as an example of a 'curious practice' that 'both characterises and reveals the everyday'.[55] The commitment to curiosity is defined by Phillips as 'a quality of attention, with a strong visual element'.[56] As he holds up Perec's work elsewhere as an example of curiosity-driven work in its best sense,[57] I would submit Meades as an illustration too of the importance of maintaining a space for curiosity in examining cities and other geographies. In *An Encyclopaedia of Myself*, the younger Meades castigates his familiar adults for, above all other failings, their incuriosity.[58] Elsewhere, the older Meades keeps faith with his allegiance to curiosity and his commitment to the undervalued and overlooked in the built environment: the banal, he reminds us, 'is a thing of joy. Everything is fantastical if you stare at it for long enough, everything is interesting.'[59] This is an argument Perec understood well, despite the cold in October in place Saint-Sulpice, and it is an argument we do well to observe in our own field-working – not by slavishly repeating his empirical working practices per se,[60] but by responding in kind to his instruction that we look and see things anew.

Notes

1. See Lee, 'On Not Staying Put', for a discussion of inter-disciplinarity in Perec's work.
2. See Phillips, 'Space for Curiosity', for a discussion of curiosity-driven writing and research.
3. See Meades, *Filthy English*, for examples of his early short stories, and Meades, *Pompey*, for his first novel.
4. Meades, personal communication.
5. Sutcliffe, 'Interview with Jonathan Meades'.
6. Doyle, 'Brought to book'.
7. Phillips, 'Space for Curiosity'.
8. See Miller, *Stuff*, on the importance of material culture in the shaping of our personal and social experience.
9. Wilson, 'Winklepickers', 36–7.
10. Meades, *An Encyclopaedia of Myself*, 89.
11. Perec, *Species of Spaces*, 132.
12. Meades, *Encyclopaedia of Myself*.
13. Lejeune, 'W or the Memory of Childhood', 166.
14. Perec, *W*.
15. Meades, *An Encyclopaedia of Myself*, 231.
16. Perec, *I Remember*, 15.
17. Perec, *I Remember*, 12.
18. Perec, *I Remember*, 9.
19. Wilson, 'Winklepickers', 37.
20. Meades, *An Encyclopaedia of Myself*, 208.
21. Meades, *An Encyclopaedia of Myself*, 107.
22. Meades, *An Encyclopaedia of Myself*, 242–55.
23. Perec, *Things*.
24. Meades, *An Encyclopaedia of Myself*, 19–20.
25. Meades, *An Encyclopaedia of Myself*, 45–6.
26. Matless, *Landscape and Englishness*, 16.
27. Meades, *An Encyclopaedia of Myself*, 227.
28. Becker, 'Georges Perec's Experiments', 69.
29. Adair, 'The Eleventh Day', 179.
30. Sheringham, *Everyday Life*, 275.
31. Perec and Mortley, 'The Doing of Fiction', 100.
32. In Perec, *Species of Spaces*, 128.
33. Becker, 'Georges Perec's Experiments', 68.
34. See Ponge, *Mute objects of Expression*.
35. Hatherley, 'Joe, Jerry and Bomber Blair', 27.
36. Meades, *Museum without Walls*, xiii.
37. Meades, *An Encyclopaedia of Myself*, 65.
38. Matless, *Landscape and Englishness*, 15.
39. See Highmore, 'Georges Perec and the Significance of the Insignificant', for an extended discussion of this point.
40. Perec, *An Attempt*, 3.
41. See, among others, classic and recent commentaries such as Becker, 'Georges Perec's experiments'; Sheringham, *Everyday Life*; Highmore, 'Georges Perec and the Significance of the Insignificant'; Licoppe, 'An Attempt at Exhausting an Augmented Place in Paris'; Phillips, 'Georges Perec's Experimental Fieldwork'.
42. Walker and Virilio, 'Paul Virilio on Georges Perec', 17.
43. Adair, 'The Eleventh Day', 180.
44. Leak, 'Paris Created and Destroyed', 28.
45. Perec, *Species of Spaces*, 176.
46. Meades, 'Pidgin Snaps'.
47. Meades, 'Pidgin Snaps'.
48. Perec, *Species of Spaces*, 210.
49. See Becker, 'Photography and Sociology', 7.
50. See Becker, 'Photography and Sociology', 7.

51. In Perec, *An Attempt*, 50.
52. Hatherley, 'Joe, Jerry and Bomber Blair', 27.
53. See Phillips, 'Georges Perec's Experimental Fieldwork', 189.
54. Walser, *The Walk*, 28.
55. Sheringham, *Everyday Life*, 275.
56. Phillips, 'Curiosity', 158.
57. See, for example, Phillips, 'Georges Perec's Experimental Fieldwork'.
58. Meades, *An Encyclopaedia of Myself*, 232.
59. Meades, *Museum without Walls*, xiii.
60. See Phillips, 'Georges Perec's Experimental Fieldwork', 189.

Bibliography

Adair, Gilbert. 'The Eleventh Day: Perec and the Infra-Ordinary', *Review of Contemporary Fiction* 29, no. 1 (2009): 176–88.

Becker, Howard S. 'Photography and Sociology', *Studies in the Anthropology of Visual Communication* 1, no. 1 (1974): 3–26.

Becker, Howard. 'Georges Perec's Experiments in Social Description', *Ethnography* 2, no. 1 (2001): 63–76.

Doyle, Martin. 'Brought to Book: Jonathan Meades on the Trial and Execution of Tony Blair', *Irish Times*, 24 June 2014. Accessed 9 May 2019. https://www.irishtimes.com/culture/books/brought-to-book-jonathan-meades-on-the-trial-and-execution-of-tony-blair-1.1842517.

Hatherley, Owen. 'Joe, Jerry and Bomber Blair', *London Review of Books* 35, no. 5 (2013): 27–30.

Highmore, Ben. 'Georges Perec and the Significance of the Insignificant'. In *The Afterlives of Georges Perec*, edited by Rowan Wilken and Justin Clemens, 105–19. Edinburgh: Edinburgh University Press, 2017.

Leak, Andrew. 'Paris Created and Destroyed', *AA Files* 45/46 (2001): 25–31.

Lee, Joanne. 'On Not Staying Put: Georges Perec's "Inter(in)disciplinarity" as an Approach to Research', *Literary Geographies* 3, no. 1 (2017): 11–26.

Lejeune, Philippe. 'W or The Memory of Childhood', *Review of Contemporary Fiction* 29, no. 1 (2009): 163–75.

Licoppe, Christian. '"An Attempt at Exhausting an Augmented Place in Paris": Georges Perec, Observer-Writer of Urban Life, as a Mobile Locative Media User'. In *The Afterlives of Georges Perec*, edited by Rowan Wilken and Justin Clemens, 205–25. Edinburgh: Edinburgh University Press, 2017.

Matless, David. *Landscape and Englishness*. 2nd ed. London: Reaktion Books, 2016.

Meades, Jonathan. *Filthy English*. London: Jonathan Cape, 1984.

Meades, Jonathan. *Pompey*. London: Jonathan Cape, 1993.

Meades, Jonathan. *Museum without Walls*. London: Unbound, 2012.

Meades, Jonathan. *Pidgin Snaps*. London: Unbound, 2013.

Meades, Jonathan. 'Pidgin Snaps – A Boxette'. Unbound, November 2013. Accessed 9 May 2019. https://unbound.com/books/pidgin-snaps/.

Meades, Jonathan. *An Encyclopaedia of Myself*. London: Fourth Estate, 2014.

Miller, Daniel. *Stuff*. Cambridge: Polity Press, 2010.

Perec, Georges. *Things: A Story of the Sixties / A Man Asleep*. Boston: David R. Godine, 1990.

Perec, Georges. *Species of Spaces and Other Pieces*, edited and translated by John Sturrock. London: Penguin Books, 1999.

Perec, Georges. *An Attempt at Exhausting a Place in Paris*, translated by Marc Lowenthal. Cambridge, MA: Wakefield Press, 2010.

Perec, Georges. *W, or The Memory of Childhood*, translated by David Bellos. London: Vintage Books, 2011.

Perec, Georges. *I Remember*, translated by Philip Terry. Boston: David R. Godine, 2014.

Perec, Georges and Kaye Mortley. 'The Doing of Fiction', *Review of Contemporary Fiction* 29, no. 1 (2009): 94–101.

Phillips, Richard. 'Space for Curiosity', *Progress in Human Geography* 38, no. 4 (2014): 493–512.

Phillips, Richard. 'Curiosity: Care, Virtue and Pleasure in Uncovering the New', *Theory, Culture and Society* 32, no. 3 (2015): 149–61.

Phillips, Richard. 'Georges Perec's Experimental Fieldwork: Perecquian Fieldwork', *Social and Cultural Geography* 19, no. 2 (2018): 171–91.

Ponge, Francis. *Mute Objects of Expression*, translated by Lee Fahnestock. New York: Archipelago Books, 2008.

Sheringham, Michael. *Everyday Life: Theories and Practices from Surrealism to the Present*. Oxford: Oxford University Press, 2006.

Sutcliffe, Jamie. 'Interview with Jonathan Meades', *The White Review*, March 2015. Accessed 9 May 2019. http://www.thewhitereview.org/feature/interview-with-jonathan-meades/.

Walker, Enrique and Paul Virilio. 'Paul Virilio on George Perec', *AA Files* 45/46 (2001): 15–18.

Walser, Robert. *The Walk*, translated by Christopher Middleton and others. London: Serpent's Tail, 2013.

Wilson, Bee. 'Winklepickers, Tinned Salmon, Hair Cream', *London Review of Books* 38, no. 14 (2016): 36–37.

14
Perecquian fieldwork: Photography and the fairground

Ian Trowell

Photographs and photography have languished on the margins of Perecquian scholarship and practice. This chapter brings them into focus, exploring the place of photography in Perec's writing and in Perecquian fieldwork, and fleshing these out through a Perecquian field project: an investigation of travelling fairgrounds.

The fairground world of speed, thrill, colour, high saccharine content, frantic movement and cacophony appears, on the surface, un-Perecquian. Richard Phillips argues that Perecquian fieldwork is primarily concerned with ordinary places.[1] Seemingly at odds with this definition, the fairground is a place of illusion, spontaneity, hedonism and polymorphous jouissance. And yet, as I argue and demonstrate in this chapter, fairgrounds (like other places within Perec's field of vision) are underpinned by codes, conventions, circumscribed actions, movements and modes of being, doing and seeing. I consider the conventional photographing of the fairground as a field in itself, flattened through the taken-for-granted of what to look at and document. A playful and experimental approach to this field of photography – developed through my own photography – enables a new reading of the field of the fairground.

I begin by situating photography as a response or final stage to fieldwork, such that it serves a purpose of 'fixing' through visual documentation the outcomes of such fieldwork. I follow this by considering the possibility of using photography to record not only the seen but also the seeing of fieldwork. I then propose a radical shift by thinking of photography as a space in itself, a space of rules and conventions, and applying a Perecquian shift to this space, such that the potential original fieldwork is further disrupted, to open new possibilities of understanding and interpretation. This proposed relationship between Perecquian fieldwork and photography is developed through three phases of enquiry: firstly, a historical consideration of Perec's use of photography (with particular regard to the *Lieux* project, Perec's extensive, playful and obscurely systematic study of Paris); secondly, a critical overview of recent self-identifying Perecquian fieldwork that calls upon photography; and thirdly, an introduction to theories and practices around challenging the understanding and undertaking of photography.

Described as a 'paratactic litany' reciting experience rather than imparting knowledge,[2] much of Perec's fieldwork writing evokes strong images of determinate and material objects as opposed to indeterminate and interiorised thoughts, bringing the work into a 'visual economy'.[3] For example, his recording of time passing refers to a stated moment – 'it is five past two' – instilling in the reader an image of a watch face or the swipe of a screen of a mobile phone to reveal a digital display of 14:05.[4] In similar visual invitations, Perec details the discrete objects associated with nostalgic bus travel,[5] discusses weather through the visual index of gathering clouds[6] and documents his own project workflow with a description of envelopes being sealed with wax.[7]

Perec's work around seeing more flatly and questioning the habitual is framed in terms of the actions of looking, observing, seeing, noticing and acknowledging. These are terms often used interchangeably or demarcated around a doing or not doing, in turn generating descriptive terms such as the over-looked, or value-laden terms such as the quality of being noteworthy.[8] Thus, a first task is to set out these terms as a processual ontology or observational chain that forms a flow of Perecquian actions of the visual and an associated set of residual descriptions of visual failures (see Table 14.1). The action of photographing (or the decision to not photograph) is not so easily inserted into the observational chain, as it needs to be registered as both intent and action.[9] For fieldwork purposes, we can initially consider the photograph as an epiphenomenal documentary response to the output of the process of seeing through the fieldwork, and so intent and action coincide at the conclusion of the chain. However, outside of fieldwork, a place may also be approached with the primary intention of taking a photograph and so the photographic intent, registered at the start of the chain, impacts down the chain.

This observational chain provides a supporting framework for a first typology of how Perecquian fieldwork and photography work together: techniques are applied throughout the forward flow of the chain to see more flatly or to embrace the infra-ordinary, and the results of this

Table 14.1 Observational chain for Perecquian fieldwork. © Ian Trowell

Mode of visibility	Mode of exclusion	Notes
In sight through conscious framing	Ignored, hidden, outside the frame	Banished aspects and the accidentally invisible
Seen or noticed	Unseen or unnoticed	Hindered or discouraged by trace nature within a complex whole
Acknowledged in the moment	Overlooked	Knowingly seen but then chosen not to be seen
Acknowledged beyond the moment	Forgotten	Knowingly seen but later chosen not to be seen
Recorded and recalled (written, verbal, visual)	Unremarked	The archived visual document haunts the chain of excluded aspects

seeing are recorded within an accepted understanding of photography (the photographic object or event is identified, composed within the viewfinder, captured and then collated and presented as part of a browsable documentation). Here, the photograph has a parallel evolution and function to making a written note. For the photograph itself this is as an a priori process, in that the object photographed is pre-determined by a way of looking and seeing. A second typology is defined by attempts to visually record the stages of the chain, rather than the eventual results of those processes. This more complex task is not to be confused with the involvement of a third party with photographic intent, effectively stepping outside the frame of activity of observational fieldwork to render the researcher as photographic object. Instead, the aim is the researcher subject (or a possible third-party photographer in a shadow capacity) recording their own seeing *in media res*. Fixing this action of observing is in itself problematical, as the camera has no sense of cognition nor direct link to our own cognitive movement through the observational chain.[10] This method of attempting to observe-the-observing is a feedback iteration of the chain, shifting the ground of potential photographic objects. A third typology is also possible as a significantly more radical step, anticipating a break with photography in terms of methodological conventions and the visual and presentational consensus that is partially glimpsed in the second typology. This is framed as a Perecquian modelling of the infra-ordinary and taken-for-granted of photography itself – acknowledging and questioning rote actions about the purpose of photography fixing the seen and applying consensus rules about how photographs arise. It is not a feedback iteration of the chain as either a whole or selective parts, but a disruptive lateral move to new, as yet undetermined, processes. This switch at the ontological rather than ontic level destabilises photography and opens a new field for Perecquian manoeuvres.

Perec, photography and the *Lieux* project

Firstly I focus on Perec's use (or non-use) of photography in his fieldwork, particularly the *Lieux* project. This project focused on 12 locations in Paris and utilised a complex mathematical constraint to create a 12-year sequence of paired reports generated from fieldwork and memory. Though the project was eventually abandoned, it is considered to be a rich source of Perec's fieldwork methodology. A special issue of the journal *AA Files* (45/46 in 2001) from the Architectural Association is devoted to Perec, and material from the *Lieux* project forms a central corpus. The journal includes photographs commissioned at the time by Perec, as well as photographs created and applied post-hoc to supplement the journal's graphic layout. It is necessary to comment on both aspects.

It is quickly revealed that the contemporaneous use of photography on a minor selection of outings in the *Lieux* project represented an out-of-character and unsteady practice for Perec. He refers to the venture (and employment of photographers Christine Lipinska and Pierre Getzler in summer 1970) as follows:

> On several occasions, I have got a man or woman photographer friend to go with me to the places I was describing who, either freely, or as indicated by me, took photographs that I then slipped, without looking at them (with a single exception), into the corresponding envelopes.[11]

This statement predominantly buttresses Perec's meticulous system of constraints as a subset of the wider complex regime of restraints defining the project whole, but also serves to establish the presence of companion photographers. The ambiguity and trepidation around photography is indicated by Getzler, a longstanding colleague of Perec from the times of the group La Ligne Générale, who recalls that 'I believe that he didn't really know what he wanted. He had his idea, which was rather literary, textual. The image for him is firstly a source of words, of word plays.'[12] Getzler's collaboration with Perec is recorded in the fieldworking circumstances of both moving through an area (making observations and notes) and a stationary staking out to observe a space, giving us a fuller insight into their thinking and actions. In the first example, while exploring rue Vilin, Getzler appears to take matters into his own hands:

> He had asked me to take the facades, but I didn't do what Christine Lipinska did, later, when she photographed facades for him where the openings had been bricked up. I never positioned myself front on, but, how shall I put it [...] so that I could imagine the movement of the city.[13]

Referring back to my typologies of photography, the above quote reveals two things: firstly, that Perec himself favoured a simple first typology, an a priori approach to visually document the results of the fieldwork (that Lipinska duly obliged with); secondly, that Getzler strove for the second typology, to document the actions of seeing. The photographs reproduced in the article fluctuate between a position behind Perec (either sharing his view or showing Perec looking at something outside the frame of the final photograph) and a seeing-in-process view characterised by a lop-sided framing and surreptitious quality. Here Getzler, avoiding the potential photographic intent in the frame outside the fieldwork, attempts to share the eyes of Perec, and documents those eyes with his camera. The rhythm is broken with a disconcerting photograph of Perec in which he has turned round and apparently sussed he is being photographed, flanked (but at a distance) by two elderly females (presumably being observed by Perec) who also confront the photographer with a resolute stare. This playful photograph implies the amplification of the influence of the observer on the observed when a camera is wielded.

The stake-out photographs taken in place Saint-Sulpice bypass this hindrance, and Getzler duplicates the invisibility-at-a-distance by taking a table near to Perec but purposely introducing obstructive elements such as pillars and decorative foliage, becoming Perecquian (a Perec clone) to observe/photograph Perec. Getzler's photographs of the scene observed by Perec beyond the windows of the café show both the seen (first typology) and seeing (second typology).[14] Getzler, however, hints at something more, an important divergence of possibilities between making notes and taking photographs:

> I therefore interpreted it using my vision of the space at that time: to show the movement, the displacement, but not like he did, in his notebooks, having the referent to mind, which is not always obvious in his descriptions [...] When he writes 'a car goes by', he

> doesn't say in relation to what. He can't describe, for example, the passage of a van in front of a shop on the other side of the road by saying that it hides it, then that a word appears behind it. For me the feeling of the space comes from the perception of a silhouette which hides something else, which modifies the triangulation, which structures the space differently.[15]

Here Getzler is almost adumbrating the important twin works from Gilles Deleuze that use cinema as a cipher for philosophy, extending the mix from time and movement (in the moving image) to seeing, describing in words, and recording with a still image. The photograph apparently captures everything, forestalling and surpassing the work of seeing flatly and writing notes. Getzler pinpoints a compromise or tension, and this tension troubles Perecquian photography in more recent projects.

Perecquian photography after Perec

Prioritising photography undertaken during and in support of self-identifying Perecquian fieldwork, I start with the visual material accompanying Perec's own work in the special issue of *AA Files*. Andrew Leak translates four texts from *Lieux* and these are presented as stylised articles to resemble typed-out fieldwork notes. Each selection is book-ended by full-page photographs taken by Cristobal Palma, with two photographs repeated for the front and back covers. A visual trope is evident in the photography, a stylised view that frames the ubiquitous street taken from a low angle such that the surface of the road occupies half of the picture space. The photographs are presented as aged, seemingly well-thumbed archival objects, attempting to be contemporaneous to the writing but immediately betrayed by the modernity of the hub-caps of the parked cars (you cannot fool a Perecquian observer). Combinations of motifs include an offset vanishing point formed by the street and flanked by street furniture or vehicles, the inclusion of pedestrian crossing markings geometrically stretched by the low camera angle, and motion indicated by the blur of vehicles and feet on crossings.[16] As they do not form a direct index to any Perecquian fieldwork (from *Lieux* or otherwise), it is questionable as to what these photographs achieve aside from a metonymic role that signals a fashionable and edgy Perecquian approach.[17] They fall outside of my categorisation since they do not relate directly to fieldwork, and instead are examples of strong photographic intent. They involve not only a pre-formed imaging of the street, but a clear purpose to fit with the architectural remit of looking a certain way and embodying strong design, the quest for 'memorability as image'.[18]

Dedicated photographic fieldwork projects from the street form a large part of the *AA Files* special issue, with a notable contribution from Richard Wentworth. The artist works at the intersection of exploring urban space and photographic documentation through his ongoing photographic project *Making Do and Getting By*. His piece for *AA Files* typifies this intersection, and shifts towards my third typology of both disrupting the seeing and the conventions and consensus of photographic recording. Wentworth multiplies photographs of the surface of the urban ground, producing overhead photographs that barely shift from first image to final image, such that their collaging disorientates sense of position and sense of order. His work resembles a mash-up between the overhead surveillance techniques employed by Google and the street-view images sourced and (seemingly haphazardly) stitched together from their 9-eye 10-images-per-metre mounted cameras.[19]

In more general work the notion of the everyday and the infra-ordinary has become a dominant trope of photography, exemplified by projects such as the Caravan Gallery. While this body of work could be claimed post-hoc as a Perecquian push to discipline ourselves to regard the unnoticed, it is driven more by the creation of a fashionable aesthetic of banality to be viewed in the gallery or coffee-table volume. The cultivating and curating of the photographic banal is taken further with artists such as Thomas Ruff repurposing his jpeg trawls of the internet and Christian Boltanski with his museum and gallery presentations of banal archives and archived banality. Again, these projects fail to acknowledge the ideas of Perec and it is not their outstated intent to support an expanded understanding of either fieldwork in action or the nuanced reading of a place.

Moving beyond endless uncontextualised reams of the everyday street scene is important, and Kaji-O'Grady offers the artist Doug Rickard as a Perecquian photographer. Rickard's street is the virtual-visual everywhere of Google Street View with photographs procured 'as found'. Further, Rickard uses Perec-inspired word-games and constraints to navigate and gather resources:

> Rickard's *New American Picture* (2012) crosses Oulipian methodology with photographic social documentary. Rickard's initial search criteria was 'Martin Luther King', yielding all those streets, boulevards and parks named after the black activist, almost all of which were in poor black neighbourhoods. From Google Street View, Rickard extracted around 10,000 images. Selected images

were rephotographed, cropped and Google's proprietary markers removed in Photoshop.[20]

Perec's 'Approaches to What?', and the search for 'the rest', informs the photographic fieldwork of Gabrielle Bendiner-Viani, mapping the 'proximal, quotidian, and in-between neighborhood places'.[21] Photographs are of the second typology, recording the act of seeing, but are used to draw out the unnoticed and overlooked, effectively Perec's 'the rest'. The photograph-as-act-of-seeing extends beyond the moment of the seeing it captures, allowing it to be reconsidered – or revisited as the site-to-be-seen – as a tool to help us appreciate both 'the rest' and the process of assigning to 'the rest'. Bendiner-Viani's methodology sets this out:

> I begin by asking inhabitants to take me on 'tours' of their everyday places, later photographing the places that my 'tour guides' have taken me to and finally showing them photographs I make of their familiar sites [...] Hence how we know place through our bodies, through physically being there, is placed in conversation with a process of photographic production and reflection, exploiting photography's peculiar relationship to the real as a prompt for storytelling.[22]

There is an unstated nuance on how such photographs might function; as the aforementioned second chance to revisit the to-be-seen of the original site, or as a tangible prompt to mark our own failure to see and potentially equip us for future encounters. Echoing the dilemmas of the role of fieldwork, we acknowledge the resurfacing of Getzler's tension around the photograph forestalling and surpassing the work of seeing more flatly *right-here-right-now*. Firstly, the photograph unsettles its time of production; both the deictic time – or 'locus of utterance' – and the compressed moment of the shutter opening and the photograph forming.[23] John Berger was fascinated with the photograph defying the bounding of its apparent instantaneity, arguing that 'true content is invisible, it derives from a play not with form, but with time. [...] It isolates, preserves and presents a moment taken from a continuum.'[24] The photograph then steps outside of this time and creates new temporal regimes, the 'abduction of the object out of the world into another world, into another kind of time'.[25] The viewer of the photograph has time of their own, to pore over the frozen moment of a frozen scene, to imagine the living subjects captured in the image, possible viewers past, present and future, and the photographic object itself.[26] This substitutes the scene of fieldwork and the action-space of seeing more flatly from the physical to the mediated image. The unnoticed and overlooked can be picked out, such that 'as photography shows us more, it also shows us how much we don't see, how much ordinary seeing is blind'.[27] Here the photograph takes on a 'context between familiarity and strangeness', effectively becoming its own scene of Perecquian fieldwork.[28] Photographic theorists, however, caution against this potential eternity of deconstructive unravelling, bluntly stated by James Elkins as 'deliberate eccentricity [...] a self-consciously aberrant pensiveness [...] the tourism of the overlooked'.[29]

Photography beyond photography

As stated above, my final consideration is the radical shift by thinking of photography as a space of rules and conventions and applying a Perecquian shift to this space, to unground the thoughtfully composed or controlled instantaneity of photography. Though the examples here are a selection from many experimental projects, an outset connection to Perec is not identified in any of this work. What I consider here are pointers towards opportunities for new fieldwork.

Martha Rosler's *Passionate Signals* project, in which she records the everyday spaces and places of airports and underground stations, strives to acknowledge and understand the separation between the encountered and recorded.[30] Moreover, her photographs can be considered as doubly heterotopic: firstly, they destabilise the usually unrecorded – beyond tired representations in action films or news footage – physical space of the non-place, such as an airport lounge;[31] secondly, they destabilise the familiar visual modes of recording and re-presenting movement through everyday life by setting the camera out as if it is our actual eyes lugubriously moving along. They give the impression of the camera being separated from the photographing subject, producing wrong views of wrong places.

The unseen of the city, its exposed social structures, is explored through the unseen of the photograph for the artist Elisabeth Neudörfl, with this unseen calling into question not only the Perecquian overlooked but also the conventions of photography:

> Each photograph shows a very exclusive section of the world – spatially and temporally. The picture is clearly cropped by the frame and the exposure is only a moment in time. In spite of this spatio-temporal detail that excludes so much more than it shows, we can see things in photographs that we cannot see in our continuous perception of reality.[32]

For Neudörfl, the photograph as place-memory encourages its own ontological auto-dissolution, but other artists try to imagine things from the other side. Rutherford gives a consciousness to the camera as it creates things and events not seen, what he calls a 'something else going on' hindered by the popular conception of photography.[33] This is not Perec's assertion of 'the rest' which is photographed conventionally by Bendiner-Viani (see above), but a different 'the rest' of photography. Rutherford's work converges with the challenging 'non-philosophy' of François Laruelle, who has now proposed a 'non-photography' that hinges upon an ontological switch between the subject and object.[34]

Fairground fieldwork

My own fieldwork concerns the British travelling funfair, a historically rich and highly visual environment that has dominating characteristics: the repurposing of everyday spaces, transient and temporary occupation, the offering of strange objects (pleasure machinery, sweet and sickly foods, pulsating music and lights) brought by a community of outsiders, an enclosed space and time to act out and loosen the bindings. On the surface this is not an ordinary and everyday space, but it is also possible to gauge codes of behaviour and rituals that can be interpreted as a kind of everydayness of the pseudo-extraordinary. Furthermore, the fairground is a predominantly visual environment, drawing you in with lures and directing the flow of movement and emotion with cues, forcing you to see certain things and ignore others. In buttressing this, fairground art combines the garish colours of a fantasy world with themes and styles from everyday visual culture, and the modern fairground machine encompasses what Nye calls the 'technological sublime'.[35]

Thus, an approach towards the fairground space as a photographic object of fieldwork has to disentangle the 'obvious' lines of visual attraction and engagement that pre-situate the framing of the photograph. In addition, these photographic codes are understood as audience-specific, manipulating the time and space of the fairground itself (enthusiasts arrive before the fair is open for business to observe and photograph transport arriving and rides building up).[36] At the outset, the Perecquian photographic encounter with the fairground has to get beneath the dominant panoply of attention-grabbing surfaces that divert our eyes and our lenses, to undertake a heteromorphic disarticulation between the visually engaged and the visually recorded, to rethink photography to rethink the fairground.

Figure 14.1 acts out an over-determined Perecquian directive, seeking the letter 'A' as an inverted lipogramatic constraint and delivering a first typology photographic task that simply documents the

Figure 14.1 One form of Oulipian constraint involves either excluding or concentrating upon particular letters of the alphabet. This constraint, which Perec and his translators adopted in writing, is applied here to photography, where it leads to distinctively focused observations, as shown here in the context of the fairground. © Ian Trowell

observed. Playfully setting out to record an abundance of in-your-face signage, I am clearly within the rules of the fairground as regarding where to look, these letters painted brightly or illuminated to attract attention as part of the to-be-seen. However, isolated and presented as a grid, there emerges a connotative excess of the visual language that moves away from the function of spelling out meaningful words. This echoes W.J.T. Mitchell's concept of the unresolvable intersign in visual culture, an attempt to disrupt textuality through illegibility by 'break(ing) down the letter as the smallest graphemic unit in alphabetic writing systems, thereby introducing a literal textual illegibility', in turn creating a 'text/image in-betweenness in the illegible letter'.[37] Consequently, the combination of Perecquian fieldwork, photography and presentational arrangement reveals the regimented visual substrate of nurtured hedonism.

Once again, looking more flatly, Figure 14.2 shows a different set of 'A's, stripping back from the glare of the intersign between text and art to unearth the mundane. Here I seek out and present informational letters from catering menu boards, customer warnings, registration plates and trademarks – the pervasive output of advertising

Figure 14.2 The photographs shown here follow the same constraint as those in Figure 14.1 focusing upon the letter 'A' – but here the photographer is endeavouring to see more flatly. © Ian Trowell

and instruction manuals. Perec relished and often recycled such *Le 3e secteur* material as 'neither literary nor paraliterary'.[38] To see and acknowledge these letters meant both looking again and looking elsewhere, understanding the space of the fairground as its own figure and ground with areas either closed off with obstructions (cables, cannisters) or encouraged to be overlooked. The stimulatory excess is strictly demarcated, and encountering these muted spaces within the fairground is disorienting, sharing the surface with vomit, urine and transgressive couplings, and drawing in to fieldwork indicators of an 'evolving physical and mental state'.[39] While these photographs conform to the same criteria as Figure 14.1, classifying them as first typology, there is also an indication of change. Drawing a parallel to Deleuze's work on the movement image, such that actual movement can only ever be indicated as lying between the frames, the cognitive space *between* the grids of letters in Figures 14.1 and 14.2 indicates a looping back in the observational chain, to go back and see more flatly. In this sense the photography is second typology, indicating a movement in seeing.

Finally, there is an attempt at the third typology, to break with a visual-photographic consensus and convention, and undermine the taken-for-granted of photography itself. I am back on the authorised fairground but seeking out both the overlooked and non-photographed that hide in plain sight. While the fairground of the past involved showpeople as an important part of the spectacle, drawing your attention to themselves in order to focus attention on the shows and games on offer, the modern-day showperson blends into the background.[40] The balloon vendors (hawkers as opposed to showpeople) are engulfed by their product (see Figure 14.3), a rooted talismanic and totemic outpost. Seldom seen on the occasion as people, it is necessary to shift behind and capture the convergent forms of dress and necessitated stance and, in doing so, immediately create and capture a dynamic backdrop of radiating vinyl twine and shimmering balloons shaped and printed to a culturally commodified excess. The showpeople minding the juvenile rides (see Figure 14.4) blend into the scenery, becoming invisible and acting invisible, sharing a convergent dress, stance, posture and expression. This is not a pose of the to-be-seen or to-be-photographed, resisting the classic contrapposto and exemplifying a planimetric composition as identified by the art historian Heinrich Wölfflin. It is here where a Perecquian approach to the field of photography creates a new reading of the field itself.

Figure 14.3 Perecquian photography involves seeking out both the overlooked and non-photographed that hide in plain sight. These balloon vendors, unlike the showpeople who draw attention to themselves, are engulfed in the objects they are attempting to hawk. Their products are visible, while they are not, though Trowell's Perecquian lens brings them into the field of view. © Ian Trowell

Conclusion

In this chapter I announce an intent to visit the fairground as a fieldwork exercise. Our potential excitement is tempered when I stress that this is a Perecquian endeavour, and we must struggle amidst the visual excess to see more flatly. Things become more uncertain when I propose to bring a camera, placing an emphasis on visual documentation and calling on Perec to decentre the rules of photography and expose a taken-for-granted of fieldwork. This goes against an unreflective assumption that we can simply 'graft' photography on to Perecquian fieldwork.

Figure 14.4 Perecquian photography offers a new reading of the field. These photographs draw attention to workers who mind the juvenile rides, blending into the scenery, otherwise unseen figures in the fairground. © Ian Trowell

Perec had a rich and playful relationship with visual material in his novels and essays. Sharing similar techniques to Jorge Luis Borges, he used visual artefacts such as paintings, photographs and even jigsaws as portals into other stories to structure a Leibnizian monadology of worlds-within-worlds. However, as I show by reviewing material from the *Lieux* project, Perec was cautious and uncomfortable in introducing photography into his fieldwork. With this in mind I set out an increasingly symbiotic relationship between Perecquian fieldwork and photograph: of recording the seen, to recording the seeing itself, and to finally shift the field of photography with a Perecquian impetus. In reviewing and analysing a series of self-identifying Perecquian projects I explore how photography can be utilised in Perecquian fieldwork. With this insight gained, I encounter and engage the fairground as both a rich and vibrant visual realm and a challenging opportunity to develop Perecquian fieldwork.

Notes

1. Philips, 'Georges Perec's Experimental Fieldwork', 173.
2. Sheringham, *Everyday Life*, 265.
3. Rowe, *Popular Cultures*, 13.
4. Perec, *An Attempt*, 24.
5. Perec, 'Species of Spaces', 52.
6. Perec, 'Species of Spaces', 70.
7. Perec, 'Species of Spaces', 55.
8. Perec urges us to set about seeing 'more slowly, almost stupidly', asking of us 'Do you know how to see what's worthy of note?' (Perec, 'Species of Spaces', 50).
9. Campany, *Photography and Cinema*, 62, acknowledges an indeterminacy in describing the photograph between 'taken and made', a vacillation between document and picture. While I sidestep either term here, the photograph as an equal partner in Perecquian fieldwork embodies this vacillation.
10. The camera and photograph records the scene in total, not what the observer-researcher is making sense of, prioritising, discerning, overlooking, etc. This is emphasised when viewing scenes of overwhelming detail, confusing patterns and colours, or simple bi-stable optical illusions such as a Necker Cube. Technologies such as eye-tracking devices recording directional glances and focusing cannot convey this information.
11. Perec, 'Species of Spaces', 55.
12. Depaule and Getzler, 'A City in Words and Numbers', 124.
13. Depaule and Getzler, 'A City in Words and Numbers', 119.
14. Perec's activities at place Saint-Sulpice are documented in Sheringham, *Everyday Life,* 261–5.
15. Depaule and Getzler, 'A City in Words and Numbers', 124.
16. Perec, 'Species of Spaces', 49, indicates Perec's observation of the pedestrian crossing vernacular.
17. Ribière, 'Georges Perec's Enduring Presence in the Visual Arts', 36, states: 'The name Georges Perec has become a byword for idiosyncratic innovative art, often in relation to works that have to do with the everyday as a subject matter or the use of self-imposed rules, in which case it functions as little more than a convenient peg', while Highmore, 'Georges Perec and the Significance of the Insignificant', 105, warns against 'cherry-picking useable aspects of the work'.
18. Zimmerman, 'Photographic Images from Chicago to Hunstanton', 23.
19. Wentworth, 'Accidentally on Purpose', 129–35.
20. Kaji-O'Grady, 'The Architecture of Constraint and Forgetting', 185.
21. Bendiner-Viani, 'The Big World in the Small', 708.
22. Bendiner-Viani, 'The Big World in the Small', 711–12.
23. Bryson, *Vision and Painting*, 87.
24. Berger, *Understanding a Photograph*, 90.
25. Metz, 'Photography and Fetish', 84.

26. Berger, *Understanding a Photograph*, 90.
27. Smith, *At the Edge of Sight*, 94.
28. Gordon, *Ghostly Matters*, 103.
29. Elkins, *What Photography Is*, 38.
30. Rosler, *Passionate Signals*.
31. The non-place is derived from Augé, *Non-Places*.
32. Neudörfl, 'Photography vs. Visibility', 13.
33. Rutherford, 'Is This Photograph Taken?'
34. Laruelle, *The Concept of Non-Photography*.
35. Nye, *American Technological Sublime*.
36. Trowell, 'Contemporary Photographic Practices on the British Fairground'.
37. Rinaldo, 'Between Paint and Ink', 145.
38. Sheringham, *Everyday*, 282.
39. Sheringham, *Everyday*, 270.
40. Trowell, 'Spiel, Patter or Sound Effect' documents the backgrounding of showpeople from the perspective of the audible voice.

Bibliography

Augé, Marc. *Non-Places: Introduction to an Anthropology of Supermodernity*, translated by John Howe. 2nd ed. London: Verso, 2009.

Bendiner-Viani, Gabrielle. 'The Big World in the Small: Layered Dynamics of Meaning-Making in the Everyday', *Environment and Planning D: Society and Space* 31, no. 4 (2013): 708–26.

Berger, John. *Understanding a Photograph*, edited by Geoff Dyer. London: Penguin Books, 2013.

Bryson, Norman. *Vision and Painting: The Logic of the Gaze*. London: Macmillan, 1983.

Campany, David. *Photography and Cinema*. London: Reaktion Books, 2008.

Depaule, Jean-Charles and Pierre Getzler. 'A City in Words and Numbers', translated by Clare Barrett, *AA Files* 45/46 (2001): 117–28.

Elkins, James. *What Photography Is*. New York: Routledge, 2011.

Gordon, Avery F. *Ghostly Matters: Haunting and the Sociological Imagination*. Minneapolis: University of Minnesota Press, 2008.

Highmore, Ben. 'Georges Perec and the Significance of the Insignificant'. In *The Afterlives of Georges Perec*, edited by Rowan Wilken and Justin Clemens, 105–19. Edinburgh: Edinburgh University Press, 2017.

Kaji-O'Grady, Sandra. 'The Architecture of Constraint and Forgetting'. In *The Afterlives of Georges Perec*, edited by Rowan Wilken and Justin Clemens, 171–88. Edinburgh: Edinburgh University Press, 2017.

Laruelle, François. *The Concept of Non-Photography*, translated by Robin Mackay. Falmouth: Urbanomic, 2011.

Metz, Christian. 'Photography and Fetish', *October* 34 (1985): 81–90.

Neudörfl, Elisabeth. 'Photography vs. Visibility: Seeing Unseen Aspects of a City', *Visual Resources* 26, no. 1 (2010): 13–29.

Nye, David E. *American Technological Sublime*. Cambridge, MA: MIT Press, 1996.

Perec, Georges. 'Species of Spaces'. In *Species of Spaces and Other Pieces*, edited and translated by John Sturrock, 1–96. London: Penguin Books, 1997.

Perec, Georges. 'Approaches to What?'. In *Species of Spaces and Other Pieces*, edited and translated by John Sturrock, 209–11. London: Penguin Books, 2008.

Perec, Georges. *An Attempt at Exhausting a Place in Paris*, translated by Marc Lowenthal. Cambridge, MA: Wakefield Press, 2010.

Phillips, Richard. 'Georges Perec's Experimental Fieldwork: Perecquian Fieldwork', *Social and Cultural Geography* 19, no. 2 (2018): 171–91.

Ribière, Mireille. 'Georges Perec's Enduring Presence in the Visual Arts'. In *The Afterlives of Georges Perec*, edited by Rowan Wilken and Justin Clemens, 23–44. Edinburgh: Edinburgh University Press, 2017.

Rinaldo, Mikey. 'Between Paint and Ink: Cy Twombly, Steve McCaffery and Textual Illegibility in North American Art and Poetry 1950s–1970s', *Journal of Visual Art Practice* 17, no. 2/3 (2018): 144–59.

Rosler, Martha. *Passionate Signals*, edited by Inka Schube. Ostfildern-Ruit: Hatje Cantz, 2005.
Rowe, David. *Popular Cultures: Rock Music, Sport and the Politics of Pleasure*. London: SAGE Publications, 1995.
Rutherford. 'Is This Photograph Taken? The Active (Act of) Collaboration with Photography', *Journal of Visual Art Practice* 18, no. 1 (2019): 37–63.
Sheringham, Michael. *Everyday Life: Theories and Practices from Surrealism to the Present*. Oxford: Oxford University Press, 2006.
Smith, Shawn Michelle. *At the Edge of Sight: Photography and the Unseen*. Durham, NC: Duke University Press, 2013.
Trowell, Ian. 'Contemporary Photographic Practices on the British Fairground', *Photographies* 10, no. 2 (2017): 211–31.
Trowell, Ian. 'Spiel, Patter or Sound Effect: Tracking the Residual Voice on the Travelling Fun-Fair', *Journal of Interdisciplinary Voice Studies* 3, no. 1 (2018): 7–20.
Wentworth, Richard. 'Accidentally on Purpose', *AA Files* 45/46 (2001): 129–35.
Zimmerman, Claire. 'Photographic Images from Chicago to Hunstanton'. In *Neo-Avant-Garde and Postmodern: Postwar Architecture in Britain and Beyond*, edited by Mark Crinson and Claire Zimmerman, 203–28. New Haven: Yale University Press, 2010.

15
'Force yourself to see more flatly': A photographic investigation of the infra-ordinary

Joanne Lee

In *Species of Spaces* Georges Perec suggests various 'Practical exercises' as a means to explore the street. The instructions propose attention to what would be most obvious, common and therefore usually of no interest, with investigators told to go about things 'more slowly, almost stupidly'.[1] In order to reveal and understand the infra-ordinary, in 'Approaches to What?' Perec makes clear that the purpose of such activity is to wrest 'common things […] from the dross in which they remain mired', and to give them a tongue, to 'speak of what is, of what we are'.[2] As an artist-scholar researching everyday places through an essayistic approach involving photography, I am drawn to Perec's specific injunction: 'Force yourself to see more flatly'.[3] This reflects for me the medium's ultimate translation of dimensional space into picture plane, through what photographic theorist David Campany has described as a 'heightened interest in the surfaces of the world'.[4]

In what follows I take literally Perec's suggestion to see more flatly and I investigate, via the constraint of black and white image-making, the material surfaces encountered daily along the 12-minute walk from my Sheffield home to the tram stop from which I commute to my university job. That Perec makes clear his interest in 'A town: stone, concrete, asphalt',[5] and recognises the 'invisible underground proliferation of conduits', or the 'underneath' of limestone, marl, chalk, gypsum, sand and lignite,[6] encourages me to consider what lies exactly around and underfoot, and that could pass unremarked on so many daily journeys. I attempt to follow, through a practice of artistic research, certain of Perec's instructions from which this essaying of the surface of a place (given that, properly speaking, an essay is a trial, test or experiment) is excerpted to a sequence of paired images for the current context. This visual essay is followed by short passages from Perec, which prompt observational writing of my own, an inventory of sorts, developed through the aggregation of intentionally flat description; the images are intended to be read in critical and generative dialogue with the text. I conclude with a reflection upon this sort of Perecquian practice as a method of artistic research, and some remarks on what a determinedly superficial attention can reveal about the infra-ordinariness of place.

In so doing, it considers how Perec's strategies for defamiliarising the places he explores are anticipated by Russian Formalist writers and photographers, whose conception of *ostranenie* sought to make the everyday strange, to heighten attention and thus to push aside habitual and complacent responses. Whether through the use of literary devices, unusual language or particular ways of looking, their method intended creative and critical effects that pre-figure Perec's own practices, and continue to inform my own (see Figure 15.1).

Figure 15.1 Following Georges Perec's call to 'decipher a bit of the town', Joanne Lee used her camera to observe and document a route she walks every day: the unremarkable space between her home in Loxley, Sheffield, and the terminus in Malin Bridge, where she catches a tram on her daily commute. A sequence of her photographs is shown here, in a photographic essay entitled 'The Loxley Road Sequence'; continues overleaf. © Joanne Lee

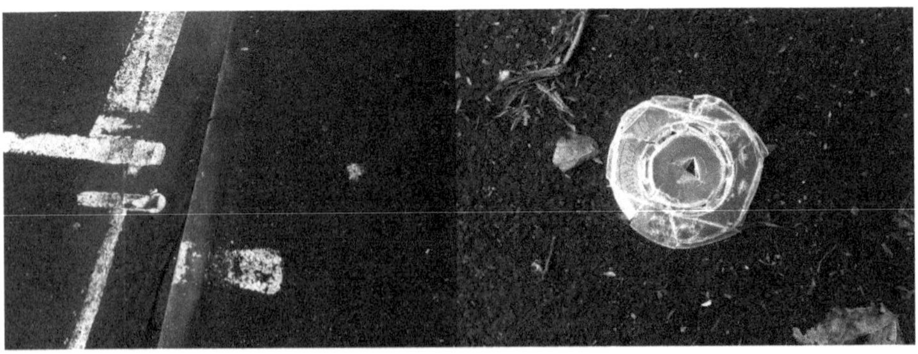

Figure 15.1 Continued

Figure 15.1 Continued

'You must set about it more slowly, almost stupidly. Force yourself to write down what is most obvious, most common, most colourless.'[7]

The roadway is a different material to the pavements, coarser. It has long white lines down the centre of the carriageway, hatched markings and directional arrows at junctions, and a segment of reddish orange separates traffic at the pedestrian refuge.

The tarmac pavement runs underfoot from my home almost the whole way along Loxley Road, bar the gravelly ingress of a lane leading down to a garage premises where domestic vehicles and taxis are repaired: there, the road surface is a patchwork of asphalt and gritty mud which holds pools of water long after the rest of the area has dried. The tarmac is far from consistent, its texture and hue change, from the darkest shade – almost black – through a patchwork of paler greys, as various interventions have been made for the installation or mending of utilities and telecoms. Some of the inspection hatches themselves bear a carapace of tarmac, though it is a poor mimic of its surroundings. After heavy rain, the botched repair to a drainage leak continues to ooze water through a seam of blacker, tarry matter.

Roundels of discarded gum pock the surface; the longer they have been there the more intricate is the craquelure of age.

Along two substantial stretches where it abuts stone walls, and behind which there are ash and poplar trees, it accrues a scurf of leaf litter and twigs brought down by the wind, which grows muddy in wet weather and gets tangled with rubbish. Woodpigeons select a particular tree in which to roost, and their guano spatters the pavement below in greenish-grey and white.

Cast yellowish concrete bears a texture of raised nipples to indicate designated crossing points for pedestrians.

'A town: stone, concrete, asphalt.'[8]

The houses here include a few stone cottages dating from the mid-nineteenth century but most are twentieth-century dwellings. The oldest are a dark gritstone; some still bear the blackened rime of Sheffield's industrial pollution, though many have been sandblasted to restore their original appearance. Newer houses have been infilled in different decades and vary between a blond sandstone and red or cream brick. Some, my own included, are pebble or spar-dashed: in this climate, the once silvery surface has become stained and grubby, so a few home-owners have decided to overpaint with a fresher grey or golden yellow. There are boundary walls of old stone, elegant mid-century metal fences, hedges of conifer and beech, and bright reddish-orange contemporary larchlap panels. Two houses built at the same time have chosen entirely different window treatments, twins determining to be as distinct from one another as possible. One stone cottage must once have been restored but is now falling back into disrepair: grass flourishes in its unmaintained gutters, and the roof is entirely moss covered; an algae-coated caravan lurks in the shade of unmanaged woodland to the rear. At night, only dim lights are visible through deep red curtains that are never opened. It has such a traditional symmetrical façade that it is just the sort of house drawn by young children but, with its gloomy outlook, it's more like the location for a horror movie. Approaching it the temperature seems to drop, the street around recedes and the tangle of surrounding woods encroach.

'What we need to question is bricks, concrete, glass, our table manners, our utensils, our tools, the way we spend our time, our rhythms.'[9]

The bus stop glass is incised with an intricate web of *sgrafiti*; the work is, by the look of the handwriting, that of the schoolchildren who regularly wait or hang out at this stop for buses home after school. One panel has had rougher treatment, the result of being abraded by someone seeking to clean off more traditional sprayed graffiti, and is now murky, almost opaque.

The nearby Academy school is the reason for a tidal passage of young people through this neighbourhood morning and afternoon. The Supper Spot does a roaring trade as the school day finishes, with clusters of kids scoffing hot chips from styrene trays, while the nearby minimarket has to employ extra people to stand at the door admitting only a few children at a time in order to combat shoplifting.

There's a tricky junction at which cars and kids are involved in a sort of twice daily choreographic negotiation with one another, each trying to dodge the other.

'Make an effort to exhaust the subject, even if that seems grotesque, or pointless, or stupid. You still haven't looked at anything, you've merely picked out what you long ago picked out.'[10]

It's almost impossible to exhaust the litter. Every day there are new deposits. The main culprits for this seem to be the patrons of local fast-food outlets. Very often it's from McDonalds: white opaque plastic discs, the lids from their soft drinks, are always distinct against the dark tarmac, while the brown paper bags with their yellow and red branding linger for a while before turning to pulpy mush in the rain. There are orangey-yellow styrofoam containers that contained the burgers or kebabs bought from smaller caterers, and the white trays smeared with leftovers from the nearby fish and chip shop, which sometimes come paired with the chip forks in blue plastic. The most numerous items are bottles for squash, juice and fizzy pop which come in clear plastic, opaque purple, orange and green, and there are many cans of energy drinks with their vivid graphics. While some appear on the pavement, many have been dropped over the adjacent wall and litter the margin of the woods that line the valley bottom.

Lager and cider cans proliferate too. The cans mark the route home from a night out, or the wanderings of the teenagers unable to drink legally who stock up with booze and head down into the woods to party. The strong smell of weed, and flashes of silver on the pavement (containers of nitrous oxide), indicate that alcohol is not the only drug.

Also common are the flaccid black bags of dog shit, slipped casually over the wall by owners who have decided to rid themselves illicitly of their pet's leavings; occasionally these catch on the spiny bushes and hang for a while before slumping into the leaf litter. In other places the bags hang more assertively from branches, decorating the woods with a collection of abject baubles.

The fly tipping of building materials and waste from DIY projects occurs where it is less overlooked by houses, particularly over the wall next to the care home: here dumps of household rubbish appear periodically too, including old duvets rolled up and cinched with parcel tape, stuffed tightly into black bags. This is macro-scale waste, but kneeling on the ground and looking closely, there are fragments and particles of much tinier stuff: scraps of paper and card, pieces of plastic, shards of glass and metal.

'Read what's written in the street: [...] posters, traffic signs, graffiti, discarded hand outs, shop signs.'[11]

There is so much to read. A road sign reminds motorists (with little effect it seems) that the speed limit here is 30 miles per hour. Pages ripped from a young person's exam revision diary are scattered for many metres, either the joyful result of the examination period ending, or the actions of a bully? Childish graffiti is spray-painted on the pavement. A small flyer for a local handyman pleads for attention and the text asks politely that it is not binned but passed on to those who might need his services. The monthly farmers' market further up the valley is advertised with distinctive yellow signs cable-tied to lamp-posts. New management is announced at the fish and chip shop, as well as its capacity to take card payments; quite often though, it's not open when it should be and apologies for the inconvenience are posted in the window via scribbled handwritten notes indicating an unexpected appointment or a family crisis. An informational board on the exterior wall of a pub tells of the major flood in 1864 when a dam burst at the head of the valley and inundated much of the area, leaving six dead in the wrecked establishment's cellar.

The faded paint of an advertisement for Condor Flake tobacco endures amid the more contemporary signage for the current Nail and Beauty Lounge that plies its trade on the corner above the hairdressers. A series of early twentieth-century hoardings made in concrete and surrounded with moulded frames are now crumbling, grown over with ivy they are mute ghosts of a previous era of advertising. Across the road, graffiti on the metal shutters of a long-closed shop front proclaim 'FED UP' in large capitals.

There are messages of strength and persistence that seemingly come from a time with different values: one manhole cover carries the name 'Valiant', another 'Savage', and yet another 'Dreadnought'; this last is positioned opposite a section of terraced housing with a stone plaque inscribed 'Perseverance Terrace'. Rather unaccountably, one inspection cover for a cable television installation is titled 'DANELAW'.

> 'Or again: strive to picture yourself, with the greatest possible precision, beneath the streets, the tangle of sewers, the lines of the Métro, the invisible underground proliferation of conduits (electricity, gas, telephone lines, water mains, express letter tubes), without which no life would be possible on the surface.'[12]

There is so much to see at the surface that tells of what is, or what will be sent underground. Triangular flaps marked CATV punctuate the street, and reveal where cable television has been installed. Square covers with the sign YW Water, or sometimes simply a W, conceal the meters for Yorkshire Water: they are inserted higgledy-piggledy in the pavement, the hinge facing in different directions.

The larger utility inspection hatches and their varied titles and logos tell a history of public and private services: there's the old Sheffield Corporation, and the different incarnations of GPO (General Post Office), Post Office Telephones and BT (British Telecom).

Most of the terraced houses have coal holes in the pavement adjacent to their front elevation; this is where, before the installation of mains gas, the fuel for domestic heating would be delivered into the cellar. They are now sealed shut with rusted metal plates and grilles; some are screwed or bolted, others tied with ad hoc lengths of wire.

When it's quiet, especially in the evening, one can hear the sewers beneath rushing with water; when it's very quiet, one can also hear the river flowing in the valley below. There have been problems with surface drainage here: water spreads in sheets across the road, bringing a tide of dirt, sticks and other debris, which remain along the gutters for a long while, sometimes blocking them and causing still further problems.

Blue boxes and black bins linger on the street outside the prescribed times for the collection of recyclables and waste: since a number of the houses have steps down to the road that are both steep and narrow it must be challenging to drag them back and forth each week.

'What's beautiful and what's ugly in a town? How do you get to know a town? How do you get to know your town?'[13]

One length of stone wall is topped with a crusty black coping, so-called 'crozzle', the repurposing of a material once used to line steel cementation furnaces. It's not uncommon in the city and its presence delineates distinctively that one is here rather than elsewhere; that said, no doubt many current residents barely notice it. It isn't exactly beautiful: even after all these years it is burnt-looking, and so rough and sharp as to deter people from clambering over (as was the original intention), but weathered a little and set against mossy stone walls, it takes on a craggy rightness here, almost a black sort of tufa. Noticing and knowing about the crozzle signifies long-term residence, or a mark of inclusion for those who have sought to know the city's industrial past. This is one form of knowing, but the many activities that go on today about which the older, long-resident generation understand little or nothing suggest that none of us quite know the same town as one another.

'Decipher a bit of the town.'[14]

In 'Species of Spaces' Perec twice instructs us to do so.

1. In trying to decipher a bit of the town, even a single area can be unfathomably complex, its different users seeing and enjoying the same place in very diverse ways. For example, the lanes leading off the main road here are variously places for the more able-bodied residents from the local care home to get some air, for teenage drinking and drug-taking, for parents strolling with their kids, for dog exercising, gay cruising, and off-road motorcycling. Some users and activities remain separate by virtue of the day or time – dog walking mainly takes place before and after work, and the off-roading seems to be largely at a weekend – but others must occupy the same space at the same time, whether or not they are aware of one another.

2. A pierced steel panel is affixed to a crumbling brick wall: it carries the graffitied words Tranquil and Euphoric, which appear in a rounded script produced by a silver marker pen, as well as three, maybe four, other tags, one of which has been buffed and overwritten. There is also a sticker printed rather unaccountably with the name of the Polish city Nowa Huta. (It too was a place of significant steel manufacture like Sheffield, though of much younger vintage having been built in the mid-twentieth century as a model communist city to accompany the huge New Foundry from which it took its name.) For whom are these messages designed? Why are they here? What is their intended meaning? What can be inferred?

'To cover the world, to cross it in every direction, will only ever be to know a few square centimetres of it, a few acres, tiny incursions into disembodied vestiges, small incidental excitements, improbable quests congealed in a mawkish haze a few details of which will remain in our memory.'[15]

In the small traffic-blighted front garden of a mid-century semi-detached house stand a variety of hand-built bird tables and nesting boxes. It gives the impression of a small village for birds, and their similar-but-different styles and colours offer a sort of miniature mirror to the wider neighbourhood. Several laminated notices inform passers-by that they are for sale, giving prices and the repeated instruction to ring the doorbell if wanting to make a purchase. There's a mobile number to call too, also given repeatedly, in case the occupants are out. It's a modest spectacle, and friends who pass this way for the first time often take a photograph; maybe it is what they will remember most from their visit.

'[I]n spite of yourself, you're only noting the untoward, the peculiar, the wretched exceptions; the opposite is what you should be doing.'[16]

A particular telegraph pole repeatedly catches the eye as it has an enduring pale blue-ish waxy splatter on its lower reaches that evokes drunken vomit or an alien sort of gunk: despite close inspection the material constitution of this stuff remains uncertain. Was it vandalism or the product of some sort of maintenance? For many months, the post opposite carried the tattered remnants of a bouquet placed at the site of a cyclist's tragic death in collision with a car. The road surface was sprayed too with fluorescent orange dots, markers delineating evidence as police investigators sought to understand what took place; while an arrest was initially made, no charges were ever brought. Sadly such occurrences remain far from 'wretched exceptions'; what remains horrific and exceptional for the cyclist's family and friends is merely another number in the statistics of daily life and death on the city's roads.

– –

Almost every working day I walk the same route from my home in Loxley, Sheffield to the Malin Bridge tram terminus from which I commute into the city. I've lived here for approaching three years, though the area wasn't entirely unknown to me when I was resident in the city 15 years earlier. In some ways Loxley is unremarkable: it is an ordinary suburb on the north-western flank of Sheffield, neither especially poor nor particularly rich, a predominantly working-class district. In others, it is rather distinctive. It is, for example, one of the valleys where the Industrial Revolution can be said to have begun, with the construction of many waterwheels driving the workshops in which Sheffield's early blade industry was established; a good deal of industrial archeology endures here, as well as many small enterprises that continue to make and mend. It was also the site of a major disaster when the dam of Dale Dike Reservoir failed catastrophically and the resulting flood laid waste to the valley and the city downstream. Since the city repeatedly frays here along footpaths into woodland, pasture and eventually the moors of the Peak District, it immediately calls into question Perec's demand to establish 'what is the town and what isn't the town'.[17] It has such an unusual mix of the urban/rural and the domestic/industrial that it never quite seems as other places.

My assertion of Loxley's special qualities is of course entirely to miss the Perecquian point. When Perec exhorts 'Carry on / Until the scene becomes improbable / Until you have the impression, for the briefest of moments, that you are in a strange town, or better still, until you no longer understand what is happening, until the whole place becomes strange, and you no longer even know that this is what is called a town, a street, buildings, pavement',[18] he didn't have in mind the distinctive historical claims, or other sorts of categorisation I made above, which might figure a place to be unusual. These are much too grand, or are the ready-made terms, the sort of thing town planners and sociologists will already have said: precisely the stuff he tells us to forget. Rather, his instruction to make strange is to enable us to really see the everyday places and habits to which we pay too little attention, to reveal that with which we have become too familiar.

Perec asks: 'How are we to speak of these "common things", how to track them down rather, flush them out, wrest them from the dross in which they remain mired, how to give them a meaning, a tongue, to let them, finally, speak of what is, of what we are.'[19] For him the answer was in a sort of writing that could be described as defamiliarisation through the practice of listing. His listing is generative, excessive, a piling up of connected and disparate details. Witness the 'Index of some of the words used in this work'.[20] And take as an exemplar the paragraph about moving into and renovating a new home, where he gathers a host of verbs (without punctuation) to describe the activities involved in so doing: 'cleaning checking trying out changing fitting signing waiting imagining inventing investing deciding bending folding stooping sheathing fitting out stripping bare splitting turning returning' and so on for another 38 lines.[21] Perhaps 'Species of Spaces' can be considered fundamentally a project of list-making?

Perec asks in 'Approaches to What?', 'How should we take account of, question, describe, what happens every day and recurs every day' and the method in his practice seems to be by noting, by responding to observational rules and by pursuing suggested exercises.[22] Listing is directly offered as a means of investigation: in the section headed 'The Town', he says, 'make an inventory of what you can see. List what you're sure of.'[23] While it is excessive, it is also knowingly partial. Perec's method for attending to a city street begins with: 'Observe the street, from time to time, with some concern for system perhaps. Apply yourself. Take your time.'[24] I note particularly the phrase 'with some concern for system perhaps', which introduces a permissive inconsistency to the investigative approach right at the start. Whatever his love of constraint and generative rules, the projects he pursued not infrequently failed to adhere to them, or to be completed in quite the way intended at the outset.[25] This is the messy territory of practice, rather than the more formal project design of academic research that is set out and carried through, with minor scope for fundamental change once under way.

When Perec writes about looking and noting 'until the whole place becomes strange' he is clearly using a process of defamiliarisation. The idea was particularly powerful in the theory and practice of those Russian Formalists whose neologism *ostranenie* suggests the dual actions of making strange and of pushing aside. Viktor Shklovsky describes it thus: 'The technique of art is to make objects "unfamiliar," to make forms difficult, to increase the difficulty and length of perception, because the process of perception is an aesthetic end in itself and must be prolonged.'[26] For the Formalists, the intention was to create a sort of literariness or poetry that would prevent habitual sorts of judgement and instead induce a heightened state of attention where different responses might be possible. When photographers of the time pursued defamiliarisation, as in the work of Aleksandr Rodchenko, the effect occurs through unexpected camera angles, the use of shadow, and the focus on small parts or details, as well as the repetition of particular formal motifs explored through series. It's an approach that reappeared much later in the century in photographic practices such as those of Lewis Baltz, who photographed banal American industrial buildings, suburban housing developments and wasteland. Here, while there are no odd angles – most of the photographs are shot head on – the type of architectural structures he repeatedly pictured in series such as the *Prototype Works* (1967–76) are defamiliarised to the point that they become abstract, minimal forms and material surfaces. But emptied out as they are, and isolated from the wider townscape in which they are located, they sustain a sort of interest that would rarely have been provoked by the buildings themselves. As we contemplate the pictures, these buildings seemingly become something more fully as images, the result of a wholly photographic way of seeing that mobilises the formal qualities of focal length, framing, tone and texture in order to translate the world two-dimensionally.

Both practices have been instructive for my own photographic investigations, which are a species of visual listing and note-making. But in getting to know a place through photography I often get much physically closer to the surfaces of things in which I'm interested than these predecessors, in some cases almost having my nose pressed up right against my subject matter. Dwelling on interior or exterior surfaces – attending to the forms, textures and tones of ordinary floors, pavements, roads, walls and ceilings – I hover close with the camera so that when I'm finding where I am at, I am simultaneously getting lost from the bigger picture. Even when I step back, there is rarely a horizon line by which to tell quite where the things photographed might actually be situated. Just as Perec begins 'Species of Spaces' with the modest page and various domestic locations before expanding out into the wider world, my early spatial investigations began at home, with photographs of found scraps of paper on my desk, and of the looming shadow cast by a nondescript lampshade on the ceiling above the bed. I stared repeatedly though a camera lens at condensation dribbling down windows or the speckled patches of light reflecting off windows onto roads and other buildings and considered that with this sort of looking it seemed as if I was photographing what was barely 'photographable' at all.

Once the photographs are taken, they are usually set aside for a while, which distances me further from the time they were shot, and the specific ideas I had at that point; I want to see them afresh, the images as they are, rather than as I had intended them to be. The distinct activities of photography and reflection on the photographs enable me to see again, and see differently, the subjects I had been looking at. A further act of defamiliarisation is in the practice of creating sequences: sometimes it is a series of single images, but often I pair pictures, or produce triptychs to set within the sequence. The sequences may draw together pictures made at different times or across a long duration, bringing them into unexpected conversations with one another, shaped by formal or conceptual aspects.

This same approach has been applied to the making of the images essayed and excerpted for the current article. The photographs deal intentionally with the most common things to be encountered: manhole covers and hatches for coal; litter; mud; graffiti; the linear forms of tram tracks; pipes and conduits; white lines and arrows marking the road; tarmac, concrete, bricks and masonry; fencing, plastic bins and metal shutters. I photographed repeatedly, on multiple days, walking to work, as the changing light and different types of weather affected the street, illuminating, darkening or making material reflective. Sometimes I focused on the shadow rather than the thing itself, looking obliquely, or at the effects of what I noticed. When, at various stages during the making process, I reflected upon the collection of photographs and started to sequence them, I could see how the repeated translation of the street into two-dimensional space was informing how I looked and what I saw on subsequent occasions. My daily walk became increasingly strange to me as the previous images changed what I attended to and how it appeared to me. The street became ever changing; the harder I looked, the more infinitely various it became, and the less possible it was to ever be able to represent it adequately. The street was nearer than ever in terms both of the quantity of photographs in which it was depicted and in the close-ups of specific sections, yet it seemed simultaneously to always be pushed further away from me. This happened too in the image pairs as the formal qualities of the picture plane (light and shadow, shape and texture, framing of or within the image) also worked to defamiliarise each photograph, making the world tilt, slide and rear up, or reveal the formation of visual links and patterns. I sought to pursue this through textual practice, to approach the subject from yet another direction, using a mechanism where modest forms of narrative became more prevalent, and where emerged a more 'human' voice, as opposed to the formal, apparently dispassionate, photography. This written element could be thought of as another two-dimensional plane to that of the photographs, reflecting or refracting what can be seen in this specific location. Bringing together text and image in such a way sees them align at points, while elsewhere they jar, speaking of things in a different register. The effect is not to 'pin down' the place, but rather to keep response in motion, to produce still more un-definitive findings, and indeed to make me increasingly less certain.

For artistic research, this becoming less known is not the negative it might be in other disciplines, and can in fact be considered a state in which to linger. As Elizabeth Fisher and Rebecca Fortnum make clear in their preface to the edited collection *On Not Knowing: How Artists Think*, artists use strategies 'to "think" in ways that stray beyond the methods of other disciplines', and their research occupies 'a kind of liminal space where not knowing is not only not overcome, but sought, explored, and savoured'.[27] Indeed, as Rachel Jones, one of their contributors puts it, working 'without knowing where one is going or might end up is a necessary condition of creation', since what's needed is 'the generation of difference rather than the reproduction of the already known' and thus it might be said that the quest for knowledge 'understood as a desire to reduce the strange to the familiar' runs counter to this.[28]

There is a sense here that this sort of artistic research practice is about keeping things strange and generating further possibility, rather than delivering conclusive findings, as might be the case in other disciplines. For Perec too, this exploratory, experimental movement is palpable: 'Even if what I produce seems to derive from a programme worked out a long time ago, from a long-standing project, I believe rather that I discover – that I prove – the direction I am moving in by moving.'[29] He goes on to say that his books are 'describing point by point the stages of a search, the 'why' of which I can't tell, only the 'how'.[30] While Perec talks of wanting to 'lay hold on our truth',[31] his *practice* of attention to the most infra-ordinary aspects actually becomes a sort of continual mechanism for creating strangeness and pushing aside what is known at each stage;

as a result, definitive conclusions are delayed and responses are kept in motion.

By paying attention to mere surfaces, investigating slowly, closely and repetitively, and translating these encounters via the dimensions of photography and writing, it transpires that the infra-ordinary, the very stuff that ought to be so known to us – so familiar – turns out to be infinitely strange. Just a little flippantly, I find myself conceptualising this is as a sort of quantum cultural studies, an exploration at a much smaller scale than that of the macroscopic world, and where as a result the 'normal' rules of research do not work … However, more properly, I would propose this as a key mode of artistic research, suggesting that the specific methods of this field allow for or enable other types of results. I agree with artist and philosopher Jyrki Siukonen, who has argued that art offers a different form of knowing: 'I find it difficult to be interested in works that tell us only those things we could learn from other sources – from historians, sociologists, psychologists, etc. If there is any point in discussing artistic knowledge, it is when it also tells us something different, something that could not be told in any other way.'[32]

For the Formalists, what was important in the process of defamiliarisation was experiencing the artfulness of an object, the object itself being unimportant. This is not my position, since the specific subject matter is clearly crucial in my investigations, but the aesthetic effects and qualities of image-making and writing produced for and through artistic research are capable of generating responses that enrich or amplify the subject, telling us something different than would ever be possible with other approaches. Ultimately this making strange is about creating and sustaining a state of wonder where final judgement is suspended, and one is encouraged to remain open to alternative interpretations: for Rachel Jones, 'Learning to see as strange makes us un-at-home in the everyday, and thereby restores it as a potential place of marvel, where we might become other than what or who we are.'[33] Experiencing the everyday in this way, through wonder, is critically transformative, since as a researcher it makes things less certain and it questions, too, the methods by which research might actually 'lay hold on our truth', offering instead a more durational prospect by which multiple realities and affects can sustain, held in complex relation.

Notes

1. Perec, 'Species of Spaces', 50.
2. Perec, 'Approaches to What?', *Species of Spaces*, 210.
3. Perec, 'Species of Spaces', 51.

4. Campany, 'Architecture as Photography', 28.
5. Perec, 'Species of Spaces', 61.
6. Perec, 'Species of Spaces', 54.
7. Perec, 'Species of Spaces', 50.
8. Perec, 'Species of Spaces', 61.
9. Perec, 'Approaches to What?', 210.
10. Perec, 'Species of Spaces', 50.
11. Perec, 'Species of Spaces', 51.
12. Perec, 'Species of Spaces', 53–4.
13. Perec, 'Species of Spaces', 61.
14. Perec, 'Species of Spaces', 51, 52.
15. Perec, 'Species of Spaces', 78.
16. Perec, 'Species of Spaces', 53.
17. Perec, 'Species of Spaces', 60.
18. Perec, 'Species of Spaces', 53.
19. Perec, 'Approaches to What?', 210.
20. Perec, 'Species of Spaces', 93–5.
21. Perec, 'Species of Spaces', 35.
22. Perec, 'Approaches to What?', 210.
23. Perec, 'Species of Spaces', 60.
24. Perec, 'Species of Spaces', 50.
25. For more on this, see the discussion of 'project' and 'essay' forms as methodological tools in relation to ideas of emergence through practice in Lee, 'On Not Staying Put', 11–26.
26. Shklovsky, 'Art as Technique', 12.
27. Fisher and Rebecca, 'Preface', *On Not Knowing,* 7.
28. Jones, 'On the Value of Not Knowing', 16.
29. Perec, 'Notes on What I'm Looking For', 142.
30. Perec, 'Notes on What I'm Looking For', 143.
31. Perec, 'Approaches to What?', 211.
32. Siukonen, *On Artistic Knowledge*, 3.
33. Jones, 'On the Value of Not Knowing', 18.

Bibliography

Campany, David. 'Architecture as Photography: Document, Publicity, Commentary, Art'. In *Constructing Worlds: Photography and Architecture in the Modern Age*, edited by Alona Pardo and Elias Redstone, 27–40. Munich: Prestel, 2014.

Fisher, Elizabeth and Rebecca Fortnum. 'Preface'. In *On Not Knowing: How Artists Think*, edited by Elizabeth Fisher and Rebecca Fortnum, 7. London: Black Dog Publishing, 2013.

Jones, Rachel. 'On the Value of Not Knowing: Wonder, Beginning Again and Letting Be'. In *On Not Knowing: How Artists Think*, edited by Elizabeth Fisher and Rebecca Fortnum, 16–31. London: Black Dog Publishing, 2013.

Lee, Joanne. 'On Not Staying Put: Georges Perec's "Inter(in)disciplinarity" as an Approach to Research'. In *Literary Geographies* 3, no. 1 (2017).

Perec, Georges. *Species of Spaces and Other Pieces*, edited and translated by John Sturrock. London: Penguin Books, 1997.

Perec, Georges. 'Approaches to What?'. In *Species of Spaces and Other Pieces*, edited and translated by John Sturrock, 209–11. London: Penguin Books, 2008.

Perec, Georges. 'Species of Spaces'. In *Species of Spaces and Other Pieces*, edited and translated by John Sturrock, 1–96. London: Penguin Books, 2008.

Perec, Georges. 'Notes on What I'm Looking For'. In *Species of Spaces and Other Pieces*, edited and translated by John Sturrock, 141–43. London: Penguin Books, 2008.

Shklovsky, Victor. 'Art as Technique'. In *Russian Formalist Criticism: Four Essays*, translated by Lee T. Lemon and Marion J. Reis, 3–24. Lincoln: University of Nebraska Press, 1965.

Siukonen, Jyrki. *On Artistic Knowledge: Notes for a Minor Platonic Exercise*. Leeds: Centre for the Study of Sculpture, 1996.

16

When nothing happens in Huddersfield

Kevin Boniface

> *Space seems to be either tamer or more inoffensive than time; we're forever meeting people who have watches, very seldom people who have compasses. We always need to know what time it is (who still knows how to deduce it from the position of the sun?) but we never ask ourselves where we are.* (Georges Perec)[1]

When I started my job as a postal worker in Huddersfield in 1998, the streets, much as they are now, were made of asphalt, Haribo wrappers, air-punching men in hooded tops, a man in beige salwar kameez who was carrying a toilet seat, buses, butterflies, buzzards, tinny reproductions of Chaka Demus and Pliers' chart hits, double denim, dressing gowns, flip-flops, footballs, Ford Kas, Mr Mahmood and Mrs Moorhouse queueing for the cash machine, the smell of weed, bacon, dog piss, wheelie bins .... I was aware of the 'hundreds of simultaneous actions, micro-events, each one of which necessitates postures, movements, specific expenditures of energy'[2] as Georges Perec evidently had been in Paris in 1974. Perec had already identified the anaesthetic effects of the habitual and had slowly, 'almost stupidly' set about recovering the things that may have been lost as a result. He advised, 'Force yourself to write down what is of no interest, what is of most interest, what is most obvious, most common, most colourless.'[3] I too was suspicious of my habitual behaviour, my conditioning. I'd had my head turned by the work of the artists, Boyle Family, as an undergraduate in the early 1990s and taken it to heart when I read Mark Boyle quotes like this: 'The most complete change an individual can effect in his environment, short of destroying it, is to change his attitude to it. This is my objective [...] From the beginning we are taught to choose, to select, to separate good from bad, best from better: our entire upbringing and education are directed towards planting the proper snobberies, the right preferences.'[4]

Where Perec readied himself to step out into the streets and calmly execute his carefully considered plan while eating a camembert sandwich in a Parisian café and looking out of the window, I didn't. I was forced to confront the streets in the course of my job and my initial response was to have a small nervous breakdown, shout at pigeons and scrawl down angry polemics with little punctuation or time for basic grammar. In this miasma, as I perceived it, my impotent rage was far too easily stirred by unavoidable everyday encounters with cheap garden ornamentation, 'stick on' fake leaded lights, the over 60s and their casual racism, dogs and dog excrement, etc. I was, however, writing these things down, which was a start. A typical diary entry from 6 November 2003: '"I hate this fucking place because it's shit" I said aggressively. The man looked taken aback; I'd never spoken to him before. He tried to console me by saying that Bradford was shit too although he conceded that it did seem worse here.' I felt lost. I didn't know where I was and eventually I realised I ought to try and find out. I began to recollect other, more measured, voices from my undergraduate studies: Paul Klee wanting to be 'as though new born',[5] André Bazin's 'impassive lens',[6] and, most significantly, the 'motiveless appraisal'[7] of the Boyle Family. I began to consider these ideas and incorporate them into my writing in an attempt to make sense of the tangle of my unfathomably mundane surroundings. My approach became more empirical and objective. I made field notes recording what I could see at half-past every hour, I made daily lists that de-contextualised things by juxtaposing them seemingly at random: fragments of conversations and found notes, street furniture and retail signage, detritus and litter, ritualised behaviour and speech, wildlife and pets, as well as examples of conspicuous consumption/leisure, sartorial codes and, of course, garden ornamentation. I was picking away at the ordinary and what began to unravel was extraordinary.

In October 1974, Georges Perec spent a weekend in place Saint-Sulpice, Paris, attempting to discover 'What happens when nothing happens?'. From a café window, he noted everything he saw in *An Attempt at Exhausting a Place in Paris*. It's through these and similar exercises in observation that he developed his virtuosic knowledge of how a place works. Inspired by these texts, I have sought out corresponding observations of the 'infra-ordinary' from my own journals. As Perec was in Paris, and I am in Huddersfield, it would be remiss of me not to mention that in 1994, Stephen Dorrell, the then Secretary of State for National Heritage famously (famous round these parts anyway) referred to Huddersfield as 'the Paris of the north'.[8] There's little doubt that this claim was rooted in political expediency rather than empirical fact but, when it comes to cigarettes, benches, stumbling pedestrians, bags, hats, umbrellas, pigeons, buses, dogs, litter, postal vans, mailboxes, etc., the two places do indeed have much in common.

In the first of the entries, Perec records that he is in Tabac Saint-Sulpice at 10.30am on 18 October 1974. He inventories some of the things he can see, with an eye to classifications, visible in the linguistic landscape. These include letters of the alphabet, names of hotels and the wording of street signage.[9] From Perec, we turn to my notes on Huddersfield.

Date: Sunday, 13 January 2015
Location: Manchester Road–Blackmoorfoot Road, Huddersfield

> The buses are racing each other between stops. The world flies past the window in a blur: BEST CARPET BARGAINS…Klippers Hair Salon…Sambuca Saturday…Karaoke Thursday…MEGA BOXES FOR £8.99…Royal Travel and Money Transfer…iTaste…Extra Care Housing…2 For 1 on Essentials (illustrated with a photograph of a packet of digestive biscuits)…YOU CAN'T BUY CHEAPER…Gold International…LE UVST TIPE X…FREE BOTTLE OF POP. A man climbs aboard looking flustered in fake leather and Fair Isle, 'It's always bloody late, this bus! He's supposed to be five minutes in front of that other one', he says out loud as he walks down the aisle. 'Bloody rubbish!' He sits down next to me in a fug of damp and sweat. The woman in front of us with the grey perm and turquoise gaberdine coat turns around, 'These people are much more helpful than the Metro people though', she says, 'And it's 30p cheaper', she adds, her knuckles white on the handrail as the bus swings out into the middle lane to overtake its rival. 'Go on, lad!' yells the damp sweat man to the driver, pumping his fist.[10]

Perec observes that 'Most People are using at least one hand: they're holding a bag, a briefcase, a shopping bag, a cane, a leash with a dog at the end, a child's hand'.[11]

In an entry from my journals from April 2013, I note the contrast between the 'stalled mums' holding onto dogs, pushchairs and toddlers and the 'unencumbered' grey-haired men who stride about the landscape, free to create new desire paths.

Date: 17 April 2013
Location: Fenay Bridge, Huddersfield

> Out on the new estate: fake-sandstone-beige and UPVC-white with accents of grit-bin and Cold-Caller-Control-Zone-sticker yellow. The background noise of burglar alarms, wind-chimes, squabbling blackbirds, shouting PE teachers and that weird clanging from the insides of swaying metal street lamps, is occasionally drowned out by the engine of the JCB whose driver is concentrating so hard that his tongue is poking out. The fake ornamental bay trees have blown over onto the plastic lawn where the high-pitched cat deterrent is repeatedly triggered by the swirling leaves and bobbing daffodils. There are sea urchins and highly glazed period folk on windowsills and solar panels on roofs. And there are dogs: people without shoes open doors while holding dogs by the collar. There are unencumbered and determined grey-haired men in navy blue fleeces pounding the streets. Teeth gritted, they march up hills, arms outstretched for extra balance along uneven nascent desire lines – past the stalled mums with their hoods up against the drizzle, pushchairs and retrievers in one hand, they reach out for their straggling toddlers with the other.[12]

By 12.40pm, Perec has moved on to the Café de la Mairie, from where he observes 'conversations between two people, conversations between three people, conversations between several people: the movement of lips, gestures, gesticulations'.[13]

Below, I've listed a few examples of such observations from the streets of Huddersfield over the last 15 years.

Date: 2 March 2004
Location: St Peter's Gardens, Huddersfield

> 'Hey! it's Brooky's bitch, soft cock!' he said, whilst making a wanker gesture with his right hand.[14]

Date: 9 July 2011
Location: Daisy Royd, Newsome, Huddersfield

> He shouts to me above the noise of his dog barking from behind the gate, 'Don't worry!' he says, 'She's all this' and he makes a C-shaped

gesture with his right hand, opening and closing his thumb and fingers to signify talking. 'Just like all women', he adds with a wink.[15]

Date: 18 May 2012
Location: Huddersfield Bus Station

At the bus station, a group discussion is underway about sandwich filling preferences. The large woman in her fifties says she could never eat peanut butter and cucumber because she doesn't like 'sweet and sour stuff'.[16]

Date: 17 April 2013
Location: Primitive Street, Huddersfield

In Primitive Street, a gust of wind blows an empty lager can from one kerb to the other while two drunks discuss the whereabouts of Amber. 'Where is she?' asks the one in the faded blue anorak with the saggy pockets. 'I don't know', says the other, 'she spat in my face about two years ago'.[17]

Date: 2 November 2014
Location: Leeds Road, Huddersfield

I walk down Leeds Road behind a girl in skinny jeans and a black puffer jacket. She's talking loudly on her phone in Polish, emphasising key points with wild, histrionic hand gestures.[18]

Date: 13 December 2015
Location: Station Road, Lepton, Huddersfield

'What is it?' says the customer, cleaning a stripe through the greasy dust that coats it with her thumb and wiping the residue on her bulging pocket. 'It's wine', explains the proprietress. 'Is it dry?' 'Yes, I think so.' 'I don't really do wine, what's it like?' 'Apparently it's very nice; it's what everyone has now.' 'I'm not sure, I don't really do wine.' 'No, me neither, it makes me drunk.'[19]

Date: 20 December 2017
Location: Park Drive South, Huddersfield

> An old man who smells of weed stops me in the street to wish me a happy Christmas. He puts his hand on my shoulder and hums a short tune. 'What's that then?' I ask. 'Music' he says, and he wanders off over the road.[20]

Still at the Café de la Mairie, Perec notes, 'A young woman is sitting on a bench, facing "La demeure" tapestry gallery; she is smoking a cigarette.'[21]

This puts me in mind of the following scene from February 2015 in Huddersfield and I freely admit to enjoying the irresistible contrast between Gallerie La Demeure, a mid-century modern tapestry gallery in the centre of Paris, and Lockwood Taxis, a 'highly affordable' taxi hire operation in a run-down back-to-back terrace on the outskirts of Huddersfield town centre.

Date: 24 February 2015
Location: Lockwood Road, Huddersfield

> Things are slowly drying out in the first real sun of the year. Snowdrops and crocuses are appearing on the verges. The big woman in a dirty pink onesie on the bench at the side of the main road inhales from her cigarette with her eyes closed. She adjusts her posture, unfurling like an enormous pink fleecy rose, stretching out her arms across the backrest. She tilts her head back to absorb the warmth of the sun on her face and exhales a long thin wisp of white smoke vertically up and over Lockwood Taxis.[22]

In between his meticulous documenting of the comings and goings of various bus services, Perec notes, 'People stumble. Micro-accidents,'[23] and I'm reminded of his quote: 'To live is to pass from one space to another, while doing your very best not to bump yourself.'[24] Below, I've listed some of the stumbles and micro-accidents of the people of Huddersfield (myself included) as they try to navigate life and space.

Date: March 2004
Location: Market Street, Paddock, Huddersfield

The wobbly, 1980s New Romantic man who hangs about outside the phone box on Market Street is looking particularly wobbly today. He's trying to show off in front of his younger, Burberry wearing companion by walking along a row of concrete bollards but he keeps falling off. His waistcoat is cool though.[25]

Date: September 2005
Location: St Peter's Street, Huddersfield

I trip over a yellow plastic cone with a silhouette of a man tripping printed on it.

Earlier, in Bradford I saw a similar cone wedged under the wheels of a roll container.[26]

Date: September 2006
Location: Heatherfield Road, Marsh, Huddersfield

A drunk couple with grey hair, blotchy skin and bleached-out black jersey and denim are trying to help their companion up from the floor of the children's playground where he's fallen. After several attempts they give up. They hand him a cigarette and sit on a bench a few yards away while he lies on the floor, smoking.[27]

Date: 16 November 2010
Location: Lea Lane, Netherton, Huddersfield

I trip over the wellington boot belonging to the man who is practising the drums with the window open and Mrs Sykes says she's glad it's a nice day and that junk mail is a bit of a pain but she supposes it keeps me in work.[28]

Date: 12 December 2010
Location: Moor End Road, Crosland Moor, Huddersfield

A woman in a big black coat rounds the corner and crashes her buggy into my ankles. She doesn't say anything or even look up, she just reverses a bit and goes around me.[29]

Date: 2 January 2011
Location: John William Street, Huddersfield

5.30am: I follow a tall thin man in a hooded top down John William Street, his hands deep in his pockets. He's drunk, and on several occasions staggers the full width of the generous pavements and trips off the kerb into the road.[30]

Date: 22 June 2014
Location: Walpole Road, Crosland Moor, Huddersfield

Two fifteen year old Vauxhall coupés driven by young snapback wearers sped past. The silver metallic one in front hit the speed-bump by the bus stop too quickly and its wide-arch body-kit came off in one piece. The following coupé, a red one, ran over the body kit and dragged it up the road for about a hundred yards, smashing it to pieces. The elderly man with the Scottish accent and the spaniel asleep in the basket attached to his walking-frame said, 'There're some right fucking idiots about, aren't there?'[31]

Across the road, an old man in synthetic fibres rustles past the upturned push-chair. The sun has yet to coax him from his tightly secured drawstring hood, despite its low glare turning his Reactolite lenses black, opaque. His vision must be impaired because he almost bumps into the woman in the grey hooded top, black tracksuit pants and enormous pink fluffy slippers as she comes out of the off-licence.[32]

Date: 15 August 2016
Location: Acre Street, Lindley, Huddersfield

The weeds between the flags on the narrow pavements are knee deep on some of the back streets; mainly long grasses and ragwort. I graze my knuckles on a concrete lamppost as I squeeze past the man with the slicked back nicotine hair. He falls backwards into a hedge but rebounds upright again and continues on his way.[33]

Date: 6 November 2016
Location: Quarmby Road, Paddock, Huddersfield

A single rubberised reddy-brown glove with off-white cuffing lies in the gutter: by far the most commonly discarded style of glove

> in the Huddersfield area. I once saw one fall from the back of a builders truck as it rounded a corner which perhaps explains the phenomenon.[34]

Perec observes the sartorial: 'Two men with pipes and black satchels [...] A man with a black satchel and no pipe.'[35] Black satchels were evidently a common accessory in central Paris in the autumn/winter of 1974 whereas, in spring/summer 2016, Breton caps are the season's must-have accessory in the small town of Holmfirth, seven miles to the south of Huddersfield.

Date: 28 April 2016
Location: Holmfirth, Huddersfield

> In Holmfirth where the streets are lined with cars and enormous laurel hedges, there are ducks in the car park, dippers in the river, and men in Breton caps.
>
> The notice attached to the ticket machine blows off in a squall as I approach. I ask the woman in the purple anorak whether she knows what it said. She tells me it was about paying for your parking with your phone. She says she doesn't know about me but she's not going to be giving them access to her phone and all her bank details.
>
> The cherry trees are in blossom.
>
> The young women in windcheaters and fluorescent trainers are running three abreast in the road.
>
> Bamforth's postcards building is still being derelict and there's a big hole where John Gill's garage was too.
>
> The line of yuccas next to the post office has gone.
>
> Outside the public toilets, there are pansies in pots, a defibrillator, a needle bin, and the stone memorial to the eighty-one who died in the flood of 1852.
>
> I carry on, past the grey pony-tailed man in the Breton cap.
>
> Past the hi-vis builders with their white paper-bag sandwiches at 10.15am.
>
> Past the suit of armour on display outside Lionhart boutique.
>
> Past another man in a Breton cap.
>
> Past the painted purple charity shop filled with women in purple anoraks.
>
> Past the navy blue railings with gold tips outside the solicitor's office.

Past another man in steel toe-capped boots who is carrying white paper bags full of sandwiches.

Past another man in a Breton cap.

Past the shop selling nautical gilets; photos of a smiling salt-and-pepper beard man modelling all the colourways.

Past another man in a Breton cap.

Past the cow in the trailer at the traffic lights.

Past the shop selling appliqué felt owls.

Past the woman with no socks and ballet pumps who is saying it's sad that the cat has died.

Past the ironmonger's shop where the man in the boiler suit is asking for a lock for his gate: 'Nothing too fancy, mind'.

Up the aubretia hill past the vertiginous hard-standings for high-altitude Astras.

Past the steep terrace with the model boat in the UPVC window.

Past another builder eating a sandwich from a white paper bag.

Past another man in a Breton cap.

Past the hipster with the big ginger beard and the sunglasses hooked over the 'V-neck' of his Fairisle sweater.

Past the elderly couple on the bench who are eating sausage rolls from white paper bags.

Past anoraks with hood-stuffed collars, baggy corduroy and twill.

Past Clarks Nature Originals and walking-boot/trainer hybrids.

Past a black pea coat and a man-bag, too long jeans and a pair of brown chisel-toes.

Past Reactolite lenses and black slip-ons with the slightest heel – ' … like a brogue with a sporty twist'.

Past gold-rimmed specs and a long straight bob, asymmetrical cardigans, leggings and a vest top, calf-length boots with the cuffs turned down, puffa coats and parkas with tight jeans.

And on into the park with the unusual arrangement of daffodils, where Lauren loves Shane and nothing much has changed.[36]

Perec notices an undertaker's van in front of the church and speculates that the people who are gathering there will be taking part in a funeral procession. Forty years later, I watch a funeral procession snake through the estate of park homes on the moor.

Date: 1 April 2014
Location: Hill Tree Park, Crosland Moor, Huddersfield

> A funeral cortège led by a man in a top hat and a cane passes through the estate. Mrs Perkins adjusts her vest top and puts out her cigarette, 'I don't know who that was', she says, 'but you should always pay your respects, shouldn't you?'[37]

Still located at the Café de la Mairie, Perec watches as 'in splendid unity, the pigeons go round the square return to settle on the district council building's gutter'.[38] He wonders what triggers their regular unified tours. In 2007 in Huddersfield, I watch as a council worker scatters a flock of pigeons that have gathered outside the home of an elderly man.

Date: 3 October 2007
Location: Broomroyd, Milnsbridge, Huddersfield

> An elderly man in a thick woolly hat stands on the the front step of his small terraced bungalow throwing birdseed out onto the grass. A flock of fifty or so pigeons gather before a council worker on a green ride-on mower comes around the corner and scatters them. The old man looks up and shouts to me 'You got owt for 'ere?' I say I haven't and he goes back inside without saying anything more.[39]

Perec moves on to La Fontaine Saint-Sulpice (Café). Another sartorial commentary. This time, there is more variety:

> A priest in a beret (another one)
>
> Capes, turbans, boots, sailor-like cap, short or long scarves, policemen with kepi, furs, suitcases, umbrellas.[40]

Over the last weekend of September, 2014, I made an inventory of the sartorial preferences of the residents of the suburb of Netherton who were engaged in outdoor chores on or around their property.

Date: The last weekend in September, 2014
Location: Netherton, Huddersfield

> Sartorial preferences of those carrying out outdoor chores in the last week of September:
>
> Male, 40s, watering potted annuals: t-shirt, jeans, sandals.

Male, 70s, scrubbing hose reel with stiff brush: t-shirt, trousers, sandals.

Male, 60s, clipping fingernails: t-shirt, jeans, sandals.

Female, 60s, digging out couch grass: fleece jacket, jogging pants, walking boots.

Female, 70s, taking seedlings round to a neighbour: blouse, trousers, sandals.

Female, 40s, walking Labrador: t-shirt, jeans, trainers.

Female, 70s: weeding between driveway setts with special long-handled tool: fleece jacket, trousers, sandals.

Male, 60s, loading garden cuttings into a Fiat Punto: fleece jacket, jeans, black shoes.

Female, 40s, re-pointing a garage wall: fleece jacket, tracksuit pants, slippers.

Female, 70s, walking Highland terrier: fleece jacket, knee-length pleated plaid skirt, flat black shoes.

Male, 60s, re-pointing wall: polo-shirt, jeans, black shoes.

Female, 30s, putting out bins: large knitted striped jumper, jogging pants, one slipper, one bare foot.

Female, 70s, popping to shop 'to get bits': knee-length skirt, knitted cardigan, flat black shoes.

Male, 60s, sweeping yard: fleece jacket, trousers, welly shoes.

Male, 60s, washing Fiat Punto: navy-blue overalls, black shoes.

Male, 60s, clearing guttering: shirt with collar, v-neck sweater, suit trousers, slippers.

Female, 60s, sweeping pavement outside house: cardigan, trousers, slippers.

Male, 80s, polishing Kia Picanto: shirt with collar, v-neck sweater, suit trousers, black shoes.

Female, 70s, sweeping driveway with brand new yard-brush: sweatshirt embroidered with floral display, trousers, welly shoes.

Male, 70s, re-applying window putty: knitted cardigan, jeans, slippers.

Male, 50s, shouting abuse at a neighbour in the street, 'Don't fuck with me!': t-shirt, jeans, socks.

Male, 70s, telling the postman that a neighbour has died, 'Yep, they've buried her and everything': baseball cap, cardigan, jogging pants, trainers.

Male, 20s, hiding door key under mat, 'You never saw that, did you? There's nowt worth nicking anyway, it's a right shit-hole': motorcycle helmet, tracksuit, trainers.[41]

5.10 pm on 18 October 1974: Perec has made his way back to the Café de la Mairie from where he continues his close reading of place Saint-Sulpice.

> A yellow postal van stops in front of the mailbox, which a postal worker relieves of its dual contents (Paris/Out of Town, including suburbs)
> It's still raining.[42]

In October 2005, I am relieving the mailbox on Mountjoy Road of its contents.

Date: October 2005
Location: Mountjoy Road, Huddersfield

> I was crouching to empty the pillar box on Mountjoy Road when I noticed a Royal Mail van parked on the other side of the street. I waved as I dislodged some stubborn flats from the cage of the box. When I stood up again I realised I'd been waving to my own van; I'd pulled up on the opposite side of the road to usual.[43]

The next day, Saturday 19 October 1974, Georges Perec is at the Tabac Saint-Sulpice making a note of the distribution of litter outside his window compared with the day before.

> Weather: Fine Rain, Drizzle
> Yesterday, there was a metro ticket on the sidewalk, right in front of my window; today, not exactly in the same spot, a candy wrapper (cellophane) and a piece of paper difficult to identify (a little bigger than a 'Parisiennes' wrapper but a much lighter blue).[44]

Below are the results of the litter survey I undertook in Huddersfield in June 2015.

Litter Survey
Fitzwilliam Street to Church Street, via Greenhead Park, Heaton Road, and Branch Street
Date: Wednesday, 17 June 2015

> Weather: Warm, dry, still
> Duration: 24 mins
> Costa take-out cup.

Coca-Cola plastic bottle
Mayfair cigarette packet
Greggs take-out plastic cup
Richmond cigarette packet
Greggs take-out paper bag
Benson & Hedges cigarette packet.
Kinder Bueno packaging
Train ticket
7up drink can
Pile of cigarette butts of indeterminate brand
Coca-Cola plastic bottle
Polystyrene takeaway container
Dairy Milk wrapper
Haribo sweet packet
Benson & Hedges cigarette packet
Wheat Crunchies packet
Richmond cigarette packet
Rizla packaging
Kelloggs Coco Pops Snack Bar wrapper
Ribena plastic bottle
Benson & Hedges cigarette packet
Benson & Hedges cigarette packet
Expired DVLA tax disc
Capri Sun carton
Till receipt
Pages from The Huddersfield Examiner
Polystyrene cup
Capri Sun carton
Two wet wipes
A child's seaside fishing net
Mayfair cigarette packet (20)
Mayfair cigarette packet (10)
Pile of cigarette butts of indeterminate brand
Coca Cola can
Costa portion control sugar wrapper
Boost Energy Drink can
Pepsi can
Maoam sweet wrapper
Mr Freeze packaging
Rubicon mango drink can
Walkers Cheese & Onion crisp packet
Mayfair cigarette packet

Plastic fork
Polystyrene cup
Polystyrene cup
Paper serviette
Plastic water bottle (indeterminate brand)
A hair roller
Snickers wrapper
Lucozade bottle
Wrigley's Extra chewing gum wrapper
Paracodol packaging
Lambert & Butler cigarette packet[45]

After a brief spell on a bench among the pigeons in the square, Perec is back in the Tabac Saint-Sulpice from where he makes this observation: 'A man walks by with his nose in the air, followed by another man who is looking at the ground.'[46] And I remember the time in 2010 when I harassed the poor man with the tartan Thermos with my persistent early morning greetings.

Date: 23 September 2010
Location: Branch Street, Paddock, Huddersfield

> The man with the tartan Thermos, the pea-coat and the all-year-round woolly hat has started crossing the road when he sees me. We pass each other at 6am every morning and he's often the only other person I see as I walk into work. After a few weeks of ignoring each other, I let on and said 'Morning'. He didn't reply. As time went by and I persisted, he started to respond but never seemed very comfortable with it. His eyes would start flickering nervously at me from about twenty yards away, I'd say 'Morning' and he'd emit an awkward choking sound accompanied by a twitchy sideways glance. Now he crosses the road and keeps his eyes fixed on the pavement.[47]

Still at the Tabac Saint-Sulpice on Saturday 19 October 1974, Perec observes 'A woman with two baguettes under her arm'[48] and I am immediately reminded of the time in March 2015 when I saw 'A woman in a pinny with four bottles of squirty cream under her arm'. I'm always cautious not to read too much into such comparisons but this one seems significant in the way it exemplifies social and economic differences over time and geography.

Date: March 2015
Location: A646 Mytholmroyd–Hebden Bridge

> The geese on the canal are overtaking the traffic on the A646.
> The big-bum lycra cyclist is overtaking too – on the inside, past the builder's tipper truck with the upturned wheelbarrows in the back and the plastic pipes strapped up over the cab like rocket launchers.
> The man in the silver Espace is picking his nose.
> The reenforced concrete fence has been repaired with bailing twine.
> There are spaces to let on Moderna Way.
> Hugo has defaced the bus shelter.
> The sensors on the traffic lights are pointing at the floor.
> The heavy-set man at the bus stop with the match in his mouth is wearing a black biker jacket, black jeans, black steelies, black beard, and a black wide-brimmed leather hat. Next to him, the short woman with the highlighted crop has a leopard skin coat, boot-cut distressed denim jeans and chunky black heels.
> In Hebden Bridge there's a group of small men with paint on their trousers.
> A Morris Traveller.
> A woman in a pinny with four bottles of squirty cream under her arm has just come running out of the Co-op.
> The briefest jackdaw picks over the lawn in the methodist garden.[49]

On Sunday 20 October 1974, Perec is back in the Café de la Mairie (it had been closed on the Saturday) eating a camembert sandwich. On Friday 17 March 2017, I am in the Co-op car park eating peanuts.

Date: 17 March 2017
Location: Crosland Moor, Huddersfield

> Mouldy windfall apples line the slippery stone steps to the back-to-backs. I walk head first into the hanging basket of dead twigs next to the front door with 'fucking crack bitch' scrawled across it in marker pen. I curse and make my way back out to the Co-op where I sit in the car park eating peanuts while the man with the Father Christmas bag-for-life hugs a spaniel.[50]

Perec notes the 'Rarity of complete lulls: there is always a passerby in the distance, or a car passing by'.[51]

9 July 2017: I pause for a moment in a quiet semi-rural spot on the outskirts of town when it occurs to me that I can see nothing moving. It's a warm, still day with no breeze to move even the leaves of the trees. It's as though the world has stopped, except:

Date: 9 July 2017
Location: Healey House, Huddersfield

> An idling diesel engine.
> The amplified telephone bell from the office of the cardboard box factory.
> Distant power tools.
> Crows, starlings and sparrows.
> Distant traffic from the main road.
> The Labrador's bark echoing around the new builds.
> A distant police siren.
> The reversing alarm of a wagon in the yard of the cardboard box factory.
> An aeroplane rumbling overhead.
> The bleating of sheep and lambs.
> The sound of flowing water draining under the manhole cover.[52]

Georges Perec's vigil in place Saint-Sulpice concludes hopefully at 2.00pm on Sunday 20 October 1974 when he observes simply 'Four children. A dog. A little ray of sun'.[53]

The last line of my journal entry of 25 February 2016 is perhaps a little more ambiguous.

Date: 25 February 2016
Location: Burton Acres Lane, Highburton, Huddersfield

> As they walk into the early sun, both the man in the lumberjack shirt and his golden retriever, are haloed by its glare. The dog stops to piss on a holly bush and the resulting cloud of vapour rises to combine with the mist of their breath, swirling around them until they almost disappear from view.[54]

Notes

1. Perec, *Species of Spaces*, 83.
2. Perec, *An Attempt*, 10.
3. Perec, *Species of Spaces*, 50.
4. Locher, *Mark Boyle's Journey*,16.
5. Haftmann, *The Mind and Work of Paul Klee*.
6. Bazin, *What is Cinema?*
7. Boyle, *Beyond Image*, 18.
8. *Huddersfield Examiner*, 7 July 2011.
9. Perec, *An Attempt*, 1.
10. Boniface, *Round About Town*, 80.
11. Perec, *An Attempt*, 8.
12. Boniface, *Round About Town*, 60.
13. Perec, *An Attempt*, 10.
14. Diary entry (unpublished).
15. Boniface, *Round About Town*, 36.
16. Boniface, *Round About Town*, 43.
17. Boniface, *Round About Town*, 59.
18. Boniface, *Round About Town*, 78.
19. Boniface, *Round About Town*, 97.
20. Boniface, *Round About Town*, 123.
21. Perec, *An Attempt*, 11.
22. Boniface, *The Most Difficult Thing Ever*.
23. Perec, *An Attempt*, 12.
24. Perec, *Species of Spaces*, 6.
25. Diary entry (unpublished).
26. Diary entry (unpublished).
27. Diary entry (unpublished).
28. Boniface, *Round About Town*, 16.
29. Boniface, *Round About Town*, 19.
30. Boniface, *Round About Town*, 20.
31. Boniface, *Round About Town*, 73.
32. Boniface, *Round About Town*, 82.
33. Boniface, *Round About Town*, 105.
34. Boniface, *Round About Town*, 108.
35. Perec, *An Attempt*, 12.
36. Boniface, 'Recorded Delivery'.
37. Boniface, *Round About Town*, 71.
38. Perec, *An Attempt*, 14.
39. Diary entry (unpublished).
40. Perec, *An Attempt*, 20.
41. Boniface, *Round About Town*, 76.
42. Perec, *An Attempt*, 27.
43. Diary entry (unpublished).
44. Perec, *An Attempt*, 31.
45. Boniface, *Round About Town*, 87–8.
46. Perec, *An Attempt*, 38.
47. Boniface, *Round About Town*, 10.
48. Perec, *An Attempt*, 38.
49. Boniface, 'The Rookery'.
50. Boniface, *Round About Town*, 115.
51. Perec, *An Attempt*, 47.
52. Boniface, *The Most Difficult Thing Ever*.
53. Perec, *An Attempt*, 47.
54. Boniface, *Round About Town*, 99.

Bibliography

Bazin, André. *What is Cinema?*, translated by Hugh Gray. Berkeley: University of California Press, 2004.

Boniface, Kevin. *The Most Difficult Thing Ever*. Huddersfield: West View Study Centre, 2017.

Boniface, Kevin. 'The Rookery' (film). WVSC/Hebden Bridge Arts Festival, 2015.

Boniface, Kevin. 'Recorded Delivery' (multi-media project). Yorkshire Festival, 2016.

Boniface, Kevin. *Round About Town*. Axminster: Uniformbooks, 2018.

Boyle, Mark. *Beyond Image: Boyle Family: Hayward Gallery, London, 1 November 1986–25 January 1987*. London: Arts Council of Great Britain, 1986.

Haftmann, Werner. *The Mind and Work of Paul Klee*. London: Faber and Faber, 1954.

Locher, J.L. *Mark Boyle's Journey to the Surface of the Earth*. Stuttgart: Mayer, 1978.

Perec, Georges. *Species of Spaces and Other Pieces*, edited and translated by John Sturrock. London: Penguin Books, 1997.

Perec, Georges. *An Attempt at Exhausting a Place in Paris*, translated by Marc Lowenthal. Cambridge, MA: Wakefield Press, 2010.

INDEX

www.ingramcontent.com/pod-product-compliance
Lightning Source LLC
LaVergne TN
LVHW052017300826
846742LV00020B/78

9781787354425